SEP 1 5 2023

"Every parent needs Sissy Goff in their corner. Her grace-filled advice always reminds me of what's at the heart of my worries—my desire to be the best mom I can be. This book gave me the tools to be exactly that."

Emily Ley, bestselling author of *Grace, Not Perfection*

"In this well-researched and deeply practical book, Sissy Goff serves as a trusted guide and counselor to help you overcome the crushing weight of worry and move into more freedom and peace as a parent. Whether you are just stressing a little over minor things or feeling suffocated and strangled by fear of the present and future, Sissy's words of encouragement will be a balm of hope and hands-on help for your weary heart!"

Crystal Paine, *New York Times* bestselling author, podcaster, founder of MoneySavingMom.com, and mom of six

"My friend Sissy has done it again. Drawing on years of clinical practice and extensive research, Sissy wrote a book specifically to support parents. Parents are living busier and more distracted lives. When meeting with parents who express worries about their kids (or themselves), I first offer encouragement and then a resource—a tool to help them feel calmer and more equipped. This gem of a book does both. Anxiety plays tricks and lies. Sissy offers truth and helps parents gain mastery over anxiety by guiding us to do our own 'worry work.'"

Chinwé Williams, PhD, owner and principal therapist, Meaningful Solutions Counseling & Consulting; coauthor of *Seen: Healing Despair and Anxiety in Kids and Teens through the Power of Connection*

"Our family has been greatly impacted by the words, wisdom, and counsel of Sissy Goff. *The Worry-Free Parent* is another powerful tool that is helping my wife and me navigate the imperfect journey of parenthood. We all need help along the way, and helpers like Sissy are a gift from God."

Christian recording artist **Matthew West** and his wife, **Emily West**

THE
WORRY-FREE
PARENT

Also by Sissy Goff

Raising Worry-Free Girls
Braver, Stronger, Smarter
Brave

Coauthored with Melissa Trevathan and David Thomas

Are My Kids on Track?
Intentional Parenting

Coauthored with Melissa Trevathan

Modern Parents, Vintage Values
Raising Girls
The Back Door to Your Teen's Heart

THE WORRY-FREE PARENT

LIVING IN CONFIDENCE
SO YOUR KIDS CAN TOO

Sissy Goff, LPC-MHSP

BETHANY HOUSE
a division of Baker Publishing Group
Minneapolis, Minnesota

Published by Bethany House Publishers
Minneapolis, Minnesota
www.bethanyhouse.com

Bethany House Publishers is a division of
Baker Publishing Group, Grand Rapids, Michigan

Printed in the United States of America

Library of Congress Cataloging-in-Publication Data
Names: Goff, Sissy, author.
Title: The worry-free parent : living in confidence so your kids can too / Sissy Goff, LPC-MHSP.
Description: Minneapolis, Minnesota : Bethany House Publishers, a division of Baker Publishing Group, [2023] | Includes bibliographical references.
Identifiers: LCCN 2022061161 | ISBN 9780764241024 (paper) | ISBN 9780764241871 (casebound) | ISBN 9781493442201 (ebook)
Subjects: LCSH: Parenting—Religious aspects—Christianity. | Anxiety—Religious aspects—Christianity.
Classification: LCC BV4529 .G637 2023 | DDC 248.8/45—dc23/eng/20230221
LC record available at https://lccn.loc.gov/2022061161

Cover design by Dan Pitts

Interior illustration by Connie Gabbert

The author is represented by Alive Literary Agency, www.aliveliterary.com.

Baker Publishing Group publications use paper produced from sustainable forestry practices and post-consumer waste whenever possible.

23 24 25 26 27 28 29   7 6 5 4 3 2 1

This book is dedicated to
my wonder of a little sister, Kathleen Weber:
I admire you more than you know. I learn every day from
the way you offer such beauty . . . through your smile,
your present-in-the-moment-ness, your lovely
sense of hospitality, and of course, your style.
I want to be more like you when I grow up.

Contents

Introduction

"I need you to tell me two things: First, that what I'm feeling is normal. And second, that I'm doing a good job."

It was a first for me. Never before had a parent sat down in my counseling office and told me right off the bat what she needed. Usually, there are a few more pleasantries. "Hi," "Hello," "This is a really cute office," maybe a short description of her children. But this brave and honest mom cut right to the chase. Why? Because she needed to hear truth.

We all do. But especially those of us who are worriers.

Let me stop for a second to introduce myself. My name is Sissy Goff, and I'm the director of child and adolescent counseling at a magical place called Daystar Counseling in Nashville, Tennessee, where I've had the privilege of counseling kids and their families since 1993. If you were going to take your kids to counseling, this is the kind of place you'd want to to go. We're in a little yellow house with a white picket fence. We have popcorn popping in the afternoons after school. Our offices look like living rooms. And our most beloved therapists are dogs. Daystar is about as warm and inviting as you can get when it comes to counseling offices—on purpose—but we'll get back to that idea later.

Because I meet with kids, I also spend a lot of time with parents. In the past few years there has been one issue I've talked about most with both: anxiety. You may have read the statistics already. At the time I'm sitting down to write this book, one in four kids is dealing with anxiety. Because I've been seeing more and more kids facing this issue, I've tried to do a deep dive to help. At this time, I've read thirty-five books on the subject, become certified as an anxiety specialist twice over, and written three books about it already. Those books are about your kids. One is for the elementary-aged girls in your life, called *Braver, Stronger, Smarter*. One is for the middle and high school girls, titled *Brave*. And one is for you and about all of those girls, *Raising Worry-Free Girls*. This book, however, is the first one specifically *about you*.

Of all the things I've learned about anxiety, potentially the most important is this: Anxiety is an isolator, but it's certainly not an isolated issue. It has an amazing ability to spread. In almost every situation in which I've had an anxious child or teen in my office, they have had at least one anxious parent. Now, that's from my observation. The research says that if you have anxiety as a parent, your child is seven times more likely to deal with it themself.[1] We'll talk more about who gave it to whom later. But it's a little like other things we've experienced recently—if one of you has it, another is likely to get it too. And this book is meant to help us stop the spread.

I'm getting ahead of myself. As I said, I've been counseling kids since 1993, but that also means I sit with a lot of parents—a lot of worried parents whose primary concern is their kids. In fact, these days I probably spend about half of my time in what we call parent consults, which are sessions with parents whose kids might or might not be in counseling. These appointments are a little like the well visits you do with your pediatrician. I have folks who come in yearly, or even quarterly, just to touch base about how their kids are doing. They're asking the "Are my kids on track?" types of questions (which is also the title of another book I cowrote). "Is this normal?" "What do we need to be doing specifically with this child at this age?" "Could there be more to this behavior?" "How do I help them work through this situation?" They're asking the questions every intentional parent has along the way.

My guess is that you're that type of parent too, just because you picked up this book. I would also guess that you love your kids deeply. That you try hard. That you're thoughtful and probably really smart too. That you're at least a little bit of a worrier (thus, buying a book called *The Worry-Free Parent*), *and* that you have the same two questions as the mom you met at the beginning of this introduction, who happened to be in my office for a parent consult.

So I want you to consider this book your own parent consult at the Daystar house. Actually, this will be a few months' worth of parent consults. We're going to do just what we'd do if you were sitting in my office. We'll talk some about your kids and talk even more about you. I'm going to ask you a few questions throughout these pages. In fact, I'd love for you to grab the workbook that goes along with this book. You could even have a friend read the book with you and talk through the questions together. We're going to talk about your past. We're going to talk about what's happening now with the kids you love. And then we're going to talk about the future—for you as a parent and for you as a person. My hope is that you'll gain a lot of practical help in the present, a lot of understanding about the past, and a lot of hope for your (and your child's) future. We're going to be talking about all three timeframes because worry impacts all three. Worry uses the past to define us. Worry distracts us in the present. And worry defeats us in the future . . . and we're not even there yet. Oh, and one of the most important things to establish is that worry lies. He uses the past, present, and future to lie to you about who you are and who you can be as a parent. He tries to make you believe those same lies that I believe that mom was believing. So let me tell you two of the most important truths you'll find in this book:

1. What you're feeling is normal. You are going to find yourself in the pages of this book often as you listen in on conversations I've had with other parents who feel just as overwhelmed and as anxious as you do.

2. You're doing a great job. Just the fact that you're reading this book helps me know that you're trying hard as a parent. You want to do all you can to love your kids. And you're brave enough to look at how your life impacts theirs. I truly believe from all my years of counseling that to look at your own life and deal with your own stuff is one of the very best gifts you can give your children.

I'm honored you'd invite me on the journey with you. Together, we're going to find a whole lot of truth and a whole lot of freedom for you as a parent *and* as a person.

For now, I want you to imagine that I've just walked down the stairs of the Daystar house to greet you for your first appointment. You've got a cup of coffee in hand, and we're heading upstairs for our first conversation together.

Worry-Free Takeaways

1. All of us need to hear truth, but especially those of us who worry.
2. Anxiety is an isolator, but it is not an isolated issue.
3. If, as a parent, you have anxiety, your kids are seven times more likely to deal with it themselves. My experience is that most kids who are anxious have at least one anxious parent.
4. The fact that you picked up this book means you're a parent who loves your kids deeply, tries hard, is bright, is conscientious, and is all the things that not only make you a good parent but also lend themselves to your being an anxious parent.
5. What you're feeling is normal.
6. You're doing a great job.
7. To look at your own life and deal with your own stuff is one of the best gifts you can give your children.

Understanding the Past

1

Understanding Worry and Anxiety

Let's take a little inventory here:

As you're reading this, do you feel worried?

Do you have a stress level you'd rate higher than a six out of ten?

Are your shoulders hunched up around your neck?

Is your jaw clenched?

Have you gotten frustrated with any of your children in the past twenty-four hours?

Have you reacted with the same emotion and intensity as your child?

Have you had a hard time falling asleep?

Have you had flashes of thoughts of your children being hurt?

Have you had intrusive, irrational thoughts?

Have any of those thoughts felt like they got stuck on a loop in your mind?

Have you had a worried reaction that was bigger than the situation warranted?

Have you had worst-case scenario thoughts regarding your kids?

Have you felt like a failure as a parent?

My guess is that you answered yes to at least one of these questions, if not most or all of them. The reason I know is, again, I sit with parents who are much like you every single day. They're parents who have come to my office to talk about their child's level of anxiety. But inevitably we end up talking about their own worry and anxiety. For some parents, that anxiety has been in place for quite some time, so they recognize it; but for others, it seems to have caught them by surprise.

I was a guest on a podcast recently, and the interviewer made an interesting statement: "We're the first generation of healthy parents." How does that statement land with you? As a counselor with over three decades of experience, I believe it's *mostly* true. Of course—and thankfully—there are the exceptions among us who grew up with parents who were ahead of their time in helping kids understand and process emotions, but I don't believe most of us were passing feelings charts around the dinner table or coming up with family coping skills lists. The great news is that, like this interviewer, I do believe most parents today are prioritizing the mental and emotional health of their kids in a way previous generations didn't have the understanding or maybe even the motivation to do. But perfectionist that I am, I would rephrase her statement. Maybe "the first generation of healthy parents" is a little too far. I'm not sure if you're anything like me, but I'm a person who tries to prioritize mental and emotional health. Much like I'm a person who tries to prioritize physical health—and I still eat a little too much queso from time to time. Just can't help myself. I'm also a person who gets frustrated more than I'd like. Who gets caught in looping thoughts and reacts bigger than the situation warrants. I'm trying, but still can't help myself sometimes. So why don't we say "the first generation *pursuing* mental and emotional health"?

Pursuing health is different than *are healthy*. I'm just not sure any of us will be fully healthy this side of heaven . . . although we can certainly try for ourselves and for the kids we love. Plus, it takes a little pressure off to think of it more as pursuit than arrival, don't you think? I want you to hear me say over and over in this book that giving yourself grace is more important than trying harder. More on that later.

Basically, all of this pursuing and arriving and first-generation lingo mean we're forging a new path. We desire to help the kids we love have tools we never had when we were growing up. And we know enough, for the first time, to try. Maybe we've even been in counseling for a season ourselves, or at least have been curious about it. We're aware of the things we wish didn't happen in our parenting—that something inside us is triggered when our kids are triggered. We know we can match their emotion and intensity and do so more often than we'd like. We know we can get stuck in the what-if spiral. We know we get angrier than we wish we did. We realize it can sometimes be hard to let go of our need for control and simply enjoy our kids. The desire is there. We're just not sure how. Where do we even begin to start?

We always want to start with where we are—specifically, we want to start with an understanding of what's happening inside us. There's a reason you get triggered and angry more than you wish you did. There's a reason you go to the worst-case scenario when it comes to these little people you love. There's a reason you even wonder, from time to time, if something is wrong with you that you can't seem to be the parent you long to be. And it's not because you're a failure as a parent or as a person. And we're going to circle back to that idea too, over and over throughout this book.

Let me interrupt here to say something about the rest of our time together: I know you're busy. You are trying hard to get this parenting thing right, *and* you're likely meeting yourself coming and going. Remember, I talked to you yesterday—or a mom who's a lot like you. She managed to come see me in between dropping off her son's forgotten soccer cleats, picking up the dry cleaning, leaving her third business meeting of the day, and driving the carpool. (Makes me anxious just thinking about it.) I have a sneaking suspicion you have just as many balls in the air.

As the lives of parents have gotten busier and more intense, my messages in counseling parents have gotten simpler. In each session, I try to leave parents with a few takeaways that are not only practical but are easy to remember. And so it will be with the next few chapters. Five things. I want to give you five things, for now, that I believe can help you understand what is going on inside you. These are five things I know to be true about anxiety that I think are particularly important for parents to hear—and can shed a little more light on this journey that you and, as a result, the kids you love are on.

Five Things True about Anxiety

1. *The more we understand about worry and anxiety, the easier they are to fight.*

Sun Tzu was a Chinese general, writer, military strategist, and philosopher who lived in ancient China somewhere between 544 and 496 BC. His most important and well-known work was a little book called *The Art of War*. It is still one of the most influential works of literature to impact military strategy across the globe. It's also applicable to the emotional (and even social) battles we fight on a daily basis. For example, Tzu said, "If you know the enemy and know yourself, you need not fear the result of a hundred battles. If you know yourself but not the enemy, for every victory gained you will also suffer a defeat. If you know neither the enemy nor yourself, you will succumb in every battle."[1]

For our purposes—and for the purposes of your parenting and your kids, we're going to consider worry and anxiety our enemy. To understand that enemy is the goal of this chapter. We'll talk more about ourselves in the next. As philosopher Sir Francis Bacon said, "Knowledge is power." Understanding this enemy of worry and anxiety is one of the most important tools in your fight. The more we know, the easier this battle will be. And so I want to start with some basic questions I am asked regularly by parents.

▪ What is anxiety, and how is it different from worry?

In *Raising Worry-Free Girls*, I talk about a "worry continuum." It starts with fear, moves to worry, then to anxiety, and then to what is considered an anxiety disorder. Fear is completely normal and, in fact, helpful. Fear keeps us alive when faced with a life-threatening situation. And fear is specifically tied to a certain object or situation. I'm afraid of spiders, but only if I happen to find one crawling on or near me. We usually only have a reaction to our fears when presented with the feared object or situation itself. We're afraid *of*. As a parent, I would imagine you are fearful of a variety of things happening to your child—pain, loss, injury, to name a few. But when fears are truly fears, they don't have the power to impact our emotions unless we come face-to-face (or at least in near proximity) with them.

Worry is different. Worry is more pervasive than fear, but it's also more abstract. We worry *about*. We don't necessarily worry about objects, but we do worry about situations. Most of those situations are either past or future oriented. We worry we might have irreparably damaged our child's level of confidence with our angry words getting to the car. We worry other parents are judging us or our child for one reason or a million others. We worry that our child might be struggling to make friends. We worry about almost anything bad we can imagine happening to the kids we love. A lot of parents tell me they worry they're storing up reasons for their kids to be in counseling later . . . and might as well start saving for it now. Worry comes in all shapes and sizes and is a normal mode of thinking for most parents. Not helpful, but normal. For some parents I see, I truly believe they consider worry a prerequisite to parenting.

As we already established, fear is an adaptive learning mechanism that helps us survive. Fear causes our sympathetic nervous system, our body's God-given EMS system, to kick into gear to help us avoid an imminent threat. We'll come back to that idea later. Anxiety, on the other hand, is maladaptive. It misinterprets threats, distorts our thinking, and often causes our sympathetic nervous system to react without sufficient evidence. Anxiety also causes our worried thoughts or images to get stuck. With kids in my office, I talk about anxiety being like the single-loop roller coaster at the fair. A worst-case scenario thought pops into your mind, and no amount of reasoning or rationalizing can get it out. And the worst-case scenario quickly becomes a real-life perspective. Your teenager isn't home fifteen minutes past curfew, and the wreck you're certain he was in plays on repeat in your mind. You see a photo of your daughter at summer camp sitting alone on her bunk, and rather than thinking she's enjoying a minute of downtime, you've already got her abandoned by all her friends and feeling lonely and depressed. The teacher stops you after class to tell you that your three-year-old son pushed another boy on the playground, and you immediately believe not only that he's struggling to make friends today but that he will do so forever and will likely be the class bully. You get the idea. My guess is you've gotten the idea thousands of times since your parenting journey began.

An anxiety disorder is different from anxiety in that it (1) is more intense, (2) lasts longer, and (3) interferes with daily life.[2] For anxiety to be categorized as a disorder, it typically needs to be present for at least six months. There are a myriad of anxiety disorders, with the five most common being generalized anxiety disorder, obsessive-compulsive disorder (OCD), panic disorder, post-traumatic stress disorder (PTSD), and social phobia or social anxiety disorder. The following descriptions of them are offered by the US Department of Health and Human Services:

> *Generalized anxiety disorder*, also known as GAD, is "characterized by chronic anxiety, exaggerated worry and tension, even when there is little or nothing to provoke it."
>
> *Obsessive-compulsive disorder*, OCD, is "characterized by recurrent, unwanted thoughts (obsessions) and/or repetitive behaviors (compulsions)." The behaviors can include hand washing, checking (on items like locked doors), cleaning, and counting. These compulsions "are

performed with the hope of preventing obsessive thoughts or making them go away. Performing these so-called 'rituals,' however, provides only temporary relief, and not performing them markedly increases anxiety."

Panic disorder is characterized by what most of us consider panic attacks, "unexpected and repeated episodes of intense fear accompanied by physical symptoms that may include chest pain, heart palpitations, shortness of breath, dizziness, or abdominal distress."

Post-traumatic stress disorder (PTSD) can develop after experiencing a traumatic event, defined as "an event or ordeal in which grave physical harm occurred or was threatened." Traumatic events can include accidents, military combat, natural or man-made disasters, and violent personal assaults on ourselves or another that we have witnessed.

Social phobia, or social anxiety disorder, is signified by "overwhelming anxiety and excessive self-consciousness in everyday social situations." Social phobia may occur anytime a person is around others, or may be specific to a situation such as speaking or eating in front of people.[3]

Let me say clearly that this book is not meant to serve as a diagnostic tool for you to determine if you have an anxiety disorder. If you suspect that you might by the end of this book, I recommend finding a trusted therapist who specializes in anxiety. My desire, however, with this book and all the anxiety books pertaining to kids, is to help you not need to go to the counselor's office. My hope is to provide you with tools to use at home that can make a difference not just for you, but for the life of your family. However, if the tools in this book don't seem to make a difference, or enough of one, I'd recommend seeing a professional. Sometimes we just can't get enough perspective on our own to make sense of our worried thoughts and we need that extra support. I've certainly done it myself numerous times over the years—as has almost every person I know who is *pursuing* mental and emotional health. Don't be afraid to ask. There are kind, deeply compassionate, and profoundly helpful counselors all over the world. We're a pretty good bunch. I think you'd like us.

For now and for our purposes, I'm going to use the words *worry* and *anxiety* interchangeably. If you consider yourself a worrier, I believe you're probably operating with some degree of anxiety. And I would venture to guess that because you picked up this book, you're likely a worrier.

■ **How much anxiety are you seeing today? Among adults? Among kids?**

Let's talk about the kids first:

- At some point in their development, 30 percent of children and adolescents will experience anxiety; 80 percent never receive help.[4]
- One in three teenagers is struggling with anxiety.[5]
- Girls are twice as likely as boys to suffer from anxiety,[6] but boys are taken in for treatment more.[7]
- Again, if you have anxiety, your kids are seven times more likely to deal with it themselves.[8]

Which brings us to you:

- 31.1 percent of adults will experience an anxiety disorder at some point in their lifetime.[9]
- Women are more than twice as likely as men to develop an anxiety disorder.[10]
- Only 36.9 percent of adults suffering from anxiety receive treatment.[11]
- Half of those diagnosed with depression are also diagnosed with an anxiety disorder.[12]

In other words, anxiety is the most prevalent disorder among both kids and adults, but it's also the most treatable.

▧ **Why is it so prevalent?**

According to the Anxiety and Depression Association of America, "Anxiety disorders develop from a complex set of risk factors, including genetics, brain chemistry, personality, and life events."[13] That would pretty much describe all of us, wouldn't it? We've all experienced a complex set of risk factors. Many of us have some sort of family history for anxiety, which we'll talk more about in the next chapter. We potentially have a personality that's wired for tension and stress. And we all have lived through a pandemic—which will go down in history as one of the most traumatic events of this century, for children and adults alike. In fact, after so many years as a therapist, I truly believe that all adults today live with some degree of anxiety, whether they know it or not.

One definition of anxiety I read stated that anxiety occurs when "our thinking and planning brain spins out of control because it doesn't have enough information."[14] Truth be told, most of us don't feel like we have enough information—about our futures, about our pasts, about ourselves, and especially about the lives and futures of the kids we love. So there again, we are—all of us—living, walking, breathing incubators for anxiety. Those are the generalities. We'll talk more about the specifics for you in the next chapter.

2. *Anxiety left untreated only gets worse.*

Statistically speaking, there are likely a lot of us who fall into the 63.1 percent of adults who never receive treatment. Maybe this is even your first attempt at some kind of help. I'm honored if this book is the beginning of your journey to battling worry and anxiety. But I certainly don't want to diminish the impact your untreated past has had. The average age of onset for anxiety is seven.[15] Take your age and subtract seven. That is likely how long this anxiety storm inside of you has been brewing. And I believe becoming a parent strengthens the storm significantly.

Our brains develop and strengthen neural pathways based on use. The scientific term is *neuroplasticity*, defined as "the brain's ability to change and adapt as a result of experience."[16] In fact, some theorists call it a "use it or lose it" phenomenon. Doctors and authors Daniel Siegel and Tina Bryson say that "where neurons fire, they wire, or join together."[17] Basically, we create well-worn paths in our brain. The paths that are used most frequently become easier to use. That circuitry strengthens in our brain. It's why you likely have no idea which pant leg you put on first each day, but my guess is that if you paid attention, it would be the same leg. Getting dressed is a well-worn neural pathway in your brain. As are brushing your teeth and making coffee. And, for many of us, worry has also become a well-worn path.

Worry is not only a well-worn pathway, but it works for us. Or so we believe. Worry often serves a purpose. Many of us try to use worry as a coping skill. We overthink because we believe we're coming to a more helpful conclusion. Or maybe we believe worry motivates us. It energizes us to do the task in front of us. Maybe we worry to keep ourselves from being blindsided by bad news. Worry makes us, somehow, feel more in control. And, in some families, it can even be a way of showing that we care.[18]

I often told my mom not to worry when I was growing up. It could have been about any situation. She was quite the worrier. It didn't matter if it was telling me to call her when I arrived at my destination, keeping tabs on me if I was sick, or even asking if I was okay when I coughed from the next room. With all the independence I could muster at six and sixteen, I'd tell her I was fine. Her response, however, was always the same: "It's a mother's job to worry."

You may feel the same way. You may subconsciously wonder, *Where would I be without my worry?* Or even, *Who would I be without it?* Worry can eventually become a way of life. But the truth is that worry interferes with our lives much more than it enhances them. In fact, I'd like for you to think of three ways you might have believed worry helped in the past. What are three ways it interferes with who you want to be as a parent and as a person today?

Anxiety left untreated only gets worse. The same is true for worry. The neural pathways are strengthened, and we spend more time worrying than we do experiencing. We feel anxious more than we feel confident—or even brave. In order to beat worry and anxiety, the truth is pretty plain: We have to fight. And we've got to fight on all levels. It's why this book (and all my books on anxiety) offers practical tools in three areas: help for the body, help for the mind, and help for the heart. Worry tries to defeat you in all three places, so we've got to fight it in each of those places.

The bottom line is that this book is for the parent who wants to change. Not just change your kids, although I believe that will come as a result. This book is for those of you who are tired of the sleepless nights, the emotional ups and downs, and the defeat that comes at the hands of worry and anxiety. You can do this. You're already learning a great deal. And there's a whole lot more understanding of the past, help for your present, and hope for the future to come.

3. Worry plays tricks.

One of the first things I do with kids who come into my office with anxiety is have them give their worry a name. It's one of my favorite tools, and one we'll talk more about in the "Help for Your Mind" chapter. I had one girl who named hers Princess Worry because she said she was the Queen and could boss the princess around. I have had several girls who named their worry Bob—go figure! With younger girls, I typically start out calling it the Worry Monster, or Worry Bug, if they're afraid of monsters. My colleague and friend David Thomas has young boys who call theirs the Hulk because they often get angry when they get worried. In my book for teens, however, I called it the Worry Whisperer. That's what it feels like . . . even for those of us who are adults. Worry whispers things in the back of our minds that feel like truth. But, spoiler alert for the rest of the book: They're not. He uses those whispers to play tricks on us. In fact, I told the teenage girls there are two primary tricks worry plays on them. He tells them,

1. Something is wrong with you.
2. You're the only one who feels this way.[19]

For you, I'd like to add a third primary trick he plays on you—or lie he tells you. We could certainly call it either.

3. You're a failure as a parent.

At this point, I have no idea how many thousands of parents I have sat with in my counseling office. They're parents of kids of all ages and all circumstances who have come for help. I believe every single one of those parents has one thing in common: At their core, they're anxious that they're failing as parents. It's not a fear *of* failure, like spiders or snakes. It's not even a worry *about* failure that hangs around a little more often. I believe it's an anxiety that undergirds every late pickup, every forgotten school note, every blown temper, and almost every normal day in between. And I would guess the same is true for you. The anxiety may not even be a conscious thought, but it's likely one that lies just under the surface and is tapped into all too easily.

Anxiety plays tricks, remember? And the tricks it plays are insidious. Its primary goal is to consume our thoughts in a way that defeats us—that keeps us from being present to our lives and with the kids we love. So the worry loops around the very things we're most afraid of. In fact, we could do a timeline from the age of onset right up through adulthood. For younger children, anxiety often loops around something bad happening to one of their parents, which is the scariest thing they can imagine happening at that age. They get a little older, and it's getting in trouble or even getting a stomach bug. A little older, and it might be a fear of getting a bad grade or getting on an airplane. A little older, and it's performing poorly in a track meet or embarrassing themselves socially. A little older (like today, for you), and it's being a failure as a parent. Worry is wise to target our fears right where we live, or think, with enough power to consume our thoughts and make us truly feel like a failure.

Let's dispel that lie right here: You are *not* a failure as a parent. Even the fact that you would read a book about your own anxiety rather than just that of your children means that you are intentional. The fact that you deal with worry and anxiety means that you care deeply, you're trying hard, and you're getting a whole lot more right than you are wrong. We'll come back to that idea later too. But for now, I want you to trust me. You're not a failure. Nothing is wrong with you, and you are certainly not the only one who feels this way. I hope that truth is starting to sink in. But I also know worry's well-worn tricky pathways, and the shame that treads upon them can be deep.

4. *Worry needs truth. And a whole lot of other tools too.*

In every book I read in my research on anxiety, there was one phrase I came back to over and over and over: anxiety distorts. It distorts our perception. It makes small problems seem medium, medium problems seem big, and big problems seem insurmountable. In fact, it's not even the problems that are, well, the problems. It's the stories we tell ourselves about the problems—in other words, the thoughts we have as a result of any given situation that might be considered problematic.

Let me give you a real-life example. I'll never forget an encounter I had with a mom a while back. Her daughter was in one of my middle school counseling groups and had been for several years. In my mind, she was a very connected part of the group. When this mom sat down in my office, however, she was angry. Not just a little angry, but *very* angry with me. (Keep in mind that anger is a secondary emotion, meaning there is always another emotion lurking beneath the surface of that anger.)

"Sissy, I'm upset about how Sophie is doing in group. She doesn't feel connected to the other girls. They walk in each week and don't speak to her. When she talks, no one asks her questions or is responsive to her. She is trying really hard and feels like the other girls just won't accept her."

Let me go ahead and say I have had almost exactly the same conversation probably ten different times with parents over the years. And almost every situation has gone the same way. I decided to do a little detective work and pay extra attention the next few weeks in group. As a side note, when I walk into group, the girls don't speak to me either. Because, you know . . . teenagers. I proceeded to overdo my own entrance in a silly way just to help them realize that they're completely unaware. And the word *unaware* is what I really would use to describe those girls. To the mom's point, some of them might be closer friends than others. But they were not purposefully leaving this girl out, or any of the girls from any of the situations. Once or twice, they may not have been as responsive to her as they were to the others. But the next week, the same thing happened to a different girl. Because, again, teenagers. But this girl whose mom came in to meet with me felt awkward. She believed that others saw externally the discomfort she felt internally. As a result, the story she told herself was that the other girls didn't like her. That they didn't want her to be a part of their group. And then she saw what she was looking for. We all do, by the way. It's a phenomenon called *confirmation bias*.[20] Confirmation bias presupposes that we see what we want to see or what we are looking for. She was unconsciously looking for confirmation of what she felt on the inside, or even what she expected was going to happen. And that is exactly what she saw. She didn't see that the girls didn't speak to me either. She didn't see the questions they did ask. She saw all of the things that confirmed her theory. And it was that theory, or the story she told herself, that was the primary problem.

Let's stop right here and look at a cognitive behavioral therapy tool called the cognitive triangle. It's one of the foundational principles of CBT, which is the most highly researched type of therapy for anxiety with the most evidence-based results.[21] The triangle is an illustration with thoughts at the top, and feelings and behaviors providing each corner of the base.

The premise behind the triangle is that our thoughts, feelings, and behaviors are all interconnected. Therefore, it's the thoughts we have (the stories we tell ourselves) that impact our feelings, which then impact or dictate our behavior. CBT asserts that if we change any part of the triangle, change will occur in the other parts as well. Most CBT interventions go directly to stopping and changing those distorted, anxious thoughts.

For this girl, the story she told herself of being left out (thoughts) caused her to feel isolated and hurt (feelings), which caused her to talk to her mom and decide to drop out of group (behavior).

We could look at the same CBT triangle with her mom, because both fell prey to confirmation bias. She was afraid that her daughter was being rejected by friends. Her mom's behavior (coming to see me) was a result of her emotion (anxiety and anger), which was a result of the story she was telling herself about the story her daughter told her. I hope you're following. She was anxious about her daughter's level of anxiety and worried that it was beginning to spill over into depression. She was doing her best to be a good, protective mom. But she missed the important fact that anxiety distorts. And anxiety often distorts our perceptions. Truth be told, I missed it the first time a parent came to me with the above situation. I didn't know as much about anxiety in my earlier years as a therapist. But I know more now. And I'm committed to helping you find the truth that I believe can set you and your kids free.

Worry needs truth. This mom needed truth too—as did her daughter. The daughter would have been much better served if we had been able to talk about confirmation bias and distorted perceptions and she had learned what to do with those anxious thoughts. Sadly, this young girl never came back to my counseling office, feeling that group had been yet another place she had been left out. I did try to present the truth of what I had seen in group to this mom. But she trusted her daughter's words and perceptions more than she did mine, with good reason. She was trying her best to help her daughter. We just didn't know enough to provide the tools and the truth that would have helped—for long after her middle school years.

Honestly, almost every time that scenario has presented itself, it has gone the same way. My hope is that together we can do something different, for ourselves and the kids we love. In the Help for the Present section, you're going to learn to be a good detective and differentiate between perceptions and reality. We're going to stop those anxious, distorted thoughts right when they start. We're going to find our way to truth. And to a whole lot of other tools too.

5. Every parent worries. Especially the good ones.

The book I wrote for elementary-aged girls is called *Braver, Stronger, Smarter*. I decided on the title based on two things: First, I love Pooh. And I particularly love the quote "You're braver than you believe, and stronger than you seem, and smarter than you think."[22] Second, as anxiety rates were rising exponentially and I was seeing more and more kids in my office battling anxiety, I noticed one primary theme that was true across the board: Every single one of those kids was really bright. It didn't matter their age or gender. Every one of them was conscientious. They tried hard. They cared deeply. They wanted to get things right. As I tell anxious kids in my office every single day, they're really the coolest kinds of kids.

The same is true of you. You worry because you care. You are conscientious. You want to be the best parent you can possibly be. But that care sometimes gets the best of you, and it's hard to turn the volume down. We're going to get there together.

Spoiler alert: The braver, stronger, smarter idea is actually another CBT tool. It's called *thought replacing*, *reframing*, or *flipping the thought*. We take the worried thought and flip it on its head. We're going to be practicing all these tools quite a bit throughout our time together. In fact, practice is another of your most important tools. The number one reason we don't work through our anxiety is we don't practice the tools we've learned that can help. So let's practice right here.

Negative thought: I'm an anxious parent, which means I'm failing myself and my kids.

Positive thought: I care so much about my kids. I've never wanted to get anything right as badly in my whole life. And I'm doing a much better job than I know. (That last sentence is my addition.)

Psychologist and author Dan Allender said in a conference I attended a few years ago that good parents get it right 50 percent of the time.[23] How's that for a statistic? Fifty percent of the time. As bright and conscientious and caring as you are, I know you're doing way better than that. And we're creating new neural pathways, even as you're reading this chapter, that are going to help you to be the parent and person you deeply long to be. You're doing great already!

Worry-Free Takeaways

1. Most parents today are prioritizing the mental and emotional health of their kids in a way previous generations didn't have the understanding or maybe even the motivation to do.
2. We always want to start with an understanding of where we are and what's happening inside of us.
3. The more we understand about worry and anxiety, the easier they are to fight.
4. Anxiety left untreated only gets worse.
5. Worry plays tricks.
6. Worry needs truth. And a whole lot of other tools too.
7. Every parent worries. Especially the good ones.

2

Understanding Ourselves

There is a well-known statement in the therapy world: We repeat what we don't repair. Or as Richard Rohr puts it, "If we do not transform our pain, we will most assuredly transmit it."[1] Gulp. Not sure about you, but I've still got some of my own pain on repeat. However, let me say this clearly at the beginning of this chapter: There is *so much* grace. This side of heaven, we will repeat. You will hear your mom's critical words coming out of your mouth at times with your kids. You'll notice your dad's flashes of anger inside of you when you feel out of control.

Our past hurts mixed with present pressure often dictate our future fear.

I think this formula is the very definition of sabotage for parents and what trips up the most well-intentioned, loving parents more than anything I know. The past and pressure can not only create more fear for you as a parent, but also hold you hostage as a person. More on that in the next chapter. But for now, please hear me again: *There is grace.* And there is also so much hope. We do *not* have to be defined by our past. The more we understand our past, the more freedom we can find from it. The more we understand the pressure we're operating under, the less power that pressure has. And the less both end up creating future fears with our kids.

I'm going to venture to say that I believe this might be the most important chapter of the book. I know . . . *I know.* You're probably like so many parents who sit in my office and make statements like "If my son only had the right tools," or "I need the right tools to help with my daughter." I do believe *tools* is the most frequently used word at Daystar these days. Tools are important—crucial, even, in this fight against worry and anxiety. And we're going to talk about *lots* of them in the second section of this book. But if we don't understand ourselves and the root causes of our anxiety, we'll keep repeating and transmitting that anxiety to the kids we love.

So let's go back to our five things. Five things about anxiety that I believe are not only true but transformational. Five things related to your past and the pressure I believe every parent is under today. And five things I believe will help you not only experience grace, but also offer more grace to yourself and to your children.

Five Ways We've Gotten to an Anxious Place

1. Anxiety is rooted in our past.

In *Raising Worry-Free Girls*, I reported this from my research:[2]

> Children of anxious parents are as much as seven times more likely to develop an anxiety disorder than children who don't have anxious parents, according to a study by researchers at John Hopkins University. [3] In their book *Anxious Kids, Anxious Parents*, psychologist Reid Wilson and psychotherapist Lynn Lyons report that "up to 65 percent of children living with an anxious parent meet the criteria for an anxiety disorder." [4] Based on these and numerous twin studies, researchers have been able to determine that anxiety is, in fact, inheritable. But, according to [Dr. Tamar] Chansky, genetics only determines 30–40 percent of the anxiety we're seeing today, with the rest related to environment and [other] factors. [5]

Anxiety is inheritable. In every parenting seminar I teach, I talk about how parents with anxiety are seven times more likely to have a child who struggles with it themselves. It's an important fact to know for the kids we love. But you are one of those grown-up kids. And if you're dealing with your own worry and anxiety now, there is a great chance it was passed to you from your parents.

What do you know about your family history? Your mom or dad's mental health? What about your grandparents? Your siblings? Remember, anxiety often doesn't look like anxiety; it can appear in many different forms, such as perfectionism, negativity, anger, or more obvious signs of worry. It also could have been at the root of a parent's alcoholism or other addiction. Remember, mental health resources weren't as accessible or acceptable when most of our parents were growing up. So many of us are still trying to piece together what was underneath the emotion and atmosphere of our families of origin.

The atmosphere certainly deserves its own conversation. Remember, genetics make up only 30–40 percent of the causes of anxiety. The rest is dictated by temperament, life experiences, parental modeling, and parenting styles.[6] We're going to talk more about temperament in the next chapter. For now, I want to address your life experiences growing up—what your parents were modeling for you and the parenting styles they employed in your home. All those factors contributed to the atmosphere of your growing-up years and continue to affect your emotional health today.

When you think back on your childhood home, was there tension? Did it seem to be emotionally charged? Was that charge more around your mom or your dad or both? How did your parents relate to each other? Were both parents present in your home? How did each of your parents relate to you? How comfortable were your parents with the expression of emotion? What emotions were expressed most often by them? What about by you? What emotions were acceptable? What were you encouraged for? What was discouraged in you? How safe did you feel emotionally as a child and teenager in your home? What was your role in the family?

Research says that many kids who grow up with anxiety have parents who

- are overly cautious of the world,
- are very critical and set unreasonably high expectations,
- are emotionally insecure or dependent themselves, or
- suppress expression of feelings and self-assertiveness.[7]

Do any of those descriptions fit your family when you were growing up? My guess is that more than a few do. I really want you to answer the questions in this chapter. I'd love for you to sit with them and even grab the workbook that goes along with this book, *The Worry-Free Parent Workbook*. I also want to point out, however, that I'm not trying to blame your parents. They were very likely doing the best they could with the resources they had and were probably doing a significantly better job than their parents before them. There is grace for them too—sometimes found more easily with a little help from a counselor. The reality is that our experiences shape us. Even from a neurological standpoint, the circuits of our brains aren't completely determined by heredity. They're also shaped by our experiences and the way we think and act[8]—which is freeing for the future, but can be limiting in the present, based on those hurtful pasts.

Basically, the way we think and act has a great deal to do with the way we were taught to think and act, as well as the ways we learned to emotionally survive our growing up years. Those old neural pathways, remember? And some of that teaching and your need for survival might have taken place at the hands of someone other than your parents.

Maybe you were bullied as a kid. Maybe you were abused by an uncle or neighbor. Maybe you had a close friend die in high school. According to the American Psychological Association, more than two-thirds of children report experiencing some type of trauma by the age of sixteen. A traumatic event is "one that threatens injury, death, or the physical integrity of self or others and also causes horror, terror, or helplessness at the time it occurs.

Traumatic events include sexual abuse, physical abuse, domestic violence, community and school violence, medical trauma, motor vehicle accidents, acts of terrorism, war experiences, natural and human-made disasters, suicides, and other traumatic losses."[9] In other words, trauma includes life experiences that alter our brain circuitry and can set us up to be more prone to anxiety. Tamar Chansky, one of the leading authorities on anxiety, states that "a child who has experienced a traumatic event is *twice as likely* to develop some type of difficulty—whether anxiety, depression, or a behavioral disorder."[10]

Again, more than two-thirds of children report experiencing trauma by age sixteen. And again, I'm not just talking about your kids. I'm talking about you. Your story is important. Your pain is important. And the way you coped with that pain has a profound impact on who you are and how you parent today.

How did you cope? By becoming hypervigilant? By trying not to feel? Trying not to need or want anything? For most of us, our natural tendency was to try to escape what hurt us. We escaped by ignoring it. Avoiding it. By watching so closely that the same kind of pain never takes us by surprise again. Driving ourselves deeper into activities or distracting ourselves with not-so-great decisions. In other words, we learned to protect ourselves. We made promises to ourselves based on our experiences of hurt.

I'll never make the same mistake.

I'll never feel that way again.

I'll never trust again.

What kinds of promises did you make? If it's hard to remember, go back to a hurtful or traumatic event or memory. How did you feel? How did you work through it? Or how did you choose to forget it? How did that event or memory change you?

Let me give you an example from a real-life parent I know.

Her dad only spanked her one time in her life. She was seven years old and had a neighbor who was more acquaintance than friend. He frequently knocked on her door and asked her to play. Something about him made her uneasy, but she was too young and too illiterate in the language of intuition to trust herself. So she played with him more than she really wanted to. On only one occasion, she told him no. She said she was too tired and didn't feel up to playing that day. It was the one time in her life that her dad spanked her.

Now, she wouldn't consider this memory traumatic, even though it was deeply upsetting to her. And the story doesn't go the way you might have imagined. The neighbor didn't go on to sexually abuse her or hurt her in any way, although her intuition was later verified in the way his life unfolded.

It was her father's anger that left its mark on her. At seven years of age, she learned that she was to set her needs and intuition aside and say yes, even if her feelings told her differently. To this day she continues to have anxiety around saying no or leaving people out. *I'll never make that mistake again.* And now she's making sure her children don't either. She struggles with every birthday party and every sleepover to make sure not to hurt the feelings of any child or any parent in their community.

Here's the backstory: This little girl's neighbor had hurdles that made it difficult for him to make friends. Her father had the same hurdles when he was a little boy. The hurdles had nothing to do with the girl's discomfort around her neighbor. She was kind and maybe even more compassionate to him because of them. But those hurdles had everything to do with her dad's reaction. He saw himself and his own insecurities and childhood rejection in the boy. The father's anger was more about himself than about his daughter.

Big or small, we make promises to avoid the same kinds of hurt and trauma we experienced when we were growing up. Those experiences and the hurt that follows shape us. They shape our brain circuitry, and they often shape our anxious view of ourselves and the world.

Anxiety is passed down . . . through the genes of our parents, through the environments of our homes, and through our experiences during our formative years. But that's not all. Anxiety is not only caused. It's maintained.

Dr. Edmund Bourne, in *The Anxiety and Phobia Workbook*, says anxiety is caused by a myriad of factors including heredity, childhood circumstances, biological causes, short-term causes, and something called maintaining causes.[11]

2. Anxiety maintains itself in the present.

According to Bourne, maintaining causes are avoidance of phobic situations, reliance on safety behaviors, anxious self-talk, mistaken beliefs, withheld feelings, lack of assertiveness, lack of self-nurturing skills, muscle tension, stimulants and dietary factors, high-stress lifestyle, low self-esteem, and lack of meaning or sense of purpose.[12] In other words, maintaining causes are living life—especially in these years. Particularly as a parent.

Which of these feel especially true for your life? We'll skip the stimulants and dietary factors for now and leave those to the physicians and nutritionists, although they are obviously significant. The muscle tension—we're all feeling more than a little tense these days. For example, how tense are your shoulders as you're reading this question? Yep. All of us. We'll talk about some tools that can help with the tension in the Help for the Present section. But for now, let's dig a little deeper with the other maintaining cause. We may not have had a lot of choice with the origins of our anxiety, but the maintenance of it is another issue entirely, and a very important one to understand if we're going to stop the spread.

Research suggests that the two primary coping strategies for anxiety are escape and avoidance.[13] It certainly makes sense in your parenting. You love your kids and don't want to see them hurt or in distress. Your job is to keep them safe in a world that doesn't feel very safe. So when they come upon those distressing situations, the most natural (and what feels like parental) response in the world is to help them escape. In addition, if you had to say what percentage of your anxiety is based on your child's potential suffering, what percentage would you assign? My guess is that it's quite high. And therefore, helping the kids we love escape and avoid doesn't just shield *them* from anxiety. It shields us as well. Or so our own worry monsters tell us. But escape and avoidance are perpetual. We calm the anxiety by escaping in the moment, but then we have to continue to escape to keep the anxiety at bay.

■ What is one thing you're avoiding in your own life or in the lives of your kids so that they (and invariably you) don't have to deal with the anxiety that follows?

When you read the words *safety behaviors*, what comes to mind? Many safety behaviors are what we think of when we envision obsessive-compulsive types of behaviors. *OCD* is a term often jokingly referenced in our culture. Not that we're making light of the disorder, but making light of ourselves. In reality, those jokes can be reflective of a discomfort we feel or even a low-lying fear that we do have obsessive-compulsive types of symptoms. According to the National Institute of Mental Health, "Obsessive-Compulsive Disorder (OCD) is a common, chronic, and long-lasting disorder in which a person has uncontrollable, reoccurring thoughts ('obsessions') and/or behaviors ('compulsions') that he or she feels the urge to repeat over and over."[14] The compulsions are considered safety behaviors, in effect meant to quiet our obsessive, anxious thoughts. Checking our locks, washing our hands, touching surfaces in a certain order. Rituals, even some routines, are considered safety behaviors. For parents, those safety behaviors often transfer to the kids we love. Now we're not only concerned about washing our hands but washing theirs as well. We certainly want to make sure we've checked and rechecked his lifejacket before getting in the water. It's not the checking that's the problem—it's the rechecking. It's the compulsion to do a certain behavior, then do it again "just to be safe." The concern with safety behaviors, for kids and for us, is that we learn to trust the safety behavior (or the compulsion) more than we trust ourselves. And, just as with escape and avoidance, we end up giving the mouse a cookie over and over again. Safety behaviors quickly become perpetual.

■ What safety behavior do you use or participate in with the kids you love that is potentially maintaining anxiety?

Anxious self-talk—how many times a day do you catch yourself talking to yourself in a negative, critical, or overly concerned way? Let's find out. Today, I want you to try to catch yourself doing this. How many times do you find yourself saying, "Well, that was stupid"? Or "You can't do that." Even "Your kids can't, so you need to step in." Research says that anxious parents use more catastrophic and threat-related language, such as "That sounds terrible" or "That's impossible," likely without even being aware of it.[15] One of the most important tools we're going to talk about in the Help for the Present section is replacing anxious self-talk. But for now, it's important to know that the anxious self-talk also perpetuates anxiety. Those negative comments don't help us. They simply create neurological paths that become well-worn, and our disbelief in ourselves only gets stronger.

> How often are you talking to yourself anxiously or negatively? What kind of language do you use? Is it harsher or more negative than you would use with a friend?

Mistaken beliefs have a similar effect. As we said before, anxiety distorts. We look for the negative (confirmation bias) to confirm the theory of our mistaken, distorted belief. We then talk negatively to ourselves (anxious self-talk), which only solidifies those mistaken beliefs. They can be beliefs about ourselves, about our kids, or about the world. "You can't do it." "Your child can't do it." "It's too hard." "You're not equipped for that." "You're not equipped for this, as a parent."

For example, you might think, *The other mothers are all talking about my child.* Then, when you see the other mothers in the hallway talking quietly, you think, *I knew it. They're talking about how she was mean to the other girl on the playground. Now they think she's a terrible kid and I'm a terrible parent.* Any one of us is operating under hundreds of mistaken beliefs per day. We're going to talk about those in the help section too. But, again, mistaken beliefs keep us caught in the perpetuity and misery of the anxiety cycle.

> What is one mistaken belief you've been operating under recently?

How are you doing with any withheld feelings? What about a lack of assertiveness? Did you read either of those on Dr. Bourne's list and think, *Uh-oh?* Withheld feelings and a lack of assertiveness can easily go hand in hand, especially for a parent. Are you familiar with the Enneagram personality types? It's a study we use regularly at Daystar in our counseling practice. If you haven't researched it, we believe it's a helpful tool in understanding ourselves and those we love. I often use the Enneagram in family counseling. When I do, I give each of the family members sitting in my office a test to determine which type they are. Beforehand, we always go over a few Enneagram-related guidelines. One of those is from *The Enneagram Made Easy* by Renee Baron and Elizabeth Wagele. The authors recommend answering the test questions based on who you were before the age of twenty-five.[16] Most parents will immediately laugh and say, "Who can remember that far back?" I'm not sure the reasoning behind that particular age cutoff for the authors, as Enneagram theorists. What I tell parents, however, is that much of who you are shifts when you become a parent. I believe that if solely based on your life as a parent, most individuals, moms in particular, would register as either a 2, the helper, or a 9, the peacemaker. As a parent, you just have to be more about the needs of others than about your own on most days. Withheld feelings and a lack of assertiveness are often nonnegotiables when you have a screaming toddler or a grumpy adolescent you're shuffling to three activities in one afternoon. There isn't much time or space for you to feel or to have your own opinion, let alone assert it, unless the assertions are in the form of consequences. Now, I agree that both withheld feelings and a lack of assertiveness do maintain anxiety. I see evidence every day in my counseling office, with children and with parents. But I understand the inherent challenges of expressing your feelings and being assertive specific to parents. I also understand that the longer we withhold feelings and don't voice our opinions, the harder those feelings and opinions can be to even access. And we've given the mouse of anxiety yet another cookie to perpetuate the problem.

Let's keep going with the mouse-and-cookie idea, because I think the last few maintaining factors certainly have their own perpetuation cycle. (I hope you've read that wonderful children's book *If You Give a Mouse a Cookie* by Laura Joffe Numeroff, by the way, and get the reference. If not, you can imagine what would happen if you did. One cookie turns into two, which turns eventually into a perpetual mouse problem—or anxiety, for our purposes.)

A lack of self-nurturing was the next idea Dr. Bourne mentioned. In a devotional I recently read called *A Rhythm of Prayer*, Sarah Bessey wrote, "Every once in a while, the best way to keep moving through your life is to do something that seems impossibly kind for your own soul."[17] When was the last time you did something impossibly kind for your own soul? My guess is that it's been a minute. Again, who has time? I sat with a group of friends who all happen to be moms the other day. One mentioned taking her child to therapy and then said, "I'm actually the one who probably needs the therapy." Another immediately said, "Yeah, right. Who has time for that?" And they all laughed in unison. You have to make time to do those things—whether it's therapy, going for a walk, reading a book, or watching a favorite show. A lack of self-nurturing quickly turns into a high-stress lifestyle, another item on the good doctor's list, and one that I would guess you're living right now. You would probably shrug it off and say, "It's just the season of life we're in right now." But if we were sitting together and you described your daily, weekly, or monthly soccer season, music lesson, play practice schedule of a life to me, I would be pretty exhausted just hearing about it. It's a lot. I don't just have a feeling that it is. I know so from sitting with thousands of parents who are just like you.

Most of us are living a high-stress lifestyle these days, not only to our detriment but to the detriment of our kids as well. It's even sometimes a reflection of status in our society. As a therapist who has watched the chaos of family life intensify over the last three decades, I happen to think it is one of the most significant contributors to the epidemic of anxiety among both parents and kids. And that high-stress lifestyle only feeds the next maintaining factor of low self-esteem. It's never enough. You can always do more. One more activity your child wants to participate in. One more round of being the room mom or dad at your child's school. All the other parents seem to do it, and they do it looking fabulous and unruffled—with organic, homemade cookies to boot. They're not losing it over lost shoes in the morning on the way to school. You're just not the parent you wish you were. And now you've perpetuated yourself through the list all the way to a lack of meaning.

▓ **Where are you in the cycle? Of all the maintenance factors, which ones are you more prone to?**

Again, I wish we were sitting in the same room. Just writing this section feels tough to me, because I would imagine it's touching on the weariness you feel. The discouragement. The overwhelmedness. The too many mice and too many cookies that not only make you feel anxious but defeated. That is not where we're going to end. You have so much purpose. Your life has meaning. You're doing a really great job as a parent, even without organic, homemade cookies. There are just a few particular challenges that come along with the path you're on and the job you've been given.

3. Anxiety is always searching for context.

In her book *Operating Instructions*, Anne Lamott recounts driving home from the hospital with her son, Sam. "The first thing happened the day my friend Peg and I brought him home from the hospital, during what for me felt like the most harrowing ride a person could take through San Francisco. The first time we hit a pothole, I thought, Well, that's that, his neck just snapped; we broke him."[18]

Do you remember the first time it hit you? Maybe it was driving home from the hospital for you too. Or maybe it was the first time you tried a swaddle before you even got home and you thought, *It's too hard. I'll never make it as a parent.* And you've had the same thought thousands of times in your parenting journey since.

I can't tell you how many parents say to me, "I never had anxiety until I became a parent." In all my research on anxiety, one of the ideas that came up repeatedly is that anxiety is always searching for context. It's certainly been true in my counseling practice. In fact, I could make a timeline of what kids worry the most about through each developmental stage.

For younger elementary-aged kids, it's typically either separation from their parents or something bad happening to a parent. For older elementary-aged kids, it's often getting sick, flying on a plane, or spending the night away from home. For middle schoolers, it usually becomes more social in nature and involves others who either don't like them or no longer want to be friends with them. For high school kids, worries often center around either their social lives or performance—whether academic, athletic, or any activity in which they're involved and could fail or embarrass themselves greatly. For every age, a child's worries center around the worst thing they can imagine happening. For an eight-year-old, it's developmentally appropriate to be afraid of losing your mom. For a thirteen-year-old, it makes sense to be afraid of tripping in the state track meet. For a fifteen-year-old, not much sounds scarier than for your friends to think you're annoying. Anxiety is always searching for context, and that context is typically what matters most to any of us at any age—which brings us full circle to you, as a parent.

In the help section, we're going to talk about the importance of naming your anxiety. What I really want you to do is personify it, like the younger kids calling it the Worry Monster and teenagers calling it the Worry Whisperer. There are a few reasons we want to separate anxiety's voice from ours and give it a name. But one reason, for now, is to understand how smart anxiety is. It's creative in its approach and tenacious in its impact. Anxiety is looking for context, the context that matters most to us, and when it finds that context, it hangs on as long and as hard as it possibly can.

4. Anxiety is a response to cumulative stress over time.

I'd like for you to do a little experiment for me. I want you to rate your current stress level on a scale of one to ten. Now I want you to think back five years. If your son is fifteen, think about when he was ten, for example. What number would you give it then? What about five years before that? When was the last time you remember having a stress level under five? My guess is that it's been at least a decade—if not back to life before the responsibilities of parenting and adulthood.

Anxiety is a response to cumulative stress over time.[19] It sounds like you've had a good deal of stress for a long time. We all have. Again, culturally, stress has become synonymous with success. Our busyness reflects our importance, in the eyes of the world. But it's too much. It's too much for you and too much for your kids.

The longer I do this work, the more I believe that the anxiety epidemic is due, in large part, to the busyness epidemic of our society, in addition to the stress it causes. When I think back on my childhood, I think about riding my bike around the neighborhood, playing outside till dark with my friends, and spending a little time (maybe) on homework. Today, kids have swim practice before school and another sports practice after. They make it home just in time for dinner and in time to spend four hours on homework. And then we don't understand why they're stressed. It's too much for them. If I could change the pressure our kids face today academically, athletically, artistically, and in every I've-got-to-get-into-the-right-preschool-to-get-into-the-right-elementary-school-to-get-into-the-right-high-school-to-get-into-the-right-college-to-get-the-right-job way, I would. I wish life, for all kids, could go back to an hour of homework a day, one practice per week, and the rest of the time just playing outside. I think they would be healthier. I think parents would be healthier too. Because not only are you watching your kids operate under that stress, but you're having to drive to the practices. You're having to help with the math homework that you weren't even doing in college. You're having to go to four performances of the play in one weekend. We're having to facilitate the lifestyle that is breeding more anxiety for the kids we love. And that's before we ever think about what's on our own plates—or in our buckets, as I typically like to think.

I love to ask kids about their buckets. If you had a bucket in front of you with all the stress in your life right now, what would be in it? What would weigh more? What would weigh less?

I don't believe you're just carrying the cumulative stress of your life. I believe you're also carrying the cumulative stress of the lives of the little people you love. And it's just too much. Too much to carry and too much pressure.

5. Anxiety breeds under pressure.

Not too long ago, I was driving through a neighborhood in Nashville and came upon a church billboard. I'm typically very entertained by church billboards. With this one, I was anything but entertained. On it was a sign advertising an upcoming parenting seminar called "Perfect Parenting." I'm not kidding. I wanted to ram my car into the sign.

You see, I sit with too many anxious parents who feel pressure to be perfect. The pressure comes from all around them . . . other parents, social media, their own parents, even their children. And it also, maybe even more so, comes from inside.

Let me remind you of something you already know: There is no perfect parent. I don't care what they look like splashed all over social media. I don't care how much your own daughter says, "If only you were more like so-and-so's mom." So-and-so's mom, who has the greatest trips in the world, doesn't feel so great inside on some days either. She feels like she's failing too. We just live in a culture that values veneer over vulnerability.

One of my all-time favorite quotes is from the renowned and highly astute theologian C. S. Lewis. In *The Horse and His Boy*, he writes, "Justice shall be mixed with mercy. You shall not always be an Ass."[20] I laughed out loud when I read that quote. Now, truth be told, the character was actually speaking to an ass—er, donkey. But obviously, Lewis purposefully phrased the sentence the way he did. I believe he was speaking to the ass inside us all, which is exactly why it made me laugh. I'm certainly grateful for his honest appraisal of me and the hope contained therein.

I posted the quote on social media, and to date, I think I've gotten more responses from that quote than any of the other thousands of things I've put up over the years. Of course, I felt I had to clarify the ass-donkey situation because . . . pressure. And only one person commented that they were glad I did. I believe every other person who hit like or share or commented on his or her own ass-ness felt known and safe—and the same kind of relieving hope I did.

Parenting is the hardest job you will ever have. It will bring out your own ass-ness more than any other job. It will also bring you more joy. And likely more sorrow. Each is inextricably linked in our humanity. But I do believe a lot of our failures stem from our own pasts, our own anxious contexts, and the pressure that pervades life these days. And I believe just as strongly as Lewis that justice shall be mixed with mercy. I won't always be an ass. And neither will you.

One of my favorite authors and psychologists, Dan Allender, says that our stories reveal both brokenness and beauty. He also says our stories are just as much about light as they are about dark. And that the fundamental human experience is limitation.[21] The most universal human experience is limitation as well. We are broken and beautiful. And the more we try to run from the brokenness, the more pressure we feel and the more our anxiety grows.

I have a small sign hanging in my office that I hope every parent—and every child—who walks through my door sees. I want to remember to see it every single day. It says what my dear friend and our executive director at Daystar, Melissa, tells the kids at Hopetown, a summer retreat program for kids in counseling at Daystar: "He doesn't ask us to try harder. He just makes us new."

We start with the past. We look back, not to dwell on the past, but to better understand where and who we are in the present. Brad Montague, in a delightful book called *Becoming Better Grown-ups*, writes, "Now and again, we could all benefit from a visit into our pasts. Light could be shed on where our insecurities came from. Where our anger began. Where our joy was lost. Bringing this understanding of who we are into the present can help shape the way we embrace everything."[22]

It helps us understand ourselves and the origins of our anxiety. It helps us understand the context created the day these amazing little people came into our lives. It helps us to look at the stress and the pressure we're living under today. Our past hurt impacts the pressure we feel in the present, which then impacts our future fear with the kids we love. In that future, we can feel defeated or we can know hope. And hope is exactly where we're heading. We won't always be asses. He just makes us new. And He is already using His Spirit and the work you're doing in this book to do that. You're doing great. Keep going. "There has never been the slightest doubt in my mind that the God who started this great work in you would keep at it and bring it to a flourishing finish" (Philippians 1:6 MESSAGE).

Worry-Free Takeaways

1. Our past hurts mixed with present pressure often dictate our future fear.
2. If we don't understand ourselves and the root causes of our anxiety, we'll keep repeating and transmitting that anxiety into the lives of the kids we love.
3. Anxiety is rooted in our past.
4. Anxiety maintains itself in our present.
5. Anxiety is always searching for context.
6. Anxiety is a response to cumulative stress over time.
7. Anxiety breeds under pressure.

3

How Anxiety Impacts You

A mom recently said to me, "I'm so worried about not getting it right with my kids that I'm not even being a parent." The mom who said these words actually is a great parent. But she's so afraid she's failing her kids that she can't even enjoy the process. You may feel the same way. In fact, I would guess that you likely do from time to time. And much more so recently. In my thirty-plus years of counseling, I've never seen parents feel as much pressure *or* as much like failures as they do today. I've never had as many parents in tears in my office. And I've certainly never seen as many parents who live in a perpetual state of worry.

How would you say worry affects you, as a parent? I certainly believe, after sitting with parents day in and day out in my office, that not only do you worry more because you are a parent, but those worries affect you differently as well.

We're about to get to our five things. But let me stress one thing that supersedes all the others. If anxiety is looking for context, it hit the jackpot when you had children. Every other anxiety-provoking context you come across in your life, you're able to take breaks from, to walk away. You are even able to *remove* certain anxiety-provoking situations (or people) from your life, when necessary. But you can't escape these little people you love so big—not the fact that they're in your life or the fact that you love them so deeply. And as we address some harder realities in this chapter and the next of how your anxiety affects you and your children, I want you to remember this foundational truth: You worry about them because you care so much.

I talked in both of my girls' books about how all the anxious children I have ever counseled have a few things in common: They're bright, they're conscientious, they try hard, and they care deeply. They're really the coolest kinds of kids. It's just that they can't turn the volume down on all of that care and trying hard. It's the same phenomenon for all of us—whatever our age. Our blessings are often our curses flipped upside down. It's true for you as a parent too. Every anxious parent I've ever met is really bright and conscientious. You try hard. You care deeply. And you love your kiddos like crazy. That trio of traits is a life-changing gift for your children. But it comes with its share of curses too. We're going to talk about some of those in this chapter and the next. Don't worry—we'll follow them up with a whole lot of practical help to get back to the blessing that you are as a parent. But for now and throughout the next two chapters, I want you to continue to remember that the reason you worry is because of your care, your conscientiousness, and your great love for these little and big kids in your life.

Five Ways Anxiety Impacts You

1. Anxiety distracts us.

One of the things I hear parents say most often is how distracting anxiety is. In fact, I've learned through my work with kids and parents that anxiety and ADHD, particularly the inattentive kind, are almost identical symptomatically. Both cause restlessness, a lack of focus, difficulty regulating emotions, and even sleep impairment. Do any of those sound familiar? Even more specifically, have you ever found yourself

- not listening to your child because you're worried about what's happening next on your schedule?
- unable to remember the conversation you had with your daughter before the birthday party because you were concerned about how she would do once she got to the party?
- unable to laugh and play with your kids, simply because of all that's pressing in on you?

There are a million ways worry distracts us on a daily basis. But maybe one of the saddest is that it robs us of time connecting with the kids we love—really connecting in hear-their-words and look-them-in-the-eyes ways. That connection is foundational not only to building but to maintaining your relationship over the long haul. And the long haul really isn't long enough. We want to be present for these long days and short years. We want to be able to let go of our worries in a way that keeps us in the moment, instead of imagining the future years based more on our anxious distortions than on reality.

2. Anxiety makes us attach future meaning to present problems.

I hear parents do it every day in my office:

"I don't think I'm preparing my child well for the future."
"I haven't had him in travel sports, and now he'll never be able to keep up at a high school level."
"I haven't had her in enough Kumon classes or tutoring, and now she won't be able to get into the right school that will help her get into the right college."
"She didn't start cheerleading at four, and now we've lost our chance for her to ever make a competitive team."

The worries can be over what we believe we haven't offered them. The sports or academics or lessons or learning opportunities we believe we've missed that will hinder our child's future in

53

some life-altering way. Or the characteristics we haven't taught. The things we feel "all the other parents" have been doing that we haven't been able to get done. We haven't started chores. We haven't been saying our grateful lists at the dinner table.

We're not keeping up, which means our children won't be able to keep up—or measure up—in all the ways that will lead to their success, our anxiety tells us. But it's simply not true.

The worries can also be over skills or traits our kids currently lack.

> "Because he can't sit still in kindergarten means he'll never make it in grade school, and there's no way he'll be able to hold a job when he's older."
>
> "How will she ever be able to function as an adult when she doesn't keep her room clean now?"
>
> "If he's not responsible enough to remember to take out the trash at thirteen, why would I ever believe he'd be responsible enough to drive a car?"
>
> "She thinks about herself all the time as a middle schooler. I'm not sure how she'll ever be able to have a healthy, caring relationship with another person."

The list goes on and on. In our worry, we become fortune-tellers for our kids. We decide what's happening now will be happening five, ten, even twenty years from now. Or what's not happening now—either what we missed or the characteristics we believe they're missing—will handicap them for the rest of their lives.

Kids are developing people. Their job is to learn under our roof while they're still home with us and we can help them learn. Our job is to eventually raise healthy, well-functioning adults. *Eventually* is the key word. They are not those adults yet.

In terms of brain development, the last portions of our brains to develop are the frontal lobes, which house the executive functioning part of our brains. The frontal lobes help develop our working memories, dictate impulse control, help us think logically, manage our emotions, and plan for the future. In the last twenty years, neuroimaging research has taught us those frontal lobes may not be fully developed until approximately age twenty-five.[1] Your eight-year-old isn't capable of managing her emotions in the same way she will be at eighteen. Your twelve-year-old doesn't yet have the skills to carry the same responsibilities he will be able to at twenty. Your fourteen-year-old is somewhat narcissistic. It's a normal and even an important stopover on the journey of development and individuation for all kids. The narcissism will fade. He will get there. And so will she.

Unfortunately, when it comes to the kids we love, our worries take over and cause our shortsightedness to become long reaching. We decide, based on their own developmental immaturity, that something is wrong. They already should be able to _____ (fill in the blank). Rather than seeing the gap as a normal part of their development, we believe it's a character flaw. And worse still, one that will mark their lives, both personally and professionally, forever.

What is one way you've been fortune-telling about your child's life? What's a future, problematic meaning you've attached to an area in which they're still growing?

Your child is growing into who God has created him or her to be. It is a journey and one that takes many unexpected and messy twists and turns along the way. Think back on your own becoming. What were some of your missteps, and how have they impacted your adulthood? What were some of the clumsier, less mature moments, and how have those contributed to who you are? My guess is that all of them have folded into the strengths, the character, and the wisdom that now mark not only your life but your parenthood. The same will be true for your kids. Trust the process. Trust your child. And trust that there is Someone in charge who is a much better predictor of the future than you or I.

3. Anxiety makes us micromanage.

When I sit with parents of young children, a few of the words they often use to describe their kids are *controlling*, *demanding*, and *inflexible*. As a therapist, my job is to help parents look underneath the behavior of their children to the reasons for that behavior. As we talk further, it almost always turns out that these little controlling and inflexible kiddos are typically anxious. The times they erupt the most often are times of transition or unpredictability. I call them my exploders. You pick your daughter up from school and tell her the schedule you had gone over (repeatedly) at bedtime the night before has changed completely. You now have to run three errands before she can go home and resume the day she had planned. And she melts down. Now, I'm not sure about you, but if someone told me at three today that my day was going to look nothing like I thought and I had no control over it, I might melt down too—and my brain is fully developed.

In lieu of other coping strategies, control often becomes a primary one for children. When they feel out of control, they explode. Here's the hard truth: We adults are not that different. For many of us (hello, any other perfectionists out there), control is still our primary coping strategy. We've just figured out how to make it work and look a little prettier. We can package our lives so that we (mostly) stay in control, can (mostly) manage our days the way we would like, and (mostly, once again) maintain our composure. That is, you could until you had kids. And then everything changed.

In the world of parenting, there is a long list of the things you can't control. You can't control their behavior. You can't control their words. You can't control their responsiveness or lack of it with their grandparents. You can't control their choices. And possibly worst on the list is that you can't control their hurts. You can't protect them from all the pain that life will inevitably bring. But we sure give it our all in trying.

When we can't control the big things, we find our own little things to control. We can't control whether other children like our kids, but we can control what play group they're a part of and which children they're in school with, and even do our best to control which birthday parties they're invited to. We can't control their grades, but we can control their school projects by stepping in and taking just a little more ownership than the teacher needs to know about. We can't control their athletic performance, but we can set them up for what we consider success with lessons every day after school and a few extra calls to the coach of the "right" team. We can't control the friends they choose in high school, but we can drop little hints about the ones we have some concerns about, thinking that maybe this time they'll listen.

Because you're a parent, you feel anxiety. Because you feel anxiety, you try to control that which you can't control. The control doesn't work. So we try harder. The anxiety gets bigger. We get more tense. We become more intense. And we micromanage.

Anxiety plus intensity equals micromanaging.

We'll talk more about what micromanaging looks like and how it impacts the kids we love in the next chapter. But for now, suffice it to say, if you know, you know.

It's hard to recount just one story of a parent who is anxious, intense, and micromanaging. I honestly see so many in my office. The micromanaging may be around grades. It may be about friendships. Or about sports. It may be about a child's weight. Or a child's faith. Decisions. Level of responsibility. I have had multiple (and usually repetitive) conversations with anxious parents over every one of those subjects and more.

You may have read the above paragraph and thought, *Well, I do worry about those things, but doesn't every parent who is intentional?* Yes. Absolutely. Worry is normal. Perseverating is not. Perseverating is finding ourselves still worrying that *maybe he's just missing it* even after the teacher told us at the parent-teacher conference, "He really is doing fine in school." Or thinking our child needs counseling, even after the counselor insists she has made a lot of progress and is ready for a break.

Just this week, I met with a dad of a fourteen-year-old girl. Within the first two minutes of our time together, I noticed his intensity. It was palpable. He was concerned about his daughter's lack of engagement with the family. He said she had recently become more withdrawn, less responsive, and more selfish. I described to him what I think typical development looks like for girls his daughter's age and why we call them the "narcissistic years" in our book *Raising Girls*.[2] I told him the story of a sixteen-year-old girl who told me that it was like she "faded" during those years. She described thinking about herself so much that she couldn't seem to get out of it to interact with others. I would only add that she did sparingly (and eye-rollingly) interact with her parents. But like with most girls in the narcissistic years, their interaction was more ambivalent and angry than positive. The same is true for the overwhelming majority of adolescent girls I've seen over the years. Every one of them could be described as more withdrawn, less responsive, and more selfish. Nevertheless, you can imagine what this perseverating dad did. He persisted. "She's lost her confidence, and she just seems like a different child." "Yes, as are all adolescents, to some degree," I tried to reassert. After fifty minutes of me trying to convince him that everything his daughter and their family were going through was normal, he still insisted that his daughter come to counseling. Perseverating. In the absence of evidence or even with evidence to the contrary, we simply can't let our concerns go.

If you have found yourself in the last few paragraphs, I want you to know that you are one of the most important reasons I'm writing this book. I have had you in my mind and heart through every page. So I want you to hear me speak very directly—and very gently—to you here.

I believe parents who micromanage have the best of intentions. I believe you are spending every ounce of your energy trying to create the best life possible for your child. I believe your heart is for them not to hurt, not to fail, not to feel the things you felt and sometimes still feel on the inside. The truth is you are not helping your child. In fact, you're doing the opposite of what you've set out to do. And my worry is that you're going to bring more damage to your relationship than help to your kids.

I want to take a minute to tell on myself here. I'm a micromanager. Remember, I'm a perfectionist, a type 1 on the Enneagram. I micromanage, both personally and professionally. I'd like to say I'm a micromanager in recovery, but I don't think I'm there yet. But I am a micromanager who is learning. And here are two of the most important things I've learned about myself in the last few years:

1. I see what's wrong before I see what's right.
2. Detail does not exist for me.

As mentioned in the last chapter, we have a summer retreat program, Hopetown, for kids who are in counseling at Daystar. I'm the director of Hopetown, which means I'm the micromanager in residence. Several years ago, I had a staff member point out to me that I could be critical with our staff. Correction: She said I was critical. So I spent some time trying to reflect on her words and not react defensively. One morning, I walked outside before the kids were awake. As I looked around Hopetown and noticed all the basketballs that hadn't been put away and the cups that were left outside, I realized that I see what's wrong first. Always. In fact, I see what's wrong to such a degree that I often don't see what's right. And I wish that were just the case with basketballs and cups. It's true relationally for me as well, and it's one of the things about myself I pray about the most and work the hardest to fight.

I also have noticed that details don't exist for me. If I'm not consciously trying to do something different, I can place the same emphasis on the one cup left out on the picnic table as on the legally required health forms one of my counselors forgot to have signed by a parent. There are no minor infractions for me. I experience the same intensity about both. And sometimes the same anger, even if I believe that anger is only internal.

I don't see details in my work life or in my personal life. I see what's wrong more than I see what's right. I micromanage because I'm worried about everything going as well for everyone around me as it possibly can. I want the kids at Hopetown to have an amazing experience. I want my staff to feel encouraged (and to do the right thing). I want my family and friends to feel loved and believed in. I really do have the best of intentions. But those intentions are missed when I micromanage. Intensity does not invite relationship. It also doesn't communicate my trust in others or give them a chance to rise up and develop their own responsibility or resilience. Instead, I sabotage relationship. I come off as critical and more angry about being out of control and things not going the way I think they should instead of being free and connected. And I would guess the same might happen for you sometimes too.

Help is coming in the next section. Help to free us from the need to micromanage, so we can breathe easier and with less intensity. But first I want to tell you the one thing I tell micromanaging parents most often in my office these days:

Let the bottom 20 percent go.

I want you to think about your top ten concerns with your child right now, whether in the area of responsibilities or homework or even relationships. What are the battles you're choosing, and what is the bottom 20 percent of those battles? I want you to start to consciously let the bottom 20 percent go. I truly believe, for both of us, that as we learn to see details and let the little things go, our intensity will lessen, as will our need to micromanage, and maybe even our anger too.

4. *Anxiety makes us angry.*

One of my favorite things about meeting with parents is when they feel the freedom to tell on themselves. It's one of the reasons I wish you were sitting on the couch in my office right now, rather than reading this book. I would want you to feel it was safe to admit some of the things you might be feeling through these pages so far. I hope you know that it is. I hope you continue to experience that you're not the only one. You're not the only parent who micromanages, and you're certainly not the only parent who gets angry. And I mean embarrassingly, lose-your-mind, full-blown-toddler-in-reaction-to-your-toddler angry.

I have worked with a family for years, and the mom is one of the kindest and most intentional I know. She has four kids, the youngest of whom was recently adopted. I counsel her eight-year-old daughter, who is thrilled to now be a big sister. We'll call her Josie. One of my favorite Josie stories is when, right before her little sister came home, she looked at her mom and said, "Mom, I don't ever want her to feel like she's different from the rest of our family. Let's not tell her that she's adopted." This wise mom looked at Josie and said, "Honey, her skin is a different color than the rest of ours is. I think she'll figure it out."

Josie is delightful . . . and can be quite a stinker. You may have a Josie at home yourself. I recently had an appointment with Josie and walked downstairs to get her. As I got to the bottom of the stairs, her mom hopped up and said, "Sissy, I need a few minutes with you first." She came into my office and said, "I need to tell you what happened the other night before Josie comes in. I wanted you to hear it from me." She described the scene of a night after dinner, when the entire family was enjoying a quiet evening together in their den. The two brothers were playing a game not far from Josie, who was reading a book. The mom said, "After about twenty minutes, Josie put her book down. She was bored, which is never a good thing for Josie—or for us. She started trying to bother her brothers. She was teasing them, and then started trying to poke them. Her brothers nicely asked her to stop. Josie didn't stop. Her brothers asked again. She still didn't stop. Then her brothers asked me to step in. I looked at Josie and said, 'Josie, your brothers kindly asked you to stop. I want you to stop now.' She looked at me—and went right back to pestering her brothers. My first mistake was that I took a step toward Josie and said, 'Josie, I already told you once. STOP NOW.' Josie, in turn, took a step toward me and said, 'Why don't you make me?'" This intentional, well-meaning (and I might say anxious) mom said, "Sissy, I have no idea what happened. But all of a sudden, I was on top of her on the floor." Oops.

Obviously, I'm not saying our anger ever needs to become physical in any way with the kids we love. But what I am saying is that we all get angry—especially when we're anxious. This mom wanted the peaceful family night to continue. She wanted her sons to keep enjoying each other and became anxious when her plan and the family peace was thwarted. Anxious, and then angry.

When was the most recent time you became really angry? What about becoming really angry and then taking it out on your kids? I believe good parents have more shame around anger than anything else that happens behind the closed doors of homes all over the world. I also believe good parents get angry.

61

If you've ever been to a parenting seminar with my friend and colleague David Thomas and me, you've heard us say that anger is a secondary emotion. In other words, there is always another emotion lurking underneath anger. More often than not, I believe that emotion is anxiety. It's what I talk about on a daily basis with parents of angry little ones. Understanding that anxiety is at anger's root can create more compassion for them instead of frustration at them. The same is true for teenagers. The reason they explode at you when asked a simple question is often that they're anxious over all the pressure they're feeling academically, socially, athletically, and in so many other areas teenagers feel they have to excel today. I also believe strongly that anxiety is at the root of your anger too.

The rage you felt recently at your four-year-old son or fourteen-year-old daughter wasn't because you're a bad parent. It wasn't because you have a problem with your temper. It was because you have a context for and tendency toward worry.

You get angry rushing out the door to school. Your emotion comes out as frustration at your kids for not moving fast enough. (Okay, it is that too.) But it's much more about not wanting your kids to be tardy, to walk into school embarrassed, or to have to do Saturday school for another late morning. You get angry when your daughter forgets to feed the dog again. But it's more that you're falling into a little parental fortune-telling, and you're worried that forgetting to feed the dog means she'll forget to go to class when she's in college, which means she'll forget to be a responsible human being.

I talk to parents every day who are ashamed of their anger. Ephesians 4:26–27 says, "'In your anger do not sin': Do not let the sun go down while you are still angry, and do not give the devil a foothold." "In your anger" assumes that you will be angry. "Do not let the sun go down while you are still angry" means, again, that you will feel anger. It's a reality for all of us, especially for those of us who care deeply. It's what we do with that anger that makes a difference. We're told not to sin, not to hurt others with it, and not to hold on to it. Anxiety makes us more prone to all three. But what I want you to understand is that your anger does not mean you're a bad parent. It simply means that you're a parent who leans toward anxiety. And there is a great deal we can do to help you experience freedom from your anxiety that, in turn, frees you from the anger that's neither who you want to be as a parent or who I believe you truly are. Help is on the way.

5. Anxiety takes away our warmth and joy.

Before I started writing this chapter, I did a survey with parents on social media. I asked, "How does your anxiety impact you, as a parent?" The number one answer parents gave was "It takes away my joy." Has that been your experience? Can you feel it when anxiety slips in and takes over? How would you describe what that's like? How are you different, when anxiety is in the driver's seat, from who you believe you are as a parent? I'd like for you to make a list with two columns. On one side, make a list of who you are as your best parenting self. On the other, list who you are as your most anxious parenting self. When do you feel more of each?

In doing the research for *Raising Worry-Free Girls*, I learned that anxiety is linked to a lack of parental warmth.[3] It's also one of the things I see repeatedly in my office. Now, that's not to say that you are not warm. I believe you are. But I believe that when that old worry monster comes in and steals your joy internally, he steals your warmth externally. He does it to me too. When I'm in my most perfectionistic place, I'm usually trying to quell my feelings of anxiety with productivity. Consequently, I lose my warmth. In fact, I prioritize productivity over relationship when I'm in that space, though I'm not even aware of it at the time. But I'll catch myself thinking, *Sissy, you have to wait until that person stops talking, or even stops laughing, until you address the next item on the agenda.* I'm like a robot in those moments, albeit a highly productive one. However, I am anything but warm, which is the opposite of who I want to be.

Many anxious parents I meet with lack the same kind of warmth. It may be that productivity is at the top of the agenda. It may be character development. It may even be wanting their children to feel happy and confident and secure. But there is something . . . something in their minds that is not only distracting them but disconnecting them in the moment. I can feel, just being in their presence, that there is an internal list and that I'm not ticking off the list quickly enough. If I feel that, I'm confident the kids in their lives do as well.

Bob Goff (not related to me, by the way) says, "What constantly distracts us will eventually define us."[4] Anxiety distracts us. Anxiety makes us attach future meaning to present problems. It makes us micromanage. It makes us angry. It causes us to lose our joy internally and our warmth externally. It makes us people and parents who we don't want to be. But there is so much hope. While it feels like anxiety defines us, that anxious parent is not who we really are. It's not who we have to be. And it's certainly not what God wants for us.

I used to have a lot of anxiety around public speaking, dating back to fifth grade. I remember the first time I spoke in front of my class in social studies at Pulaski Academy. My face became so red with embarrassment that Mrs. Bennett sent me to the nurse to take my temperature. I had, in fact, blushed my way into a fever and was sent home. That fear hung around for many, many years—well after I had started speaking in front of crowds that sometimes numbered in the thousands. For years, I had to do something to center myself, to get my mind off of my red face or the fact that suddenly I couldn't seem to remember how to swallow. And this verse was always the one that brought me back to myself:

> God wants the combination of his steady, constant calling and warm, personal counsel in Scripture to come to characterize *us*, keeping us alert for whatever he will do next. May our dependably steady and warmly personal God develop maturity in you so that you get along with each other as well as Jesus gets along with us all.
>
> Romans 15:5–6 MESSAGE

It still makes me breathe a little more deeply just to read those words. My prayer is that they can be defining for me—and for you.

God wants the combination of His steady, constant calling and warm, personal counsel to come to characterize us. Not anxious, panicky parenting. Not fortune-telling, micromanaging perfectionism. God does not feel or do any of those things. And the good news is that we don't have to either. He wants you to experience *His* warm, personal, steady, constant calling, both as a parent and as a person. And if God wants it, we know He can make it happen. He can bring us back to who we want to be. He can free you to parent with more presence, more warmth, and more of the joy He has set before you. He's got this. But first, in the next chapter, let's dig a little deeper into how anxiety impacts the kids we love.

Worry-Free Takeaways

1. In my almost thirty years of counseling, I've never seen parents feel as much pressure and worry or feel like failures as much as they do today.
2. The reason you worry is because of your care, your conscientiousness, and your great love for these little and big kids in your life.
3. Anxiety distracts us.
4. Anxiety makes us attach future meaning to present problems.
5. Anxiety makes us micromanage.
6. Anxiety plus intensity equals micromanaging.
7. Anxiety makes us angry.
8. Anxiety takes away our warmth and joy.
9. God does not want you to feel that way.

4

How Your Anxiety Impacts Your Kids

By now you know that if you're a parent with anxiety, your kids are seven times more likely to deal with it themselves.[1] As we've addressed, part of this worrisome statistic is due to genetics. But much is also due to parenting styles. We've talked about how worry and anxiety impact you, as a parent. Now I want to discuss how your worry and anxiety impact your kids.

Have you ever seen the direct impact of your worry on your kids? Have you watched them shrink back from something you're afraid of? Have you heard their words of distrust of either the world or themselves that mimic your distrust of the world or yourself? We sure saw it in our offices during the pandemic. The most fearful kids consistently had the most fearful parents.

Worry and anxiety are both taught and caught. They're taught directly through the words we use and our behavior. They're also caught from a biological standpoint through something called mirror neurons. Mirror neurons are "tiny parts of the brain that allow us to empathize with others and understand what they're feeling."[2] Mirror neurons, according to a *Harvard Business Review* article, cause us to smile when we see another smile, or yawn when we see someone else yawn. But those neurons also pick up on stress and anxiety. A study out of the University of California, Riverside, found that if you are looking at someone who is both "anxious and highly expressive," there is a significant chance you'll feel those emotions too.[3] The same is true for our kids. You never have to tell your children to be afraid of snakes. When you see one on a hike and scream, your daughter's mirror neurons take note. Snakes are scary. She not only understands, but she feels the fear with you. Maybe you shrink back from social situations and withdraw behind your more extroverted family members. If so, your son's mirror neurons learn that social situations are anxiety-provoking and best to avoid. He feels the same social anxiety you do. The reality is that your child's brain is learning from you, even when you're unaware you're teaching.

Kids also catch our anxiety through a phenomenon called *social contagion*, which is another way emotions spread from one person to another.[4] *Harvard Business Review* reported research findings that simply observing someone who is stressed caused 26 percent of people in the study to show elevated levels of cortisol, which is considered our primary stress hormone. If the person experiencing stress was in a romantic relationship with the observer, the observer was 40 percent more likely to have elevated levels of cortisol.[5] You can imagine how our stress impacts the stress levels of the little people who look to us for stability, and whose brains aren't even fully developed.

You have likely experienced the effects of mirror neurons and social contagion at some point yourself. I do so most often with anxiety, although it can happen with other emotions too. I regularly find myself meeting with a parent, or sometimes in a social situation, thinking, *Why do I feel so anxious?* It typically takes me a few minutes to realize that I don't . . . or at least I didn't until I started talking with a visibly stressed or anxious person. Their anxiety spread right over to me through firing neurons and social contagion. Yours does with your kids too.

This chapter's five things are going to look a little bit different. In this chapter, I'm going to delve into the five primary ways I believe people parent out of their own anxiety: projecting, criticizing, rescuing, magnifying, and minimizing. We're going to call them something hopefully a little easier to relate to. But first, let me go ahead and say this: I think we all lean one direction or another, or maybe even several directions at once. We're all guilty. Often, how you lean is based on either what you believe you needed growing up or how you handle your own emotions today. We're going to talk about those ideas too. The more we understand about the directions we lean and how those directions impact our kids, the greater our chances for stopping the spread.

Five Ways the Anxiety of Parents Impacts the Anxiety of Kids

1. *Sidecar parenting*

"She's just like me. I struggled in the exact same ways when I was her age." I can't even begin to count the times I've heard parents say these words in my office. It's funny . . . it's typically said out of a concerned place, a desire to help kids have tools to battle their anxiety, but also with some kind of angsty pride. She's just a chip off the old anxious, panicky block. And what I picture with those parents is the Adam West Batman show I watched after school. Batman is on his motorcycle, with Robin crammed into the sidecar next to him. Batman is speeding recklessly through the streets of Gotham, outracing danger and outwitting every criminal who comes his way. In the meantime, I can't imagine how carsick Robin had to be.

▪ The Premise: My experience will be his experience

Many parents think, *Because this child is most like me, he'll feel anxious just as I did.* So we not only recognize the anxiety, but we sometimes overinterpret behaviors as anxious that might not necessarily be. In the therapy world, it's called projection, "the process of displacing one's feelings onto a different person."[6]

I had a young girl I worked with on and off for several years. Her parents were divorced, and it was her dad who brought her in. The first time I met her and her dad, he talked about how similar the two of them were. He said, "She just has so much anxiety. I did too, at her age. She won't do certain activities that I know she would like and probably do well. Her anxiety holds her back and seems to impact her confidence the most. She doesn't seem to believe that she can or is good enough. I'm just worried that the other girls don't like her because she doesn't assert herself."

Where It's Coming From: My own anxious past

Let me say that since I met these two kind individuals, my experience has been very different from the father's description. I experience this dad as unassuming. And I would actually describe his daughter as overconfident, much more like her mom. She does have some degree of anxiety, but also has a driven personality, which I think she potentially interprets as anxious because of her dad's words over the years. She's involved in a lot of activities and seems to feel very comfortable with the spotlight. I don't think I've ever seen her hang back, whether from an activity or from engaging socially. I worry more about her sounding like she's bragging to her friends, rather than appearing insecure. If I had to guess, I would say the child the father was describing in my office that first day was much more who he was at his daughter's age than his daughter.

What It Looks Like: Projection

Because her dad saw them as similar, he assumed his daughter must be having the same emotions and experiences he did. His own insecurities, at each stage of his daughter's development, were rising up in him afresh. He struggled with friendships because of his own self-consciousness and lack of confidence. The fact that his daughter is left out must be for the same reason. And then everything he sees—or we see—is through that lens. We're back to the confirmation bias we talked about in chapters 1 and 2. For this girl and for many I see, the tragedy is that our perception of what's going on, based on our own projections, can keep us from seeing what really is going on. Her dad can't help her with what is actually wrong because he's so locked into what he perceives is wrong. And sadly, that perception has now become his daughter's too.

■ **How It Affects Them: They jump on board, shut down, or rise up to take care of us**

In the case of this girl, she sees herself as her dad does. She's aware that she struggles some relationally. But she sees it as anxiety-based, rather than unawareness-based, as I do. She thinks her anxiety sometimes causes her friends not to include her. I believe her overconfidence and unawareness of it sometimes causes her friends not to include her.

In other cases, I see kids who do the opposite. When their parents are over-identifying and projecting, those parents often have more emotion than the child does. A dad is anxious his son won't make the football team, just like his own experience in high school. So he pushes. And pushes and pushes. He gets angry at his son for not practicing enough. Or a mom has more emotion over her daughter's exclusion from a group of friends than her daughter does. In both cases, the kids just stop talking. They stop sharing their worries with their parents. I have lost count of the number of kids who've told me, "I can't talk to my mom or dad about it anymore because they make a bigger deal out of it than I do." Or even worse, your children feel the need to take care of your feelings, rather than feeling their own.

I have a two-year-old nephew who is the light of my life these days. We were outside together not long ago. He had walked around the opposite side of the car from me to get in. All of a sudden, I couldn't find him. He hadn't gone far but had wandered across the neighbor's driveway—without a glance to see if a car was coming, I'm sure. I panicked. And then totally overreacted. I grabbed him and angrily put him in time-out. "Don't ever walk across the driveway again without a grown-up watching, Henry!" He immediately got so teary, put his little hands on either side of my face, and said, "Be okay, Diddy." I melted. My anxiety was definitely bigger than his because, well, he's two. But my anxiety was also bigger than the situation warranted. And sweet little two-year-old Henry felt the need to protect me. It's not a kid's job. And it's often not even about them when we start sidecar parenting—or aunt-ing, in my case.

2. Backhoe parenting

"I just don't understand what he does with his time. He sits and stares constantly. He can't remember his chores from week to week, and they're the same chores. I can't get him to focus on homework when he comes home from school. I want him to start on it right away, and he only wants to play. I just can't get him to focus."

This mom came to meet with me because she was concerned about her seven-year-old son's lack of productivity. She felt she lived her life cleaning up after him—literally and figuratively. She was constantly reminding him about all the things, from school-work to making his bed to using soap when he took a shower. She is what I would consider a backhoe parent. Now, if any of you are professional backhoers, my backhoe knowledge is limited to what Henry has been teaching me. But according to Wikipedia, "A backhoe digs by drawing earth backwards, rather than lifting it with a forward motion like a person shovelling."[7] In layman (or non-toddler-age boy) terms, the backhoe has a bucket that digs from the rear, rather than the front.

The Premise: Her failure is my failure

Backhoe parents have an underlying anxiety that their child is missing it . . . whatever *it* is. The child is not responsible enough, like the boy described above. She's not kind enough, so I have to check on her behavior at a friend's house. He's not a good enough friend, so I've got to explain to him after most conversations with his peers how he should have handled himself differently. Digging from behind to clean up their failures because that failure is a reflection of my own.

Where It's Coming From: My own self-critical voice

I think most of us who are anxious fall into one of two catego-ries: catastrophizer or criticizer. We're going to talk more about the catastrophizers in chapter 6. But I want to talk a little about the criticizers here. I am one, so I'm afraid it doesn't take me long to know one. If you are a criticizer, here are two important things I know about you: (1) It's not who you want to be. In fact, I would guess that you get mad at yourself regularly for the ways you find yourself picking at your child. You don't mean to. But you're worried. He or she genuinely needs help. (2) Every anxious parent I've ever met who is critical of their kids is even more critical of themselves.

The way you talk to yourself will inevitably be the way you talk to your child.

We're going to come back to that idea in the last section of the book with hope for your own critical voice. I don't want you to live there one more day—for your kids' sakes and for your own sake. It's too much. It's hurting you, even if you're not allowing yourself to see it. And it is hurting these kids you love so dearly.

What It Looks Like: Control and criticism

In our Intentional Parenting seminar, my colleague David Thomas spends a few minutes specifically addressing dads about sports. He says he constantly hears boys who talk about not wanting to ride home from games with their dads. Many of those car rides are versions of the backhoe idea. The fathers are cleaning up their sons' athletic messes, in their minds, by telling them everything they did wrong and everything they should have done differently during the game. Control and criticism. Again, I realize it's coming from a good place. But the messaging is off. The sender's intention doesn't come through to the recipient. These boys don't feel helped by their fathers' instructions. They feel criticized.

Backhoe parents really do have good intentions: I don't want my child to fail, so I'm going to do everything I can not only to clean up their messes, but to make sure they don't fail again. We go over the game play by play. We stay on them constantly about responsibilities and all of the things they're not doing. We hover. We micromanage. And our frustration ends up making them feel like they're a failure.

■ **How It Affects Them: They feel criticized, like they can't measure up or please us**

When I met with the mom of the unproductive (in her eyes) son, I told her that her drive for his productivity was based more on her needs than his. This boy is very different from his mom. He actually needs just as much unproductive time as productive. He needs to be able to just stare. I talked with her about how I believe her son is highly creative and has to have time for his mind to wander. He needs time to play outside and just be a kid. His mom can create a schedule, but that schedule needs to include down time, play time, and rest time, as well as learning time and productive time. And I want her to start telling him three things he's doing right every day.

I hate to circle back around to my type A friends, but here's the deal: I think the backhoe parent describes us. And most kids I see with type A parents feel very connected to them when they're younger, but not so much as they get older. Instead, they feel like they can't measure up. They can't get it right. They feel that their parents aren't pleased with them. In fact, I think most kids with type A parents would say that they don't feel their parents like them very much. And I know that is not the message you want your kids to get. Help is on the way. I really do promise.

3. Snowplow parenting

Have you ever been snow skiing? One of my favorite parts of being in a ski resort in the winter is looking up at night on the mountains to see the lights of the snowplows going up and down the hills. They're grooming the runs by smoothing out all the little bumps and imperfections. They're making it easy on us, for which I could not be any more grateful.

The children of snowplow parents, at least initially, feel the same kind of gratitude. Anxious kids are some of the most dependent and even manipulative kids I know. They are utterly convinced (and convincing) that they can't do whatever the scary thing is in front of them . . . whether it's going to school one particular morning, running in the track meet, or doing the math problem that's included in the day's homework. They would rather you be their coping skill than develop any of their own.

▤ The Premise: I can't let my child suffer

There are a couple of problems here. Or maybe I should say issues that aren't problems on their own, but are when they come together in a snowplow's wake. One is that all children long to be independent. Another is that all parents long to help and even protect their kids from harm, as we've already discussed. You care, so of course you don't want to watch your child struggle, or hurt, or, heaven forbid, fail. Not because you're afraid of how that failure will reflect on you, but because you're genuinely afraid your child can't handle it.

▤ Where It's Coming From: My fear that they're not _____ enough

I want you to think back to a time when you thought, *My child is not* _____ *enough*. It could have been *strong* enough, *brave* enough, *social* enough, even just not *ready*. It might have been about starting school. It could have been about riding a bike or driving a car. Or it could have been regarding some type of hurt, such as not making the school play or not being chosen for the cheerleading team or soccer team. Whatever it is, our thought in those times is often *It's just too much for them to handle.*

In those moments, we technically have two options. We can let them experience whatever milestone or hurt is headed their way, or we can snowplow. We can rescue them from having to experience it by smoothing out any and all bumps in their path.

▤ What It Looks Like: Rescuing

At our parenting seminars, we talk about how we're often so busy being the resources for our kids that they don't develop resourcefulness. It's back to those two responses parents have most often in light of their children's anxiety: escape and avoidance. We want them to escape and avoid the anxiety-provoking situation, and so we become their primary resource and resort to rescuing.

In other words, snowplowing. We level the bumps and smooth the path for them so we don't have to watch them struggle and they don't even have the opportunity to fail.

You keep him home from school.

You make a phone call to the cheerleading coach to see if they might have one more spot.

You let him miss the youth retreat.

You switch her to a school where surely the girls are kinder.

You let him quit.

You don't make her do it—whatever it is. She's not ready. It's just too much.

Now, there are certainly situations where the above responses are logical. When a child is physically unable to go to school, for example, due to chronic illness. Or when the anxiety is so significant that the counselor has told you that being away for a weekend would be too much. But when we rescue kids based on our fear of their imagined hurt, rather than their true capabilities, we hurt them more in the long run.

How It Affects Them: Eventually it makes them feel incapable and hinders their growth

Psychologist Madeline Levine writes, "Kids who learn early in life that they're capable of mastering activities that at first feel a little stressful grow up better able to handle stress of all kinds."[8] I would also assert that kids who don't learn to master activities that feel stressful don't grow up better able to handle stress. Instead, two primary things happen. First, they don't believe they're capable. In all of my research on anxiety, the definition I came up with was this: Anxiety is an overestimation of the problem and an underestimation of yourself. When we rescue them, we just confirm that definition. The problem really is bigger, and they are smaller. The fear is stronger than they are. They can't do it. Or at least, they can't do it on their own.

Second, I believe that rescuing hinders a child's growth. When we don't let them try, they don't learn. It's that simple. They don't learn that they *can* do hard things, and they don't learn *to* do hard things. Stress inoculates a child against stress. In addition, from a brain standpoint, the amygdala learns only when it's activated. We'll talk more about that in the next chapter.

I do have to admit that snowplowing does initially make for an easier road for them. But snowplowing only begets more snowplowing. It creates entitlement too. We've got to keep snowplowing, as does everyone who comes after us in either authority or relationship with them.

Your kids need the bumps. In fact, have you ever seen a child tearing over moguls on skis? It's amazing to watch and exhilarating for them to experience. I love snow skiing for kids because it's adventurous, fun, risk-taking, relatively safe, and something we can do together as families. There is no choice on a mountain but for kids to go down. And, as in all things, they get better as they go.

Your child may not want to go. They may be pulling out all the manipulative stops to get you to rescue. They not only don't seem capable, but they're telling you they're not. That's where we want to have other voices. Call your pediatrician. Have a conference with the teacher. Go for a parent consult with a trusted counselor in your area and talk through the situation. Call a friend. Talk to your spouse. Have another voice, one more objective and maybe less anxious, who can help you get past your own fear to a balanced perspective on whether this is a rescue situation.

Every expert on worry and anxiety would say that for anyone of any age to work through their anxiety, they have to do the scary thing. The scary thing for them is whatever is making them anxious in the moment. The scary thing for you is likely stopping the snowplow. We're not going to do it without help, though. To continue the skiing theme, we learn by starting on the easiest slopes. We gradually move our way toward the harder hills and then the expert as we develop our skills. We're not going to stop snowplowing for kids and throw them straight onto the hardest slope. In fact, if you're feeling convicted as you read this and want to learn how to stop the snowplow effect, I'd recommend *Raising Worry-Free Girls*, whether you have girls or boys. It has specific, step-by-step instructions for how to move your kids toward doing the scary thing. And that's ultimately what they need.

All children long to be independent. Your manipulative, dependent child really does, ultimately, long to do the scary thing. It's what will teach him resilience. It's what will bring her confidence. And the more worried she is about the scary thing, the more confidence she'll gain from the task.[9]

It's time to give up the snowplow and stop rescuing. What's one area of life where you're snowplowing for your child today? What would it look like to give them more opportunity and ownership to move toward independence? They can do it . . . and so can you.

4. Helicopter parenting

The term *helicopter parent* actually originated from teenagers in Dr. Haim Ginott's 1969 book, *Between Parent & Teenager*, who were describing parents who hover over them.[10] (Not super surprising, huh?) Dr. Ann Dunnewold, in a book with a fabulous title, *Even June Cleaver Would Forget the Juice Box*, defines helicopter parenting as simply "over-parenting." She says, "It means being involved in a child's life in a way that is overcontrolling, overprotecting, and overperfecting, in a way that is in excess of responsible parenting."[11]

According to *WebMD*, these are seven signs you're helicopter parenting:

1. You fight your child's battles.
2. You do their schoolwork.
3. You coach their coaches.
4. You keep your kids on a short leash. (You stay for birthday parties, check their GPS often, etc.)
5. You're a maid in your own house.
6. You play it too safe.
7. You can't let them fail.[12]

Anyone feel a little seen with that list? It does cross over into some of our snowplow and backhoe parents as well. For our purposes, we're going to be a little more specific with our helicopter parents.

▦ The Premise: I have to protect you

There is a phenomenon happening in summer camps all over the country—maybe all over the world, but I have a feeling we may be a little worse about it in the good ole USA. It happened this past summer with our summer retreat program as well. Now, let me say again: These parents have the best of intentions. It's just the delivery that's off.

It started with an email. "I'm curious how my son is doing at Hopetown this week." Our staff purposefully doesn't communicate with parents while their kids are at Hopetown, except in an emergency. We are a teeny program with about thirty kids per week and fifteen counselors. We just don't have the manpower for someone to incessantly check emails and respond to every worried parent. In this day and age, however, parents pull out all the stops to try to contact us, from emailing to texting anyone they know who's involved to trying to direct message our staff on social media. This past summer, we happened to see such an email. And then the next: "I noticed that my son isn't smiling in many of the pictures. I need someone to respond to me." And the next: "He seems to be sitting outside of the group. I don't think my son is happy. I would like his counselor to call me immediately." And so it continued all week until she picked up her son and pulled one of our counselors aside. "What was wrong? I could tell he had a really bad week."

Again, we are a small operation. We don't have a staff member with a group roster, ticking off the boxes to make sure we have a happy photo of every child every day that we can upload to some glitzy website. We're completely focused on engaging our kids while they're with us and giving them the best, most purposeful experience they can have connecting with God and each other. Social media is not our top priority. But this mom wasn't just helicoptering. She was hovering so closely that the wind from her rotors was knocking over anyone in proximity to her or her child.

▧ Where It's Coming From: A distrust of the world, more than my child

As reported by *Business Insider*, one camp director addressed the same phenomenon in a letter to parents:

> "If your child is all the way on the right side of a photo with five campers, it does not mean they are on the 'outside' of the social group," he wrote in his missive. "If we post photos at mini golf and there are none of your children, it does not mean we have lost them! They may have been in the bathroom, or over somewhere else eating an ice-cream cone with friends." He implored parents to stop bribing their kids to appear in photos as an "incentive for some sort of earnings or award program back home," and to please avoid diagnosing medical conditions from photos in the gallery—as one dermatologist parent did of a child's mole spot (it was chocolate).[13]

Seriously? Helicopter parenting with a strong, strong wind.

▧ What It Looks Like: Magnifying

As a parent, whatever you pay the most attention to is what is most reinforced. I remember another strong-winded helicopter parent at a parenting conference. I was speaking on the subject of friendships and kids. We were talking about how to get your kids to talk—how hard it can be to get them to share what's really going on relationally at school. One father raised his hand and said, "My first question when I pick my daughter up every day from school is, 'Who was mean to you today?'" Okay. I have quite a few concerns with that question. (1) It implies that someone was mean to her every day. (2) It sets her up to see herself as the victim of every negative situation, rather than a participant, which we all sadly are most of the time. (3) It accentuates the negative—and magnifies it. It makes it bigger than it probably is.

I have a very wise friend who talks to her sensitive and worry-prone daughter about ducks. "Ducks have this outer layer of feathers that is waterproof. So when water comes, as it will, they just shake that water right off. And it never really bothers them or seeps down into who they are." Mean kids are going to happen—especially in the world of girls. We set children up much better for life when we teach them how to cope, rather than to see themselves as the victim and try to escape.

▨ How It Affects Them: Too many ways

Researchers at the University of Minnesota found that "children with helicopter parents may be less able to deal with the challenging demands of growing up, especially with navigating the complex school environment."[14] An article in *Parents* magazine listed the following impacts of helicopter parenting: "decreased confidence and self-esteem," "undeveloped coping skills," "increased anxiety," a "sense of entitlement," and "undeveloped life skills."[15]

From my own work with kids, I see those things and more. I do believe it makes them feel incapable. I think kids rise to the confidence we place in them. When we helicopter, we're communicating that they can't do it themselves. Kids who feel capable are more confident. I also see helicoptering contribute to higher levels of anxiety, entitlement, and a lack of coping skills and life skills in general. If you do it for them, they either will not do it for themselves or they'll come to resent you.

I also believe one of the most important skills for kids is a sense of perspective. And it's one they're showing less and less of today. It's so important, in fact, that we devoted an entire chapter to it in *Are My Kids on Track?* When we are helicoptering over them, watching for any possible threat, they lose perspective. We lose perspective. There are no minor threats. The chocolate on a child's face, the teacher who isn't as positive as we would like, the friend we don't believe is a good influence, and so many more. We lose perspective and cause our children to lose perspective as a result. And now, not only have we impacted them, but we've impacted our relationship with them.

In my office, kids of helicopter parents typically either lean toward an unhealthy dependence on or resent the involvement—or control—of the parent. The more dependent children are the ones who end up living with a sense of entitlement. "My parents took care of things for me . . . my teacher should too. As should my boss. And spouse. And anyone else who is in relationship with me. I deserve it." The children who resent the control look for other ways—such as risky, destructive, and sometimes deceptive behavior—to find their own sense of control. "I'm not allowed to go to parties with my friends. . . . Well, I'll show you and figure out a way." "You won't let me have social media when literally every person I know does? I'll show you and use a friend's phone and have it anyway." And so on, all the way into all the risk and deception and control they can muster.

Trust is foundational to relationships, even with your children. When we don't trust them, which is what helicopter parenting boils down to, we are essentially shutting the door to an open, ongoing, connected relationship with them as they become adults. Especially in their teenage years, when connection is tough in the best of circumstances, I believe helicopter parenting is one of the most detrimental types of relationship. Plus, we're just not that fun when we're helicoptering. We're back to losing our joy with the kids we love. We're too busy hovering to be fun. And none of us wants that.

5. Parade-float parenting

We loved our dogs in my family growing up. I had, over the course of my eighteen years living at home, two wire fox terriers and two black Labrador retrievers. Both terriers had the same name, as did both labs. My sweet mom did not want my sister or me to feel sad. Ever. So when Dixie, our first fox terrier died, Mom went out and got a new one that day. She brought it home and named it the same thing. When Blue, our lab died, a new one appeared immediately. (We could never do that now, with all the six-month waitlists for $2,500 designer doggies.) Then, it was different. As were so many things in our families. Thus, Dixie I, Dixie II, Blue I, and Blue II. I'm pretty sure my mom learned it from her mom. Patches I, Patches II. Kris I, Kris II. I come from a long line of parade-float parents.

▓ **The Premise: If I can just keep them happy enough, they won't be sad—or anxious**

I have a friend who told me recently, "I've decided my mom is the best 'go to lunch' mom around. She is delightful over lunch. But she is not helpful if I'm struggling, or when there's conflict between my brothers and me. She doesn't know how to enter into my sadness or really any feelings other than happiness. But she is a blast to laugh and have lunch with."

You may have had a similar upbringing. I don't honestly think many of us grew up in homes where we had healthy conversations around emotions. We weren't passing feelings charts around our dinner tables and choosing three emotions we felt that day. My family sure didn't. On one hand, I had new puppies to distract from any grief of losing a furry family member. On the other, my grandparents were teaching courses on "How to Win Friends and Influence People," a class based on a classic book, but not necessarily an idea to build a family around.

▓ **Where It's Coming From: My fear of reality and desire to shield my kids**

Remember that statement "We're the first generation of healthy parents"? We've circled right back around to it. I do believe you're the first generation of parents who are committed to emotional literacy in your family. Emotional literacy is simply the naming and expression of emotions. Our parents didn't know about emotional literacy to teach it to us, because their parents never taught it to them, and so on, as far back as we can trace our families. But for some of us, parade-float parenting still exists. It just looks a little different.

▓ **What It Looks Like: Minimizing**

I recently met with a highly articulate and intelligent fourteen-year-old girl who had asked her parents if she could come in for counseling. "I've been struggling with anxiety since the start of the pandemic," she said. "I used to think about getting sick some, like when my stomach was upset or I would hear about someone throwing up. But now I can't stop thinking about germs. I wash my hands a lot." When I asked her how often a lot was, she started by saying, "Three times a day." Then she quickly said, "Nine times a day." Then, "Actually, more like twenty-seven times a day, because three times nine is twenty-seven." This anxious girl was showing signs of obsessive-compulsive disorder that were significantly impacting her daily life. My heart broke for her. She was obviously bright, conscientious, kind, trying hard (all in line with our anxiety profile) and was suffering deeply. When I met with her mom afterward, she said, "We just wanted to come in proactively and because she asked for it. She's a really great kid. She was worried some a few months ago but seems to be doing great now. She's just more high-strung than her dad and I are. . . . We don't know where she got that." And she laughed. "But she's a really amazing kid." She was right. She is an amazing kid—who is struggling. When I asked about the handwashing, she said, "Oh, she is doing that some."

This mom doesn't mean to be a parade-float parent. My guess is that it's more how she engages with her own life . . . and pain. I've had other parents who dismiss their child's pain by labeling them as dramatic or overly sensitive. I've had parents who've talked about their kids' bouts of self-harm as "a phase." I even had one mother tell me she couldn't take her suicidal daughter to the hospital because she hadn't fixed her hair that day. I don't know what kind of parenting that is, but it's extremely out of touch.

I do want to say that we're living in a more dramatic time than I've ever experienced with children and teenagers. They're no longer using words like *sad* and *stressed*. They go straight to *depressed* and *anxious* instead. I think I hear the phrase *toxic relationship* at least twice a week in my office. The words these kids use with their peers and with us carry more weight and intensity than the ones we used when we were their ages. And at times it can be hard to differentiate the drama from what's real. In either case, we want to start with listening.

Perspective is an important skill for all kids to develop. Helping them understand their pain and place it in perspective. I use a one-to-ten scale in my office to help, much like the ones hanging up in the ER, but based around emotional pain rather than physical. I'll ask questions like "What's the worst thing you can imagine happening?" and "What would be a ten for you?" Then, when they're describing a situation, I'll go back to the scale. "What number was that on our scale?" Or even, "What number did it feel like?" And "What number do you think it really was?" to help them get to a place of better perspective. Kids who live at ten tend to need help developing that kind of emotional perspective. But again, we always start with listening.

When we start instead with phrases like . . .

"You're fine."

"It's not that big a deal."

"You won't even remember this happened in a week."

"You'll get over it."

"You're making this bigger than it is."

"You'll feel better tomorrow."

Or even just try to change the subject . . .

. . . and then move on without hearing them, we're minimizing their feelings. And they will either learn to distrust those feelings or get that much bigger with them to get our attention.

▓ How It Affects Them: They dwell on emotions or disconnect and distrust them

I have noticed in my counseling practice that a majority of the kids who tend to struggle with perspective have two primary types of parents. They are parents who either magnify or minimize their emotions. The children of magnifiers tend to think that the best way to connect with those parents is to magnify their own emotions. The children of minimizers feel like, unless they get really big, their parents won't notice or hear them. They end up dwelling on their emotions. Getting stuck. Using big words to describe those emotions. And they often live from crisis to crisis.

They're always sick. There is always a problem with one friend or another. They've always had a panic attack that day. No one ever listens to them. No one understands. You get the idea. Or maybe you're getting it because you're experiencing it with your child on a daily basis.

We talked before about how whatever we pay the most attention to is what's most reinforced. But maybe whatever we pay the least attention to is also reinforced. Or if not reinforced, encouraged when it arises out of a genuine need of our kids that we're not meeting. They need us to listen and to help them gain perspective. The balance between minimizing and magnifying is where the magic happens, or at least where perspective is found. More on that momentarily. But for now, it's important to be aware of the impact that both magnifying and minimizing emotions have on the kids we love. They dwell. They get stuck. And we often get stuck right alongside them.

I see other kids with parade-float parents who hear their parents' messages loud and clear—too loudly and clearly, in fact.

"My mom told me it's not a big deal. So I'm sure she's right."

"My dad told me to get over it. I guess something is wrong with me for feeling this way."

"I'm too sensitive."

"I feel too much."

"My feelings must be wrong."

When we don't validate their feelings, kids learn to disconnect from and even distrust those feelings. Our parade-float parenting keeps things fun for sure, but it doesn't leave much room for any other emotion than happiness, leaving kids believing they need to disconnect from all others. Emotional literacy isn't developed. And neither is intuition.

At Daystar we regularly see parents who are in hard situations and want help knowing how to communicate with their kids. It may be that the parents are going through a divorce. It may be that a family member has been diagnosed with a chronic illness. Or that one parent is an alcoholic. That a parent has lost his or her job. Or that there has been a tragedy in our world or country.

It can be any number of situations that are not only hard to go through, but hard to talk through with the kids we love. In those situations, when parents ask us how to talk about it with kids, our first answer is always the same: Tell the truth age-appropriately.

Kids are intuitive. They feel deeply, if left to their own emotions and without our intervening parade floating. They're aware of much more than we realize early on. If you're struggling in your marriage, your child likely knows. If you're worried about your mom's cancer diagnosis, your child has already discerned something is wrong. If your husband is an alcoholic, hiding it from your teenager doesn't help. He has likely already sensed it and is worried about you. Sometimes, in those situations, we value protecting kids over telling them the truth. We minimize issues in our own lives with responses such as "Everything's fine," "You don't need to worry," or "I don't know what you mean."

I remember a teenage boy telling me he had never realized how his grandmother treated his mom until this past Christmas. "My mom does a great job handling it, but how Nana treats her and talks to her has got to be hard." When he tried to subtly say something to his mom about it, she denied any problem. She didn't want him to think poorly of his grandmother, so she said, "It's not a big deal at all. I think she just didn't feel very well."

When we deny their feelings, we teach them to distrust those feelings and to distrust themselves. If I could give kids any gift as they grow up, I would give them the gift of intuition—of trusting their gut sense of what's happening around and inside of them. And believing that they know what to do next. More than confidence. More than courage. I believe intuition is one of the most valuable life skills any of us can possess.

This mom, like the others we've talked about, also had good intentions. She was trying to protect her son and his grandmother. But in that protecting, she invalidated his feelings. Protecting isn't worth that. It also isn't worth not telling kids the truth. Tell the truth. Age-appropriately, of course. And we typically recommend letting them ask questions and lead the conversations, as kids have a built-in sense of only asking for the information they're ready to handle. But when they ask or comment, tell the truth. Don't minimize and don't deny their emotions. They need those emotions to develop intuition and to become healthy, balanced, non-parade-float parents someday.

Finding the Balance

I recently had a parent consult with a wise couple. Neither of these parents had any kind of role model for who they want to be as parents, but both are bravely doing the best they can to figure out what it looks like to be healthy and balanced. And they're aware that they're reacting and parenting in ways that are sometimes not the most helpful to their child. I was honored to spend an hour with them.

"In my training for leadership with my company, I was told that a leader's job is to be the calmest person in the room. I guess maybe that's a parent's job too," the dad said.

Yes. Yes and yes and yes. I am fully aware that it's easier said than done. But I do believe it's possible. Balance. Non-anxious responses, not motivated by our own stuff. I had a similar conversation with one of the wisest moms I know, who is also a dear friend, just this week.

"I think I've blown it, Sissy. It's just been such a weird season we've been living in. I used to be so intentional about helping my son name his emotions and then work through them. Somewhere, in the midst of all that life has looked like in the past year, I've just stopped. I think I've gotten stuck in my sadness and overwhelmed-ness, and I've let my son do the same. I've been paying more attention to his worry than his courage. Listening more to his sadness than reminding him that he's got strength. I haven't been telling him that he can do hard things. I want to do both. And somehow, I'm very aware that this is more about me than it is about him."

A grown-up's job is to be the calmest person in the room. To allow their children to face struggles and to remind them that they're not alone. To experience all the emotions God has given them, but to learn that they are not controlled by those emotions.

To not only develop, but to trust their intuition. And to remind them that we are here for them, to listen and to help them bravely move toward and through the scary thing. As my friends Katherine and Jay Wolf tell their kids every morning, "God made you to do the hard thing in the good story He's writing for your life."[16] The same is true for you as a person—and as a parent. No sidecars, backhoes, helicopters, snowplows, or parade floats needed. Just you. Calm, non-anxious you. And now we get to talk about how in the world you do that. I surely believe you can. I want you to learn to trust your own intuition and your own skills that we're about to work on, and to remember that you have a Parent who has all of the calm and all of the grace that you need for this job.

Worry-Free Takeaways

1. Anxiety is both caught and taught, both through our brain chemistry and through the way we relate to our kids.

2. The way you parent out of your own anxiety is based either on what you believe you needed growing up or how you handle your own hurt today.

3. Sidecar parents believe their experience will be the experience of their children. They are projecting their feelings and needs onto their kids, based on their own anxious past. As a result, their kids jump on board with their parents' perspective, shut down emotionally, or rise up to be the stability for their anxious parents.

4. Backhoe parents are constantly cleaning up after their kids, believing that any failure on the part of their child reflects a failure of their own. They are parenting out of their own self-critical voice and eventually lean toward being either a catastrophizer or criticizer of their kids. Backhoe parenting comes out as control and criticism, and children are left feeling criticized and inadequate, that they can't live up to or please their anxious parents.

5. Snowplow parents have children who would rather let you do the work for them than do it themselves. And snowplow parents are happy to oblige. They do their best to prevent suffering for their child. Their underlying fear is that their child is not capable. Out of that fear they rescue the child, often communicating the very message they fear. It eventually makes kids feel incapable and hinders their growth.

6. Helicopter parenting is overparenting. Helicopter parents believe it is their duty to protect their child. They trust their child, but don't trust the world. As a result, they end up magnifying problems and creating more in their wake. Children of helicopter parents struggle with anxiety, entitlement, a lack of coping skills, and life skills in general.

7. Parade-float parents are committed to the happiness of their children at all costs. They operate under the belief that if they can just keep their kids happy, they won't be sad or anxious. It's coming both from their own fears of reality and their desire to shield their children. Kids with parade-float parents end up feeling their emotions are minimized. As a result, they dwell on those emotions or disconnect from and distrust them.

8. The way you talk to yourself will eventually become the way you talk to your child.

9. A parent's job is to find balance and to be the calmest person in the room. We are to help our kids move toward healthy risk under our safe, emotionally steady, trusting, watchful eye.

Help for the Present

5

Help for Your Body

"We need help with our daughter. It's like we're caught in this cycle of anger and frustration. She gets angry and starts yelling. We immediately start yelling back. She ends up yelling louder or longer or just falling apart. And we end up feeling like we just ruined her."

Okay, let's switch roles. You are sitting in my chair in my office, as the counselor. You have now had some version of this conversation 379 times. You know anger is a secondary emotion. What is the emotion underneath this little girl's anger? What is the emotion underneath the anger for these parents?

You guessed it. Anxiety. These are not angry parents. And they certainly are not ruining their child. The child is also not angry—or she's not intending to be. And more often than not, she feels just as terrible after the collective meltdown as they do. Only she doesn't quite have the words or maturity to express it.

Let's talk about that collective meltdown. That's what much of this chapter is about: the collective meltdowns and how to either calm them or stop them from occurring. We are again going to use our five things in the Help for the Present section of this book. But I'm going to complicate it a bit. We're going to have two lists of five things, but both fives are equally important.

We start with understanding. In *Rewire Your Anxious Brain*, psychologist Dr. Catherine Pittman and Elizabeth Karle write, "The most powerful tool in coping with anxiety reactions is having an in-depth understanding of your own unique anxiety responses."[1] Therefore it is important to start with an understanding of how anxiety specifically impacts you. Anxiety typically shows up in your body first, so we want to learn to recognize where it starts and how it tends to hijack these bodies of ours that truly are fearfully and wonderfully made. But as with kids, we don't want to stop with understanding. I promised you practical help. So we have five things to *know* about how anxiety impacts your body and five things you can *do* when it does. Let's get started with a little science—well, okay, a lot of science. But hang in there with me. The science is crucial to our understanding of both how we can help ourselves and the impact our anxiety has on the kids we love.

Five Things to Know about How Anxiety Impacts Your Body

1. Our bodies have a complex alarm system designed to keep us safe.

As we just described, the first step to regaining control is to understand what's happening. Because often, we simply don't know. We think we're overreacting. Or we think the problem is as *immediate* and *catastrophic* as our body is telling us it is. Or we might even think we're having a heart attack.

Instead, here's what actually is happening. Our bodies truly are fearfully and wonderfully made with a built-in alarm system designed to help us survive life-threatening situations. In scientific terms, it's called our sympathetic nervous system, and it begins a complex chain of events as soon as the alarm goes off.

First, we see or hear something that we (or our subconscious) perceive as a threat. Our eyes or ears then relay that message to the amygdala, whose job it is to interpret the alarm. If the amygdala believes the threat is indeed imminent, it relays the message instantly to the hypothalamus, which is considered the command center of the brain. The hypothalamus then communicates to the rest of the body, using the sympathetic and parasympathetic nervous systems. The sympathetic nervous system "functions like a gas pedal in a car," activating the fight-or-flight response, whereas the parasympathetic nervous system calms the body, much like a brake pedal, signaling the threat is gone and the body can return to a "rest and digest" state.

So once the amygdala sounds the alarm and triggers the hypothalamus, the hypothalamus kicks the sympathetic nervous system into gear. The sympathetic nervous system then stimulates the adrenal glands to pump epinephrine, or adrenaline, into the bloodstream. (Anyone besides me have the lyrics "The thigh bone's connected to the leg bone" playing in your head as you're reading this?) The epinephrine then begins multiple changes in the body, all designed to keep us safe from the perceived threat.

- Our heart rate increases, sending more blood to our muscles, our vital organs, and the heart itself, enabling us to move faster to escape the threat.
- Our blood pressure rises and pulse quickens.
- Our lungs open up smaller airways so that we're able to breathe more deeply and quickly for our escape.
- Our brain receives more oxygen as a result, increasing our alertness.
- Our pupils dilate, helping us better visualize the threat.
- Finally, our bloodstream is flooded with nutrients, giving a burst of energy to all parts of our bodies.

Our bodies truly are fearfully and wonderfully made, with the amygdala and hypothalamus working in tandem so efficiently that the entire physiological response takes place before we even realize it. In other words, our bodies have responded to the threat before we're even fully aware of that threat.[2]

The next phase of the alarm involves a hormone called cortisol, considered the body's primary stress hormone. After the initial response from the hypothalamus ends and epinephrine begins to subside, the hypothalamus releases cortisol into the brain. Cortisol itself has a variety of jobs, according to the Mayo Clinic. It "increases sugars (glucose) in the bloodstream, enhances your brain's use of glucose and increases the availability of substances that repair tissues. Cortisol also curbs functions that would be nonessential or harmful in a fight-or-flight situation. It alters immune system responses and suppresses the digestive system, the reproductive system and growth processes."[3] And all of this takes place in a matter of seconds. The amygdala is the catalyst of a highly complex system designed to keep us safe—and one that can easily get off track. But first let's talk a little more about the two ways anxiety reaches and impacts our brains.

2. There are two primary pathways to anxiety: the amygdala and the cortex.

Think back to the most recent time you had a stress response. Maybe a car veered toward you in traffic and you jerked your car out of the way. Maybe one of your children fell off a jungle gym and you raced to him before you actually thought about racing to him. Maybe you jumped when someone rounded the corner and you let out a little (but somehow still embarrassing) shriek. In each of those scenarios, we react before we have time to think about our reaction. It's automatic and happens within a fraction of a second. Those responses are created by our good old reactive amygdala.

We typically think of anxiety as driven by the amygdala, activating the fight-or-flight region of our brain. That is certainly one of the primary neural pathways leading to anxiety, and the one we're going to spend the majority of this chapter focusing on. Amygdala-based anxiety originates in our bodies and predominantly impacts our bodies as a result. But there is another pathway—one that requires a little more time and significantly more thought.

You're lying in bed one night alone. You hear a strange sound outside. *What was that sound?* you wonder. *Was it a voice? I think it might have been a man's voice.* And before long, you've already pictured the man in a hoodie on your front porch, working his way through your front door to come after you and your children. Or maybe your teenage daughter promised to call when she arrived at a friend's house. It's been ten whole minutes and you haven't heard from her yet. Her GPS app isn't working, and now you're convinced she fell asleep at the wheel, drove off the road, and got into a terrible accident. Or perhaps you had a strange interaction with a friend at the grocery store. She seemed hurried and distant and barely acknowledged you. By the time you arrive back at your house, you're convinced that you must have hurt her feelings last weekend at the Christmas party and now she no longer wants to be your friend. Our bodies aren't the only place anxiety originates. We can also think ourselves into an anxious state—or maybe overthink ourselves into an anxious state is a better way to put it. Cortex-based anxiety originates in our thoughts and impacts further thought, as well as often getting our bodies on board.

The amygdalae (yes, there are two, but they are commonly referred to singularly) are almond-shaped regions toward the back of our brains with "thousands of circuits of cells" that "influence love, bonding, sexual behavior, anger, aggression, and fear. The amygdala's job is to create emotional memories by attaching emotional significance to various objects or situations."[4]

The cerebral cortex is the large, squiggly gray matter we typically picture when we think of the brain. The cortex is made up of the left and right hemispheres and divided into sections called lobes. The frontal lobes are in charge of much of our executive functioning, anticipating and interpreting situations (the man in the hoodie, the missing teenager, and the aloof friend, for example). Because humans have highly developed frontal lobes, we have the ability to not only anticipate and interpret, but predict future events and imagine their consequences.[5] (The man in the hoodie is breaking in, the teenager is already on the way to the hospital, the friend has abandoned us, for example.) If you find yourself stuck in worried thoughts, obsessing over doubts, re-imagining ideas or images that only make your anxiety worse, or if you are preoccupied with endlessly trying to find solutions to various problems, you are likely dealing with cortex-based anxiety, according to Pittman and Karle.[6] The next chapter, "Help for Your

Mind," is all about anxious thoughts based in our cortex and how to stop them.

If, however, your anxiety comes upon you suddenly, without any logical reason or seemingly precipitating event, you're more likely dealing with amygdala-based anxiety. In fact, the amygdala takes over in less than a tenth of a second, operating much more quickly than the cortex and often without our awareness or control. The amygdala doesn't even produce conscious thoughts. It's making lightning-fast connections for what it thinks is our survival.

If we were to simplify the science, cortex-based anxiety begins in our thoughts. Amygdala-based anxiety begins in our bodies. The two are related, however. The amygdala is involved in both pathways, and Pittman and Karle describe its role as similar to that of a conductor of an orchestra.[7] "There are many connections from the amygdala to the cortex," say Pittman and Karle, but fewer from the cortex to the amygdala. Thus, it's the amygdala that has the most influential role in anxiety and the power to cause you to act before your cortex can process the action.[8] In effect, the amygdala hijacks the brain, overriding the cortex's ability to think. We can't think our bodies back to a state of calm once the amygdala has taken over. We can't use our cortex to tell our amygdala not to worry. In fact, if you've ever had a panic attack, you've experienced this very phenomenon. According to Pittman and Karle, it's almost as if the amygdala turns the cortex off in those scary moments.[9] And it's why we've got to learn to calm the amygdala down before we can learn to calm the anxious thoughts originating in the cortex.

In addition, the cortex is more forgetful than the amygdala. Remember, the amygdala acts as a storehouse for emotional memories. Therefore, our amygdala-based memories last longer than our cortex-based memories.[10] The amygdala-based memories are what we commonly refer to as *triggers*. They are events, objects, smells, sounds—basically anything that activates the amygdala's alarm system as a result of emotional learning from our past.[11]

I counsel a young girl who was attacked by her own dog. The event was traumatic and understandably would have caused her amygdala to attach an emotional, anxious memory to dogs. What it attached to even more, however, was loud, abrupt sounds. And it was her wise parents who realized that her panic over balloons bursting and fire alarms sounding was taking her back to the dog bite. She didn't understand her reactions herself. We often don't either. Many of us have certain sounds, smells, sights that can evoke memories that instantly trigger us, whether we realize it or not. When we have emotional and intense reactions that confuse us, it's often a result of amygdala-based memories. You may have heard the phrase "If it's hysterical, it's historical." That's the amygdala talking (or remembering and reacting).

In fact, I'd like for you to think back on a few times your amygdala has sounded the alarm recently. What were the triggers? What did it perceive as a threat? How did it impact your body and your thoughts? What might your amygdala have been remembering?

The amygdala remembers and then takes over. As Pittman and Karle write, it creates "something described by Joseph LeDoux . . . as a 'hostile takeover of consciousness by emotion.' . . . [with] your clearest thinking skills and personal insights . . . disabled."[12] The amygdala is immediate. It's illogical. But the good news is that it is also trainable. But first, I want you to hang in there for just a little more bad news.

3. The amygdala is notorious for false alarms.

In fact, many individuals with anxiety disorders live in a "chronic state of hyperarousal."[13] That chronic stress eventually enlarges the amygdala, making it even more vulnerable to fear, anxiety, and anger. Robert Sapolsky, Stanford University professor and stress expert, says, "Chronic stress creates a hyper-reactive, hysterical amygdala."[14] Back to hysterical and historical. Our history (life experiences and genetic makeup) often dictates an amygdala response, and then the amygdala takes over to the degree that it perpetuates itself in our future history. In other words, the more the amygdala takes over, the more likely it is to take over. It develops what is considered a hair-trigger response.

In their book *The Yes Brain*, two psychologists whose voices I trust immensely talk about how the brain is essentially rewired as we worry. "The actual physical architecture of the brain adapts . . . reorganizing itself and creating new neural pathways based on what a person sees, hears, touches, thinks about, practices and so on. . . . Where attention goes, neurons fire. And where neurons fire, they wire, or join together."[15] In essence, they create new neural pathways based on worry.

So now we've got two strikes against brains that have a tendency to worry. One is that they enlarge and develop a hair-trigger response in the amygdala. The other is that they create new neural pathways causing an even greater propensity to worry. Therefore, brains that are historically wired to worry will have even more worry in their future. I hope you're getting the picture. Worry impacts your brain in a negative way. It literally changes its structure.

What does this mean for you, as a parent? You are living in a chronic state of stress. That's what being a parent is. And again, if you've picked up this book, you're likely prone to worrying. I would imagine you've had a false alarm or two over time. You've probably gotten accustomed to living in a chronic state of stress since your parenting journey began. I sit with chronically worried parents in my office every day.

Chronically worried parents react. Their first thought is the worst thought. And then that worst thought just gets bigger and bigger and bigger until it has hijacked not only their bodies, but their emotions as well.

Something's happened.
Something's wrong.
Something is wrong with her.
He's not like everyone else.
Why is she not learning more quickly?
Is he going to turn out to be a _____?

And those alarms aren't alarming only you. They're the alarms that cause the collective meltdown and end up alarming the entire house.

4. *The amygdala gets our whole body on board. And our whole family.*

I have a saying in my office: "Amygdala begets amygdala." I think amygdalae operate a little like hormones in a sorority house (sorry, dads who are reading). I remember when I was living at the Kappa Kappa Gamma house at the University of Arkansas. Not just our room but our entire hallway of girls would all have their periods at the same time. I don't understand the science behind that, but the hormones had a ripple effect that caused all of our bodies to get on board.

Amygdalae operate in much the same way. The influence can go in either direction—from child to parent or parent to child. Most often, I hear stories of it starting with the child. "When she starts screaming like that, I have to admit that I end up getting really angry too." "It's like I become a child with him and wind up just as loud and as angry as he is."

You know, if the same is true in your house, that it doesn't help.

But it can also go from parent to child. I recently got a phone call from a parent panicked about her daughter. "She has had panic attack after panic attack this week. I can't get her to calm down. She doesn't remember or want to use the tools you've given us. I don't know what to do. Can you call me right away?" It was obvious from this mom's tone of voice that her amygdala was in the flight portion of the fight-or-flight zone. She was terrified and had no idea how to help her daughter. When I called her back, I realized that her husband had also told her just a few days before that he wanted a divorce. I believe it was her amygdala that was rippling over to activate her daughter's, and neither of them was aware of the origins. In our next session, we did go back over tools for this preteen girl. We talked about some things she could do alone and with her mom that could help. But I also brought her mom in to talk about the importance of seeing her own counselor as well. A grown-up's job is to be the calmest person in the room. And when our amygdala is setting off alarms right and left, the amygdala of our child will do the same. And vice versa. We've got to calm down our brains, bodies, and resulting emotions. And the great news is that we can.

5. Neuroplasticity works.

You've likely heard the word *neuroplasticity*. Neuroplasticity is the ability of the brain "to change its structures and reorganize its patterns of reacting," according to Pittman and Karle. [16] Neurons that fire together wire together, right? And that firing and wiring can work against us, but it can also work for us, if we do the worry work. In other words, as neuroscientist Joseph LeDoux said, "People don't come preassembled, but are glued together by life."[17] The wiring of your brain is shaped by your experiences and can change as a result of your ongoing experiences. We change our brains with practice by changing our behavior. It's how we improve our pickleball skills or learn to text faster. Even imagining practicing certain skills has the ability to create changes in our wiring.[18] This is true for our neural pathways and our cortex, and it's true for our amygdala.

The amygdala learns by experience. The amygdala isn't logical, as we said before, but the learning isn't based on the amygdala understanding. It is based on its activation. *Activate to generate* is a phrase used in many cognitive behavioral therapy circles.[19] Activate to generate simply means that to change our amygdala's stress response we have to be in the presence of what creates the stress response. We have to activate the neurons in our amygdala to generate new growth. If we're escaping and avoiding the things we're afraid of, our amygdala never has a chance to learn.

Let's look at a real-life example. You're worried about your son's grades. You've gotten into the habit of checking online daily, if not a couple of times per day, to see if he has been turning in his homework. The same could be true for checking your GPS app to see the location of your newly minted sixteen-year-old driver. Maybe you need to check it just one more time. The more we check, the more we feel the need to check. And the less our kids, who are trying to earn our trust, experience that trust.

Or, maybe you're not a checker as much as a rescuer. Your toddler son falls, and you immediately jump up to grab him. Your daughter is hurt by a friend at school, and you immediately pick up the phone and call the other parent. Your son gets an "unfair" grade on a quiz, and you instantly fire off an email to the teacher. And there we have it. You might check. You might rescue. Or it may be that you just react. Your emotions go from zero to ten with almost the same speed as your eight-year-old's do. You react and do so with great alarm and immediacy. In each of those instances, by rescuing your child you're also removing yourself from the stress-provoking and amygdala-activating situation. You're reacting, rescuing, and checking as a response to the learned, historical, and often hysterical messages your amygdala is sending your sympathetic nervous system.

There is a better way. Because the amygdala is completely functional at birth and its memories are built by emotion, it remembers forever unless we intervene. We truly can cause the amygdala to unlearn through experience. We can retrain and rewire these faulty alarm systems of ours.

Let's go back to the above scenarios and make some changes. Rather than jumping up to recue your son, you take a deep breath and respond with a calmly stated "You're okay." Rather than checking your daughter's GPS, you decide to trust her for a little longer and don't let yourself check again until she, rather than your faulty amygdala, gives you reason to. Instead of sending the email to the teacher, you start by asking your son what he would like to do to solve the problem. In each of those situations, you're creating new neural pathways that compete with the well-worn fear and anxiety pathways. The more you use them, the easier they will be to use—just like the stress response in the amygdala. But that stress response is not going to go down without a fight. My colleague David and I had the honor of having Dr. Tina Payne Bryson on our podcast, *Raising Boys & Girls*, to talk about the brain. She said that it takes four weeks for new neural pathways to develop.[20] It's important to remember that during those four weeks, your amygdala will activate its stress response often. But growth is still happening.

When you don't do the thing your amygdala is screaming at you to do, you will feel anxious. In those moments, remind yourself of the "activate to generate" phenomenon. Take a deep breath and keep going with the new behavior. (More on the importance of breathing in a bit.) The practice you're learning is called *exposure therapy*, and according to our friends Dr. Pittman and Karle, among the types of therapy for anxiety, and for panic attacks, phobias, and OCD in particular, nothing has been as dramatically successful as exposure therapy.[21] You're exposing yourself to the anxiety-provoking situation and pairing that situation with safety. We'll talk more about exposure therapy in chapter 7. But for now, know that it's going to take time and a whole lot of practice. In fact, the primary reason we don't work through our anxiety is that we don't practice the skills it takes to create new neural pathways. To work through our fear, we have to do the scary thing . . . over and over and over. Let yourself stay in the anxiety-provoking situation without escaping. The goal is not to stop feeling anxious. The goal is to learn that you can feel fear and still do the brave thing. That you are stronger than any fear that can come your way. Now, let's get to practicing.

Five Things to Do When Anxiety Impacts Your Body

1. *Listen to your body.*

In *Braver, Stronger, Smarter*, there is a drawing of a superhero. I ask the girls to color in where they first feel anxiety in their bodies. As you know, kids are amazing. They're much more aware than we often give them credit for. Any time I ask a child where they first start to feel worry, they immediately know the answer. "My face gets hot." "My tummy starts to feel fluttery." I even had one young girl tell me she felt it first in her hair bow. There you have it. We, however, are a little more disconnected from our bodies. We're moving too fast to pay attention. Doing too much. We stuff the feelings (physical and emotional) and keep moving. And it's often not until the end of the day that our anxiety and the exhaustion from it catch up with us. Or even more likely, it's not until our own angry voice at the kids we love matches the piercing siren of the amygdala that has hijacked our brain and our home.

In *The Body Keeps the Score*, Bessel van der Kolk tells us, "Neuroscience research shows that the only way we can change the way we feel is by becoming aware of our *inner* experience and learning to befriend what is going on inside ourselves."[22] I want us to do just that. Take a few deep breaths right now. Think about the different parts of your body. Where do you feel tension? Now think again about a recent time you had a stress response. Where did it start in your body? Is it in the same area? Where did it go next?

Parents often tell me that their children go from zero to ten instantaneously. They do. Sometimes we do too. Remember, the amygdala sounds the alarm within a fraction of a second. But if we can learn to stop the progression when it first begins, the less our bodies and brains will be hijacked by the alarm. Our body awareness can act as a helpful indicator light for us. As soon as your jaw clenches, your shoulders tense, your stomach starts to flutter, or even your bow tingles, you know the switch has flipped and it's time to start the de-escalation process. Sooner is stronger in this war against worry and its effect on our bodies. Now that you know where in your body the anxiety starts, let's talk about how we can immediately start to combat its effects.

2. Breathe.

I remember when I first heard about deep breathing. Even as a therapist, I thought it sounded a little hokey. Have I mentioned that I'm an Enneagram 1? In other words, I am a *fast* mover. There is not a lot of time for deep breathing when I'm trying to get as much done as possible as quickly as possible. But then I tried it.

I want you to try it with me for just a moment. Here's my favorite way to do it with kids in my office. I want you to place your hand on your leg. With your index finger, I want you to slowly draw a square. With the first line, slowly breathe out for four seconds. With the second, hold your breath for four seconds. With the third line, breathe in for four seconds. And with the last line, hold your breath again for four seconds. Repeat four times.

This method is called either square or box breathing. It's used by athletes, police officers, and Navy Seals (although Seals call it combat breathing, which sounds much more intense and Navy Seal-ish). According to the Mayo Clinic, it regulates the autonomic nervous system by stimulating the parasympathetic nervous system, which is the rest-and-digest portion of our nervous system. It is known to improve mood, reduce stress, and help with insomnia.[23]

Breathing is like nutrition for our bodies. It's something I now explain multiple times a day in my counseling office. I believe it's that important. Here is my summary of how it supplies our bodies with nutrition. When we become anxious and our sympathetic nervous system kicks into gear, our breathing quickens. When it does, it constricts the blood vessels of our brain, shifting the blood flow away from the prefrontal cortex, which helps us think rationally and manage our emotions, and to the amygdala. And there's exactly where that hijack occurs. When we breathe deeply in response, the blood vessels of our brain dilate again and send the blood flow back to the prefrontal cortex, making us capable of rational thought and self-control. It's why parents tell me constantly that their child is like a crazy person when he or she is anxious. Right. Because the rational part of his brain isn't even working in those moments. But breathing changes everything. For them and for us.

Breathing also stimulates something called the vagus nerve, particularly when we breathe from our bellies, as described in a *Women's Health* article. The vagus nerve is the longest of our cranial nerves, starting at the base of our brain and traveling down both sides of the neck to the heart and lungs, touching almost every organ on its way down the body. The vagus nerve is responsible for communication between your brain and your digestive system, as well as helping you to switch between the sympathetic and parasympathetic nervous systems. With chronic stress, the vagus nerve loses the ability to tell the body to move to the rest-and-digest state of the parasympathetic nervous system, putting you at risk for issues such as anxiety, depression, diabetes, GI disorders, and emotional exhaustion.[24] Catherine Pittman describes how the vagus nerve works: When you breathe deeply from your belly, the lungs expand and press against your diaphragm wall. The diaphragm forces your abdomen out and puts pressure on your spine. The spine puts pressure on the vagus nerve, which lowers your heart rate, blood pressure, and breathing, and it enhances brain waves and removes lactate from your blood, contributing to a sense of calm alertness. The vagus nerve even stimulates the release of serotonin, which is connected to feelings of enjoyment, contentment, and impulse control.[25]

Breathing not only calms our anxious bodies in the moment, but also has long-lasting effects on our amygdala. Studies "have shown that even a half hour of daily mindful breathing for two months appears to shrink the amygdala."[26] That is permanent hope in the form of a non-anxious brain. I believe all of us should be making mindful breathing (more on mindfulness coming soon) a daily practice in times we're not anxious, just to calm our overanxious brains and slow down our frenzied hearts.

3. Practice grounding exercises.

After breathing comes grounding. It's another one of my top three go-tos for anyone who is anxious in my office. You've now calmed your body through breathing. Your thoughts, however, are still stuck in that single-loop roller coaster we call worry. We've got to shift the focus.

Grounding techniques are another cognitive-behavioral therapy tool used for anxiety and PTSD and can provide significant help if you have a panic attack. Anxiety typically resides in the past or the future. We are not in the present moment when we're anxious, or even present *to* the moment. We're looping about something that did happen or that might happen (and probably will, in our anxious minds). Grounding is meant to anchor us to the present.

There are countless grounding techniques out there that are helpful. Anything sensory related is grounding. My favorite to use with kids is the 5-4-3-2-1 game. I use it myself sometimes too. Name five things you see, four things you hear, three things you feel, two things you smell, and one thing you taste. Other grounding techniques include these:

Name everything you see that's a certain color.

Run cold water over your hands.

Go outside barefoot and stand in the grass.

Name three things you see and three things you hear, and move three body parts.

Take a short walk.

Squeeze a piece of ice.

Describe an everyday task out loud (as if you're teaching someone else how to do laundry, make coffee, etc.).

Count backward from one hundred by ones, fives, or sevens (depending on your math skills).

Try to remember, scene by scene, your favorite movie. (*Frozen* is a fan favorite in my office.)

Visualize a place you love and feel safe.

Pet or play with your dog (or maybe cat).

Picture the face of someone you trust and try to hear their voice encouraging you.

List your favorites in several categories—food, TV shows, songs, etc.

Say three kind phrases to yourself that are true.

Memorize Scripture and repeat it out loud. In doing so, we have the double benefit of calming our anxious bodies and hiding God's Word in our hearts.

Breathing can be a grounding technique as well. One of the reasons I particularly love square breathing is that it not only activates the parasympathetic nervous system, but the drawing of the square on our leg serves as an actual grounding technique.

We start with being aware of the origins of anxiety in our bodies. We move to breathing. Then grounding, and then incorporating an idea called mindfulness.

4. *Practice mindfulness.*

For those of us who grew up hearing about the New Age movement, mindfulness can sound like a hokey holdover from that time. While mindfulness can be linked to Buddhism and other religions, Scripture also has many references to mindfulness without ever using the word.

Mindfulness is simply any intentional practice of focusing on the present. Mindfulness can include breathing and grounding techniques, as well as a host of other scientifically proven, data-driven, stress- and anxiety-reduction methods—that also happen to be scriptural. Prayer is an act of mindfulness, as are Scripture memorization and recitation and even simply spending time in God's Word.

Second Corinthians 10:5 encourages us to take every thought captive, an idea we'll circle back to in the next chapter. Romans 12:2 reminds us to be transformed by the renewing of our minds. And Philippians 4:9 encourages us to "practice" what we've heard and seen and received. We know that breath is used throughout Scripture to symbolize life as well. Job 32:8 says, "But it is the spirit in a person, the breath of the Almighty, that gives them understanding." Breathing, practicing, and taking thoughts captive are all examples of the mindfulness that is also scientifically proven to reduce anxiety and stress.

In the 1970s, Jon Kabat-Zinn, a molecular biologist, developed a new program called mindfulness-based stress reduction, or MBSR. The premise behind it is that we can "relieve suffering by focusing our attention on the present moment, as opposed to ruminating on our past or worrying about our future."[27] Since that time, research has shown the profound effects mindfulness has on our physical and mental health.

- Mindfulness leads to a decrease in worry and anxiety.[28]
- MBCT (mindfulness-based cognitive therapy) reduces the risk of depression relapse by almost half.[29]
- Mindfulness gives us greater awareness of our thoughts and emotions.[30]

- Mindfulness helps us have better control of our emotions.[31]
- Mindfulness decreases our emotional reactivity.[32]
- Relaxation training (a form of mindfulness) "almost immediately reduce[s] activation in the amygdala."[33]
- Mindfulness is especially effective in activating the parasympathetic nervous system.[34]
- Mindfulness yields short- and long-term positive effects in the amygdala.[35]

We get lost in our thoughts for almost 50 percent of our waking lives.[36] Our minds are continually evaluating our reality as either good or bad. And our minds are often drawn toward anything other than what is happening right now. It's why we miss the moment significantly more than we realize—or than we would like. Basically, with mindfulness, you choose what you pay attention to. Mindfulness is not about stopping our thoughts or emptying ourselves of something. Our thoughts and emotions are God-given and are what make us human. Mindfulness is about "changing *our relationship* to those thoughts and emotions," according to Judson Brewer, author of *Unwinding Anxiety*.[37]

What exactly is mindfulness, and how do I do it? you may be asking. My guess is that you already are doing it. Again, conscious breathing is an example of mindfulness, as are grounding techniques. If you've ever taken a yoga class, you've practiced mindfulness. Anything that pulls our focus away from our anxious thoughts and anchors us to the present is considered mindfulness. The Mayo Clinic writes, "Mindfulness is a type of meditation in which you focus on being intensely aware of what you're sensing and feeling in the moment, without interpretation or judgment."[38] It involves training our anxious minds to stay in the moment, which can be tough for any of us. The *Harvard Gazette* recounted a study from 2014 that found "individuals would rather apply electroshocks to themselves than be alone with their thoughts."[39] So there's that. The tragedy is that we are not only alone but are trapped in those looping, anxious thoughts any time we're not actively combating them.

I want to give you a few examples of mindfulness now, although the next chapter will include more. These are two of my favorites to recommend in counseling:

Progressive muscle relaxation focuses on slowly tensing and relaxing different muscle groups in your body and can be particularly helpful at bedtime. Start with your feet by tensing and relaxing the muscles in your toes. Work your way up your body to your neck and then head. Or you can reverse the order. Tense each muscle group for five seconds, then relax for thirty seconds and repeat.

The three doors technique is one I recommend constantly for kids who are having trouble falling asleep, but I recommend it for use throughout the day too—for both kids and adults. In this exercise, I want you to think of three places you know well and where you feel particularly safe. It can be a vacation spot, your home, or even your grandparents' old house. I often use the summer camp I attended and loved as a child, Camp Waldemar. Imagine each location as a separate door. Walk through the first door and enter the scene. Use all your senses to visualize yourself walking throughout the entire place. What do you see? Hear? Smell? Feel? After you have walked through the first room, exit, and enter the next door. Then the third. Most people tell me they're asleep before they ever get to the third spot.

Mindfulness can also include simple, practical exercises like going for a walk (without obsessing over all the things you need to do), coloring, journaling, saying something kind to one person a day, and focusing on one thing at a time (even simple tasks) as you notice what you see, feel, hear, and smell. There are countless apps to help with mindfulness. A few of my favorites include Calm and Headspace (which I especially love because the voices leading the meditations all sound like Mary Poppins) and Abide, which anchors us to Scripture as we're practicing mindfulness. However, technology only adds to our mindfulness when we're using a mindfulness app, *not* when we're endlessly scrolling through social media or allowing it to act as our primary form of distraction. Just putting your phone down and focusing on what's in front of you can be one of the best acts of mindfulness.

5. Take care of yourself.

After sitting with thousands of parents over the years, I believe one of the hardest things in the world for you to do is simply to take care of yourself. I can't even begin to count the number of parents I've talked with about things like going on dates with their spouse, doing fun things with friends, taking a walk, eating right, getting sleep, and even going to counseling for themselves, and the response has been the same: "Who has time for that?"

You may feel like you don't have time to walk with a friend. Or go out to dinner with your spouse. There just don't seem to be sufficient hours in a day to get enough sleep. I have a friend whose go-to lunch for years was M&Ms in the carpool line. Counseling for yourself? Where would your kids go during your appointment? And you'd rather invest the money in their counseling than in yours. There can be many obstacles to taking care of yourself. Still, I would respectfully but strongly say, "You don't have time not to." I can't speak for you, but when I'm not taking care of myself, I'm more prone not only to anxiety but also to anger. In fact, as I'm writing this, it's the day before New Year's Eve and I've been doing some reflecting on things I've learned this year. One is that my hurried self is not my best self. What about you? How are you different when you're taking care of yourself versus when you're not?

Research shows that sleep and exercise both have a significant impact on the amygdala.[40] Exercise, in fact, offsets symptoms of an activated amygdala. So if you have a panic attack, move. Get outside and walk or run. The movement burns off excess adrenaline, and the reduction in anxiety is measurable after only twenty minutes of exercise.[41] Exercise is also known to promote widespread growth in brain cells.[42] There are so many benefits to moving our bodies when anxiety tries to hijack our brains.

In terms of sleep, you may not realize that sleep is a particularly active time for your brain; it's when the glial cells of our brains clean out toxins from the day.[43] Inadequate sleep impacts our focus, impairs our memory, lessens our ability to problem-solve, and affects our insulin, causing us not only to eat more but to gain more weight from what we eat.[44] In addition, research has shown that the amygdala is more impacted by inadequate sleep than any other region of the brain.[45] Not sure about you, but that makes me want to go right to bed!

Eating right also can help our anxiety. Skipping meals can cause drops in blood sugar, which can make you feel more anxious and jittery. In addition, 95 percent of serotonin receptors are found in the lining of the gut, and research out of Harvard is pointing to probiotics as helpful in treating both anxiety and depression. Magnesium, zinc, and foods rich in omega-3s can help as well.[46] An article in *Men's Journal* lists several foods that can help reduce anxiety: asparagus (for folic acid), blueberries (antioxidants and vitamin C), milk (antioxidants, B2, B12, protein, and calcium), almonds (B2 and E), oranges (vitamin C lowers cortisol), salmon (omega-3 fatty acids), spinach (magnesium), turkey (tryptophan releases serotonin), oatmeal (linked to serotonin release as well), and avocados (because guacamole is rich in vitamin B and is good for everyone).[47]

Eat right. Get good rest. Exercise. Take care of yourself. We give out of an overflow of what we receive. When we're running on empty, we have nothing to give. And my guess is that you lean toward empty pretty often these days. Please take care of yourself. You deserve it, whether you see it or not. God sure does. He created your body with a built-in alarm system to take care of itself. And He has entrusted that body to you. Your body is what enables you to care for your kids. And, believe me, they want you to take care of it so you can care for them. You are fearfully and wonderfully made. Please treat your body and your mind accordingly.

Before Romans 12 talks about being transformed by the renewing of our minds, it talks about our bodies: "Therefore, I urge you, brothers and sisters, in view of God's mercy, to offer your bodies as a living sacrifice, holy and pleasing to God—this is your true and proper worship" (Romans 12:1). Or as *The Message* puts it: "So here's what I want you to do, God helping you: Take your everyday, ordinary life—your sleeping, eating, going-to-work, and walking-around life—and place it before God as an offering. Embracing what God does for you is the best thing you can do for him." And then it goes on to say, "Don't become so well-adjusted to your culture that you fit into it without even thinking. Instead, fix your attention on God. You'll be changed from the inside out" (v. 2). We'll be transformed . . . not only our amygdala will be, but our hearts and minds too, as we practice these important tools and fix our minds on something other than our own anxious thoughts.

Breath prayer is a contemplative form of prayer that has been around for thousands of years. Breath prayer is connected, as you might have guessed, to our breathing. Contemplative prayer, says *Christianity Today* writer Sharon Lee Song, is "focused on being with God, awakening to his presence in all things."[48] Sounds a lot like mindfulness, doesn't it? Typically, contemplative prayers are silent forms of meditation or they consist of just a few words. Breath prayer ties those prayers to our breathing and reminds us that God is with us, closer than our very breath. As Acts 17:28 says, "For in him we live and move and have our being." So let's try some breath prayers together as a way to practice mindfulness and simply be in the presence of God. It will not only calm our bodies but center our hearts.

The Jesus Prayer is a commonly used breath prayer:

Inhale slowly and pray, *Lord Jesus Christ, Son of God,*
Exhale slowly and fully, praying, *have mercy on me, a sinner.*
You can repeat the same words as you take several slow, deep breaths.

Sarah Bessey includes several others I love in her devotional, *A Rhythm of Prayer,* including these:

(From Matthew 11:28–30)
Inhale: *Humble and gentle One,*
Exhale: *you are rest for my soul.*

(From Romans 8:38–39)
Inhale: *Nothing can separate me,*
Exhale: *from the love of God.*

(From Psalm 46:10)
Inhale: *Be still*
Exhale: *and know you are God.*

(From 1 John)
Inhale: *There is no fear*
Exhale: *in your Love.*

(From Psalm 23)
Inhale: *I will not be afraid*
Exhale: *for you are with me.*

(From Philippians 4:7)
Inhale: *Peace of Christ,*
Exhale: *guard my heart and mind.*[49]

May the peace of Christ guard your heart and mind, and your body too. Through breath. Through taking care of yourself. Through practicing mindfulness and all the tools we've talked about in this chapter. He is the God of peace . . . and that peace is meant not only to fill you, but to transform you. Let's talk more about that transformation as we discover help for your mind in the next chapter.

Worry-Free Takeaways

1. Understanding the science behind anxiety is crucial to our understanding of how we can help ourselves, as well as the impact our anxiety has on the kids we love.
2. Our bodies have a complex alarm system designed to keep us safe.
3. There are two primary pathways to anxiety: the amygdala and the cortex.
4. The amygdala gets our whole body on board. And our whole family.
5. Neuroplasticity works.
6. Listen to your body.
7. Breathe. Breathing is like nutrition for our bodies.
8. Practice grounding exercises to pull yourself out of the worry loop.
9. Practice mindfulness. With mindfulness, says author Seth Gillihan, we can "relieve suffering by focusing our attention on the present moment, as opposed to ruminating on our past or worrying about our future."[50]
10. Take care of yourself.

6

Help for Your Mind

"Parenting is so hard and is only going to get harder."

"Everyone else is doing a better job."

"If I don't figure it out when they're young, they'll really struggle as teens."

"I'm not instilling enough values in them."

"It's too late to course correct."

"I said too much."

"They don't like me."

"When their behavior doesn't change, I must be the one doing something wrong."

"I'm not spending enough time with them."

"I'm screwing them up."

"I can't do it. Maybe I shouldn't have had kids."

"I'm damaged."

"I'm not equipped."

"My children will fail because I don't model Jesus well."

"My mistakes will have lifelong consequences for them."

"I'm not doing enough."

"I'm not good enough."

"I'm not equipped or wise enough."

"I'm not enough."

"I'm going to ruin my kids."

"No other parent gets as frustrated as I do or says mean things."

"I'm constantly failing."

"I should be able to do it all (work, clean, cook, self-care, be a fun parent)."

"I should be better at this by now."

"If I was a better parent, my kids wouldn't be struggling."

"It's too late."

"I'm overweight and underappreciated by my family."

"I only operate out of my wounds."

"My need for space and distance is wrong and damaging."

"I have to hold it all together for the sake of my family."

"I don't know who I am anymore and no one likes this version of me."

"I'm passing down all my fears."

"I'm always messing them up."

"Every moment is an opportunity to mess them up for good."

"I'm not the mom for the job."

"Because of me, they're going to need a lifetime of therapy."

"My child's salvation depends on how I teach/perform/live out the gospel."

"I have to be on all the time."

"I'm doing more damage than good."

"I'm harming my kids in ways I can't see now but will regret later."

"All of their struggles are because of my failures."

"I'm making everything worse."

"My kids deserve better."

Whew. That's quite a list of statements, isn't it? I don't know how it impacts you to read them, but it broke my heart when I read them for the first time. Seriously. I couldn't stop thinking about it for days, and it jump-started me into doing everything I could think of to help and encourage the parents who wrote those statements. Including writing this book.

Do you want to know who those parents were? You. Or at least, they were parents who are a whole lot like you. I put out a simple question on social media: "What are the lies you believe as a parent?" And those are just a portion of the devastating answers that came back to me from parents all over the world. Parents who are trying hard, who are conscientious enough to follow a "parenting expert" on social media. Parents who have no idea how much good they're actually doing in the lives of their kids. You.

I'd like for you to go back over the list. I want you to star the ones you have said to yourself or believed in the past year. And I want you to add to the list any thoughts that you circle back to regularly. They can be thoughts about yourself, about the world, or about your kids. But I want you to specifically identify the anxious thoughts—those that get your amygdala started if you stay with them long enough. The ones that keep you from being present with your kids and that keep you, in general, from being the parent and person you want to be. They're the ones that, given a little perspective, you know aren't true, but that somehow still have entirely too much power. And they're the ones this chapter is going to help you get rid of, or at least strip of power when they do come.

I would imagine some of those thoughts are worst-case scenario thoughts regarding your kids—what could go wrong now and in the future. We're going to tackle those kinds of thoughts too. But for now, I want you to go back to the list and pick the top three to five thoughts you have most often. Out of all the anxious thoughts I hear parents talk about in my office, I believe the most damaging—to you and to your kids—are the negative thoughts you have about yourself.

Now I want you to imagine someone you care about—an adult or a child. It could be your spouse, your best friend, even your son or daughter. I want you to imagine yourself saying those statements to that person. I know—it's hard to even picture, because my guess is those words would never come out of your mouth to anyone other than yourself. If they did, however, how would they impact that person? Specifically, what would it do to their confidence in who they are and their hope for who they're becoming? Now I want you to sit with this question for just a few moments: How do you think those thoughts impact you?

Five Things to Know about How Anxiety Impacts Your Mind

1. *We all have intrusive thoughts.*

The average person has dozens, possibly even hundreds, of intrusive thoughts per day.[1] An article published by Harvard Medical School defines intrusive thoughts as thoughts that are (1) "unusual for you," (2) "bothersome," and (3) "hard to control."[2] The article describes those thoughts:

> It seems to come out of nowhere—a strange, disturbing thought or a troubling image that pops into your mind. It might be violent or sexual, or a recurring fear that you'll do something inappropriate or embarrassing. Whatever the content, it's often unsettling and may bring on feelings of worry or shame. The more you try to push the thought from your mind, the more it persists.[3]

These intrusive thoughts impact six million Americans, according to the Anxiety and Depression Association of America. The thoughts can be connected to a mental health disorder, such as obsessive-compulsive disorder or post-traumatic stress disorder. They can be brought on by stress or anxiety and can even be associated with hormone shifts.[4] Hello, all of us. I believe they are also associated with parenting. Back to that idea of context. For you, the thoughts might not be that you'll do something inappropriate or embarrassing, but that your child will. It might be that your child will be injured or even die. Or, going back to the beginning of the chapter, the intrusive thoughts might be more related to failing as a parent.

Intrusive thoughts often take the form of the very voice in our head making the statements that started off this chapter. We all have the voice and those thoughts. Especially in this day and time, all of us have dealt with some degree of anxiety or depression, or certainly hormones. And thus, the voice that tells us that something is or will go wrong. And that maybe that something is us.

2. The thoughts that get stuck get stuck for a reason.

Here's the scenario I describe to parents in my office daily. I'm driving across a bridge in my car. I have a flash of thought: *Maybe I could drive off this bridge. It wouldn't be hard and things sure would be easier.* Then, I move on. It doesn't mean I'm suicidal. It just means I had an irrational, intrusive thought. Thirty minutes later, the bridge is no longer on my mind . . . unless, for some reason, the thought gets stuck. It's back to the old one-loop roller coaster. For kids and grown-ups, anxiety is the primary reason I see those thoughts get stuck in a loop. In that case, *I could drive off this bridge* becomes *Maybe I want to drive off this bridge.* Or, *Maybe my son isn't keeping up in math* becomes *My son isn't capable of doing math. He will fail.*

It's the same idea we talked about earlier in the book regarding kids. Their looping thoughts are predictable along the lines of their development. Development creates the context for them. Your thoughts are predictable along the lines of context (parenting), as well as another CBT concept called your *core beliefs*.

Let me give you an example. Let's say you had a really difficult time in middle school. Other kids were unkind to you. You never were a part of the group of friends you longed to be. You often felt left out and alone. Your daughter has just entered seventh grade (context on top of context). Her group of friends has gotten together a few times without her. She's seen it on social media and heard about it around the lunch table. You can barely talk to her about it because it upsets you more than it does her. Why would those girls ever leave your daughter out? They must have decided she's not good enough for them. She'll never find friends now. Her middle school years are going to be just as horrible as yours were. The only thing you can think to do is to call the mothers of those girls and beg that she be included next time—which we know will only serve to isolate her further, in the long run.

ABC is an acronym for a therapeutic model created by Dr. Albert Ellis, a renowned psychologist and researcher.

A stands for the **activating event or adversity.**

B is for your **beliefs** around the event or **your interpretation of that event.** It's based on what are considered your core beliefs, or how you see the world.

C is for **consequences,** including both emotional and behavioral responses.[5]

In the above scenario, A is your daughter being left out. B is your belief that middle school is terrible and that any shifting of friends will cause irreparable damage to your daughter. C is the devastation you feel as a result, and the action of calling the other girls' parents.

The thought gets stuck because it touches on your core beliefs. Any time thoughts get stuck for those of us who are anxious, they're related to both context and core beliefs.

Let me give you a few more examples:

Thought
My son is going to fail fifth grade.

Context
Your love for your son.

Core Belief
His ADHD makes him less capable.

If we were to break this down into the ABCs, A would be that your son with ADHD failed a quiz in the fall of his fifth-grade year.

B is your belief that kids who have ADHD aren't quite as capable. (Let me say, as a therapist who has worked with thousands of kids with ADHD, that this is in no way true.) You've read the research that disproves this belief, but you can't shake it. You love your son and want the best for him. As a result, C is your feelings of hopelessness and attempts to micromanage his academics, even when his grades disprove your theory.

Thought
My daughter is going to struggle with anxiety for the rest of her life.

Context
Your love for your daughter.

Core Belief
Your anxiety has made life significantly harder for you.

Now, let's look at the ABCs. A is that your daughter had her first panic attack in sixth grade. B is your belief that her anxiety will follow the same pattern as yours. You know there are resources that weren't available for you at her age, but you still have a nagging fear or belief that she'll be defined by her anxiety, as you feel you have been your entire life. C is that you react and pay more attention to her anxiety than to her bravery. Whatever we pay the most attention to is what's most reinforced. She needs you to pay more attention to her courage than her fear—and to get her the help that can make a profound difference in her anxiety and yours.

Thought
The other parents think I'm a bad parent.

Context
You love your kids and want to be the best parent you can be for them.

Core Belief

Everyone else is better at this.

A is that you're repeatedly late to pick your kids up for school. Or maybe it's that your daughter didn't make the competitive cheer team. Or that you don't have time, with your work schedule, to volunteer at school. It could be a million different As, and likely is. B is that you believe every other parent has got it together, they somehow make it all work. And even your best efforts come up short. I hope you continue to hear my voice say those beliefs are lies—the same intrusive thoughts that originate somewhere else, which we'll talk more about later in the book. But out of those beliefs, it's easy to live with a C of a lot of shame and, therefore, even more anger at your kids and resentment toward the parents in your community.

3. Our interpretations are what fuel our anxiety.

Cognitive fusion is another cognitive behavioral therapy term for confusing thoughts with reality. The reality is that your daughter has been left out. Your son has ADHD. Your daughter has anxiety. Or you're chronically late. The thoughts around the events are *My daughter will never find friends. My son is going to fail fifth grade. My daughter is going to struggle with anxiety for the rest of her life.* And, *The other parents think I'm a bad parent.* Those thoughts are different from reality. Our emotions and responses are based more on our anxious thoughts, or our interpretations of the event, than on reality.

With cognitive fusion, the problem is in our interpretation of the event. Our interpretation is where the thought is confused with reality. Those interpretations take place in the cortex, which is infamous for misinterpretations.[6] Have you ever noticed a firetruck in your neighborhood and thought, *OH NO! MY HOUSE IS ON FIRE!* That's the cortex working for you—or against you. Reality was that you just saw a firetruck drive down a neighboring street. The thought was, *I hope it's not going to my house.* And the misinterpretation came in when you confused that thought with reality and your core belief that *Bad things seem to follow me.*

Misinterpretations are considered negative "automatic thoughts" by Judith Beck, a preeminent psychologist, who writes that those thoughts are not random but are based on our core beliefs, which she describes as "the most fundamental level of belief; they are global, rigid and overgeneralized."[7] So . . . we've circled back around to core beliefs. Those core beliefs are what dictate our misinterpretations.

Thoughts + Context + Core Beliefs → Misinterpretations → Anxiety

We're going to talk about how to change this formula in the second half of this chapter. But we know that change isn't possible without awareness. So I want you to create this formula with a few anxious thoughts and misinterpretations you might have had recently. We specifically want to focus on the core beliefs. If we only look at the thoughts and try to change those, we'll be whac-a-moling those thoughts indefinitely. The core beliefs are where the change comes.

It could help to think of core beliefs as themes. We all have intrusive thoughts, context, and some themes in our core beliefs. If you are a student of the Enneagram, it can be a helpful place to find more of your core beliefs. I'd recommend Suzanne Stabile's book *The Journey Toward Wholeness* for more help in finding how your core beliefs might be related to your Enneagram number. *No one else ever tries as hard as I do* is one that has been particularly true for me. I have a friend who says she's always in the wrong line of life. It could also be that no one seems to notice the things you do. Our core beliefs often emerge when we're overwhelmed, tired, or struggling in one way or another.

You can also go back to your growing-up years to discover more of your core beliefs. Think back on feelings you felt regularly, thoughts you had often, or areas where you're already aware of misinterpretations. Middle school, in particular, is a breeding ground for misinterpretations. Our core beliefs usually begin somewhere in our more formative years. The reality is that our core beliefs served us well back then. They helped us survive our families or any kind of trauma we encountered. "Being good equals being loved." "Life is easier when I fly under the radar." "If I can just keep people laughing, they won't notice the things I can't do." Again, we've all got themes or core beliefs that likely started when we were young. They were necessary back then. The reality is that they don't serve us as well anymore. But just as in Proverbs 26:11, "As a dog returns to its vomit, so fools repeat their folly," we seem to keep going back to them when an activating event collides with those beliefs. The core beliefs create cognitive fusion as well as certain cognitive distortions that we're particularly prone to.

4. Cognitive distortions are interpretations based on our core beliefs.

Cognitive distortions are the specific interpretations we often fall victim to. They're negative thoughts that trigger both our anxiety and our pain. They are a byproduct of our core beliefs. We all also have certain types of cognitive distortions to which we're more susceptible, all of which are considered "distorted, illogical and unrealistic" by Dr. David Burns.[8] In his book *Feeling Great* he came up with ten types of cognitive distortions most of us deal with:[9]

1. All-or-nothing thinking. Those of us who lean toward such thinking often see the world in black and white, good and bad. *I'm a failure as a parent* would be an example of all-or-nothing thinking.
2. Overgeneralization. Once means all. Sometimes means always. A negative event becomes a recurrent pattern of failure or defeat. *My daughter had one panic attack* means *She'll battle debilitating anxiety her entire life.*
3. Mental filter. Many of us have a tendency to filter out the positive events, comments, or even thoughts and focus solely on the negative. We ignore our son's many great

qualities and think, *He has never shown any responsibility. Why would I think he could drive a car at 16?*

4. Discounting the positive. In this case, it's not so much that we filter out the positive, we just give more weight to the negative. It has more power—especially if it's about us. *My daughter doesn't even like me. All she does is tell me what I'm not doing right.*

5. Jumping to conclusions. I believe we women are a little more prone to both types of jumping to conclusions: fortune-telling and mind reading. With fortune-telling, we believe we know how things will turn out, and (spoiler alert) it's typically negative, especially when it comes to us. With mind reading, we believe we know what others are thinking—and that is most often skewed against us as well. *There is no way she'll make competitive cheer. . . . I'm a bad mom because I didn't sign her up for lessons in preschool.*

6. Magnification and minimization. We either blow things out of proportion or minimize them, including events or the way we felt in reaction to them. *She has the worst teacher in the school* or *He doesn't see anything I do for him.*

7. Emotional reasoning. Our feelings dictate our logic. I feel _____, so therefore I must be ____. *I feel like I've failed my kids* becomes *I am a failure as a parent.*

8. "Should" statements. Mental health experts talk often about our need to stop "shoulding" on ourselves. But we still do. We use words like *should, must, ought to,* or even *have to* in our efforts to make ourselves better, which ends up only making us feel worse. *I should spend more one-on-one time with my kids.* Or, *I ought to be able to manage three kids' schedules without dropping the ball.*

9. Labeling. This is another type of overgeneralization. Rather than saying, "I made a mistake," we say, "I'm a terrible person." Rather than, "I got angry with my son and yelled," we say, "My anger will ruin my son. I'm a horrible parent."

10. Self-blame and others blame. With kids, I believe both are present. *I'll never be able to do this*, whatever "this" anxiety-provoking thing is. Or, *If my parents [or whomever] would just help [in whatever way your anxious child is demanding], I wouldn't have to worry [or do the scary thing]*. I find that most anxious parents, however, blame themselves.

Other therapists have added to the list: outsourcing happiness, personalization (thinking something is your fault when you had nothing to do with the outcome), entitlement, a false sense of helplessness, and a false sense of responsibility to name a few.[10]

We all fall into at least one of the cognitive distortion categories. Which ones resonate with you? The issue with the distortions is that, particularly when it comes to parenting, we believe the thoughts are valid. After all, it's our children and our parenting that are at stake. Distortions aren't distortions to us. They're true and are thoughts that "should" be heeded. So the thought, as a result of those core beliefs, often stays stuck.

5. Rumination is the choice to stay in the distorted thoughts.

Years ago, my counselor shared a story I'll never forget. She told me about a video of a gymnast who was in a vault competition. Since then, I've done a little research on the vault. Typically, a gymnast runs down a padded runway. They then jump onto a springboard and spring onto the vault with their hands (called the preflight). In the off-flight, they twist or do some kind of maneuver before landing on the other side of the vault. The experience of the man in the video, however, was anything but typical. The video began as he was chalking his hands at the beginning of his turn. Then, he ran with all his might toward the vault. As he hurtled his body toward the vault in preflight, something went wrong with his steps. Rather than hitting the vault with his hands, he missed and slammed into the vault chest-first. After recovering, he did his best to walk gracefully to the end of the mat. As he turned to get back in line for his second attempt, he grabbed a folding chair and broke it over his own head. After finishing the story, she looked at me and said, "That's what you do to yourself constantly, Sissy." She was right. And it's called rumination.

In his book *Unwinding Anxiety*, psychiatrist Judson Brewer defines rumination as "focusing on one's distress and repeatedly thinking about it over and over."[11] It's considered a trademark of both anxiety and depression. Rumination is the cousin to perseveration, which is thinking about the same thing repeatedly. Sound familiar? It's easy for any of us to ruminate, whether it's about our failure or our fears.

A study from Harvard found that the familiarity of a mood state influences our staying in it. Our anxiety, or even our sadness, can become familiar and even comfortable, in a strange way.[12] Any deviation from that sadness or anxiety can create more anxiety. Have you ever heard the saying "Better the devil you know than the devil you don't"? It's that kind of idea.

Brewer says, "I see perseverative thinking as possibly the top issue tripping up my patients."[13] I would tend to agree. I believe one of the primary seductions of rumination is that it makes us feel more in control. As a parent, control is something you often want more of but feel you have less.

Rumination keeps us comfortable, makes us believe we're in control, and has a sneaky way of making us think that we'll finally come to the solution if we just keep thinking long enough. In effect, we're trying to solve problems that don't even exist yet. Rumination, just like anxiety, is a liar.

Rumination leads to depression.[14] It also creates negativity bias, which is the tendency to notice and dwell on negative events more than positive ones.[15] We end up developing what is often considered a worry circuit in the brain, well-worn pathways that make us even more prone to worry and anxiety. In fact, rumination has been found to strengthen the circuitry in the cortex that leads to anxiety.[16] In addition, research shows that when we continue to think about a negative event, we lengthen our emotional reaction to that event.[17]

Perfectionists are particularly prone to rumination (hello, your friend, the author who breaks chairs over my head). Perfectionists are in a perpetual loop of negative self-talk. We ruminate over all that we should be doing, all that we haven't done, and all that we've gotten wrong thus far. Plus, perfectionism has many of the same effects as rumination. Placing unreasonably high expectations on ourselves is "guaranteed" to increase our anxiety, according to research.[18] And like rumination, perfectionism is both a creator of anxiety and a response to it.

Obsessive-compulsive disorder is also linked to rumination. Obsessing is thinking perpetually about a certain situation. Compulsions are behaviors we repetitively engage in, believing they will bring relief. Behaviors can include washing, checking, counting, tapping, and various others. The issue with compulsive behaviors is that we have to engage in them more and more to find the relief we're seeking. Plus, we learn to trust the behavior more than we trust ourselves.

In the last chapter, we established that the amygdala is notorious for false alarms. In this chapter, we've learned that the cortex is known for misinformation. In other words, anxiety lies to us. Based on context and our core beliefs, we're prone to thoughts that have more to do with cognitive distortions than with reality. And then we keep those thoughts in a worried cycle through rumination. Our reactions have more to do with the misinformation than with the truth. Worry lies to us. It limits us. It keeps us from being present and keeps us from being ourselves. It also keeps us from enjoying the kids we love. But worry doesn't have to have the final word. There is good news.

Thoughts are just thoughts. We can review and regret or listen and learn from those thoughts. In fact, our very brains can learn through the same neuroplasticity that changes our amygdala. We can literally change the structure of our brains by the ways we choose to think and, therefore, act, all through a process called cognitive restructuring.

Five Things to Do When Anxiety Impacts Your Mind

After I wrote *Raising Worry-Free Girls*, one of the questions I was asked most on podcasts was "Is there a cure for anxiety?" I'm sad to say I don't believe there is a cure. Mostly because, as we've talked about, we can't change how God made us. You are anxious because you're conscientious. You care. You try hard. Things matter to you. And, as we said before, it's hard to turn down the volume on all of that caring. We can't cure anxious thoughts, but thanks to neuroplasticity, we can change our relationship with them. Anxious thoughts may still be present, but they don't have to have power. That's where cognitive restructuring comes in.

Cognitive restructuring literally changes the cortex. It's one of the most effective therapeutic tools in treating anxiety, depression, ADHD, and even issues such as substance abuse and eating disorders.[19] With cognitive restructuring, we notice and change our negative and maladaptive thoughts.

The key to cognitive restructuring techniques is not only learning to be aware of and dispute the anxious thoughts, but to replace them with new, positive coping thoughts.

1. Notice the negative.

As we've established, anxiety gets worse with certain types of thinking. The negative themes, cognitive distortions, and dysfunctional, self-defeating thoughts need to go. They don't help; they hurt. They strengthen the worry circuitry of our cortex and even scare our amygdala at times. But for those negative thoughts to stop, we first have to notice them. It's why we talked about themes and identifying specific cognitive distortions we're prone to. Anxiety is found in our thought-based interpretations of events, rather than in the events themselves. With cognitive fusion, those interpretations become our reality. And we react emotionally as if the interpretations were true. When we become aware of our interpretations and stop them, we can begin to take control of the emotional reactions the thoughts cause.[20]

What kinds of negative thoughts have you had lately? I would like you to trace the thoughts. In fact, I'd really like you to document them. In CBT, it's called a *thought spiral*.[21] I think of it like a helicopter going down. When someone in my office is in a thought spiral, I can almost hear the *whop-whop-whop* of the blades shutting down. An exercise we do in therapy uses a downward arrow. The thought starts like this:

My daughter has been getting angry a lot lately.
↓
Her behavior is demanding and manipulative.
↓
I wonder if something is wrong with her.
↓
I think she might have a personality disorder, like my mom.

Now we've quickly reached a place of catastrophic thinking.

I had a mom tell me recently that when she (the mom) was spiraling over her daughter's friend problems, her daughter looked at her and said, "Mom, it's going to be okay. It's not like I'm really sick or something."

The thoughts need to go. They don't help us or the kids we love. Recognize the negative thought and follow the thread—or arrow. The first step is always to notice when the cortex is producing negative thoughts or images. Practicing identifying, disproving, and replacing those thoughts can literally rewire the cortex to be less likely to activate the amygdala.[22]

We recognize the thought and then we stop it. Some types of therapy would even have us yell "STOP!" when it happens. My theory is that might frighten your kids. Other schools of thought would suggest a rubber band around your wrist you can snap to punish yourself when the unwanted thought surfaces. Again, sounds a little dramatic to me. We're already punishing ourselves enough. Instead, to help yourself focus on something else when the negative thoughts come, you can chew gum, suck on a cough drop, take a cold shower, sing a song, do a few jumping jacks, or even count the bumps on your steering wheel if you're waiting at a red light. I would also suggest asking your friends to help you catch yourself if you use words that sound like you're spiraling. You could have the equivalent of a cuss bucket with your spouse, where you have to put a quarter in each time you sound like you've fallen into a cognitive distortion theme. And then go to dinner somewhere fun on the earnings. You could wear a visible piece of jewelry to remind yourself what you're working on, which will bring it to mind any time you notice the jewelry. Whatever method you use, it's important to learn to catch yourself in the process. Notice and stop the thought. Then name it.

2. *Give it a name.*

In the introduction, I mentioned the importance of naming the worried voice for kids. For younger ones, we often call it the Worry Monster. Or Worry Bug, if they're frightened of monsters. We refer to it as the Worry Brain versus Smart Brain, as we teach them some of the very tools in this chapter. In the book *Brave* for teenage girls, I call it the Worry Whisperer.

One of my favorite therapy books is Jenni Schaefer's *Life Without Ed*. It is a profoundly helpful and surprisingly clever approach to one woman's experience with an eating disorder. *Ed*. Get it? She names him "Ed" for *eating disorder*. And the book chronicles her breakup with Ed.

With some of the kids in my office, I'll try to come up with clever names for the voice in their heads . . . or the thoughts they have as a result of their anxiety. In my experience, they're one and the same. One girl who becomes really angry and whose name happens to be Adeline has given her Worry Monster the name Mad-eline. I want you to come up with a name for your worry monster. When we give it a name, we (1) reduce its power and (2) start to learn that it's not us, but a voice outside of ourselves. I believe it's easier to fight that which is outside of us than what's within us.

The Anxiety & Phobia Workbook divides the voice into four categories: the Worrier (which furthers anxiety), the Critic (furthers low self-esteem), the Victim (furthers depression), and the Perfectionist (furthers both chronic stress and burnout).[23] Let's get creative. What name would you like to give your voice?

I do believe it's worth mentioning that there is a voice in all of our lives known as the father of lies. I had a critical reviewer on Amazon upset that I paired anxiety with Satan, but I strongly believe Satan does his best, especially in the time we're living in, to make us anxious. I obviously know anxiety can take on a clinical life of its own and impact us from a medical perspective, as well as a therapeutic one. But I would consider anxiety a liar, and John 8:44 says of Satan, "He was a murderer from the beginning, not holding to the truth, for there is no truth in him. When he lies, he speaks his native language, for he is a liar and the father of lies." So there does seem to be a strong relationship between anxiety that lies to us through our thoughts and the originator of those lies. I also particularly resonate with the idea of Satan being the originator of those thoughts, because I believe that what we are talking about, with noticing and naming and disputing the thoughts, is the very idea talked about in 2 Corinthians 10:5.

3. Disprove the thought.

"We demolish arguments and every pretension that sets itself up against the knowledge of God, and we take captive every thought to make it obedient to Christ" (2 Corinthians 10:5).

Paul sure seemed to understand the importance of stopping thoughts and changing them. We're taking thoughts captive by recognizing and naming them. But it's also important that we disprove them.

Our job, with our thoughts, is to be good detectives. We want to look for the evidence—first to support the thoughts and then to dispute the thoughts. We want to ask ourselves questions like (1) What is the evidence? (2) Is this always true? (3) What is the worst that could happen? (4) What is the likelihood that the worst will happen? (5) Am I looking at the whole picture, or only part of it?[24]

We want to follow the facts themselves, rather than our interpretation of those facts. Considering "If _____ then _____" possibilities can also be a helpful tool in your detective work, particularly with the worst-case scenario ideas. It's one I use in my office regularly too.

"If my son fails math, then he might have to repeat it."

"Then what?"

"He could have to take summer school."

"Then what?"

"He wouldn't get to go to the summer camp he loves."

"Then what?"

"He'd be really disappointed."

"And then what?"

"I guess he'd be okay and would probably learn better from the consequence of missing camp than my micromanaging his schoolwork."

Notice the negative. Give it a name. Be a good detective and disprove the thought. And now we get to replace that thought with something much better.

4. *Replace the thought.*

Research tells us that

> by deliberately thinking coping thoughts at every possible opportunity, you can rewire your cortex to produce coping thoughts on its own. . . .
>
> It's useful to watch for "musts" and "should" in your thinking. . . . If nothing else, replace "I should . . ." with "I'd like to . . ." That way, you aren't creating a rule that must be followed. Instead, you're simply expressing a goal or a desire—one that may or may not be met. It's a kinder, gentler thought.[25]

Those kinder, gentler thoughts can be tough, though. The negative ones not only seem to have more power, but they tend to stick around longer. An article I read recently described how negative and critical thoughts are more like Velcro, while our joyful and positive thoughts are like Teflon—they just slide right on by. It takes fifteen seconds of holding on to a positive thought for that thought to actually be imprinted in our minds.[26]

We want to replace those negative, critical thoughts with positive thoughts that build us up rather than tear us down and make us anxious. Philippians 4:8 says, "Finally, brothers and sisters, whatever is true, whatever is noble, whatever is right, whatever is pure, whatever is lovely, whatever is admirable—if anything is excellent or praiseworthy—think about such things."

We reinforce that which we pay attention to—or think about. In our kids and in ourselves. But how do we do it? How do we replace the negative thoughts with positive or coping thoughts? Reframing thoughts is another therapeutic tool we use in our offices. It's a little bit of the context we talked about in the beginning of the chapter. Remember the thought, context, core belief exercise? In every one of those situations, the context was the parent's love for their child. Rather than thinking, *My anxiety is making things worse for my kids and making me a worse parent*, I want you to think positive, coping thoughts like *I'm anxious because I love my kids. I care about them so much. My anxiety is driving me to get the help that's actually going to make me a better, more informed parent than I would have been otherwise*. Reframing is exactly what it sounds like. We take the same photo but put a new frame around it. When you bought this book, you might have been feeling some degree of shame over the way you interpreted your anxiety was impacting your kids. I want you to see it as your love and intentionality having caused you to pick up this book, and as your anxiety being a direct result of that great love. Let's take that thought captive and reframe it.

We can reframe or replace thoughts with more positive ones. We can also replace them with truth. I have kids and parents practice replacing the lies anxiety tells us with truth daily in my office. Scripture is a great place to start, with truth that speaks specifically to our worries. Philippians 4:6–7; Matthew 11:28–30; John 14:27; 1 Peter 5:7; Matthew 6:25–26; Psalm 59:16; Matthew 6:34; Psalm 55:22; Psalm 23:4; Isaiah 41:10; Joshua 1:9; Romans 8:31 (actually all of Romans 8); and Zephaniah 3:17 are a few of my favorites. Pick one verse and memorize it to act as both a grounding and reframing tool when you get anxious.

I also love the idea of a good mantra. The word sounds hokey, but it's just a statement that's true that you can go back to over and over, like "I'm stronger than any worry that comes my way." You can also think back to something brave you've done recently as a milestone.

I have an eleven-year-old girl who went on a really scary slide at a waterpark this summer. Since then, she says to herself, "If I can go down that slide, I can do this." What's your slide? What could you use as a milestone? I want you to think of a statement you can go back to when your thoughts start to spiral, one that not only brings peace but reminds you of how brave and capable you actually are.

A young woman I worked with for quite some time told me that when she comes up against something that makes her afraid, she says to herself, "Jesus and Sissy believe I can do this." I'd really love for you to be able to do the same. I certainly believe you can do this, or I wouldn't have written this book. But the trick is for you to start to believe that truth as well.

5. Stop being so hard on yourself.

I am confident you related to at least a few of the sentences at the beginning of this chapter. I also have a hunch that you connected with my story about the vaulter. In my three decades of counseling, I have never heard as many parents as weary, discouraged, and critical of themselves as I have of late. I know that the voice in your head and your thoughts turn toward self-criticism or even self-hatred way too frequently. Here's the honest truth: It never helps.

Breaking the chair over his head didn't help the vaulter. Not that I have a lot of sports references, but it makes me think of myself snow skiing. It is one of two sports I can do fairly well—water skiing being the other. I haven't let myself retire from either yet. When I go snow skiing, I typically do so with a group of friends. I have one friend who falls a good bit. When she does, she always comments about how I never fall. And I don't, for some reason. Maybe it goes back to that perfectionist idea of wanting to be in control. But I think it also has something to do with knowing the consequences of falling.

When I fall snow skiing, I get angry with myself. I push myself harder. The worry voice becomes incredibly critical in my head. I say things to myself like *That was stupid, Sissy. How could you fall on that run? Bend your knees. Keep your body facing down the mountain. Small curves in the snow with your skis. Those aren't small enough. You've got to try harder. Keep the turns tighter.* With every word, my teeth clench more and my body gets tighter and tighter . . . until I'm not skiing well, I'm even more frustrated, and I'm certainly not enjoying myself. Does that sound familiar? I believe that when we're critical of ourselves with the kids we love, we get tighter and tighter and, in reality, angrier and angrier. The anger may be directed at ourselves, but it can't help but spill over onto the kids we love. Being hard on ourselves doesn't help. In fact, I believe it only makes things worse. I want you to be honest about how you've been talking to yourself recently. I often ask the parents and kids I'm meeting with, "What's the worst thing you say to yourself sometimes?"

Remember the research that says when we think a thought repetitively, the structure of our brain changes? You're not only strengthening the worry circuitry, you're strengthening the self-hatred circuitry too. And that's circuitry none of us wants in our brains.

A study by social psychologist Thomas Curran found that there has been a 33 percent rise in perfectionism in the last few decades, with perfectionism being "broadly defined as a combination of excessively high personal standards and overly critical self-evaluations."[27] The study also found that perfectionists may be at greater risk of anxiety, depression, and suicidal thoughts, as they are chasing an unattainable goal in perfection.[28]

You're chasing an impossible goal in perfect parenting.

Proverbs 12:25 says, "Anxiety weighs down the heart, but a kind word cheers it up." I'm not sure about you, but often I'm waiting for that kind word from someone else. Maybe we're still waiting on our parents' approval that just doesn't come. Maybe we're even unconsciously seeking approval from the kids we love. That is not going to come, likely until they have kids themselves. Other people in our lives can help, and we certainly want to make sure we have people around us who encourage us. But when it comes down to it, we've got to learn to say kind words to ourselves. We've got to counter the critical voice with our own kindness. In his book *The Ragamuffin Gospel*, Brennan Manning reflects on an idea first put forward by the psychiatrist Carl Jung: When God calls us to love the least of these, maybe the ones He is calling us to love are ourselves.[29] Kind, positive self-talk is one of the most fundamental skills we learn in therapy. And it is also one of the most life changing.

If it sounds impossible to start to talk to yourself with kindness, I want you to go back to step one. Notice the negative. My guess is that you're believing more lies than you are truth, particularly about yourself. I recently read in a devotional by my dear friend Gail Pitt[30] something about God's voice versus Satan's that stopped me in my tracks; it is a message posted in various forms around the internet, shared below as a simple chart.

God's voice	Satan's voice
Stills you	Rushes you
Leads you	Pushes you
Reassures you	Frightens you
Enlightens you	Confuses you
Encourages you	Discourages you
Comforts you	Worries you
Calms you	Obsesses you
Convicts you	Condemns you

Satan is the father of lies. He speaks to us in that discouraging, condemning, worrying voice. And then we take up his voice as our own.

Instead, when the thoughts come, I want you to start by taking a deep breath. Notice the negative. Give it a name. Disprove the thought. Replace it with truth. And remember that all this anxiety is really only happening because you're trying to be the best parent you can be. And because you love those kids in your life like crazy.

Even if it's hard, just start the process. As Charlie Mackesy writes in the wonder of a book *The Boy, the Mole, the Fox and the Horse*, "'Sometimes I think you believe in me more than I do,' said the boy. 'You'll catch up,' said the horse."[31] And said our great, loving, encouraging, redeeming-all-things God. And Sissy.

Worry-Free Takeaways

1. We all have intrusive thoughts.
2. The thoughts that get stuck get stuck for a reason. Intrusive thoughts are predictable along the lines of context and your core beliefs.
3. Our interpretations are what fuel our anxiety.
4. Cognitive distortions are interpretations based on our core beliefs.
5. Rumination is the choice to stay in the distorted thought.
6. With cognitive restructuring, we can rewire the amygdala and replace the negative, maladaptive thoughts with positive, coping thoughts.
7. We want to start by noticing the negative.
8. Give the worried thought a name.
9. Disprove the thought by being a good thought detective.
10. Replace the negative thought with truth.
11. Stop being so hard on yourself.
12. God believes in you more than you could ever know. And so do I.

7

Help for Your Heart

Help for your heart. How does that phrase sound to you? It's what I want so much for you. That and the hope we'll talk about in the last section of the book. Yes, I believe help for your body is important. We won't get anywhere in this war on anxiety without it. And help for your mind is deeply valuable, as we truly can change the structure of our brains by learning to think differently. But what I want most is for you to find help for your heart. And hope. I believe both have the power not just to make you less anxious, but to transform you into a freer, truer version of the person and parent God made you to be.

If you had to pick three words to describe your heart right now, what would they be? And no, I don't mean in a cheesy, over-spiritualizing way. Several years ago, a friend I was having lunch with asked me how my heart was. Truth be told, my heart in that moment was annoyed. I'm not exactly sure what she was looking for, but her question didn't feel like it came from a place of caring curiosity, but potentially more from a desire to pat me on the head. It felt patronizing somehow—although I'm sure that wasn't the intent. I remember thinking, *If you're close enough to know how my heart is, you shouldn't have to ask.* But here I am, asking. Not

141

so much because I want to know the answer—but because I want *you* to know the answer. And I think we often don't. Especially when you're a new parent. The parent of a toddler. The parent of younger kids who are busy with practices and lessons and school and homework and all the things you help facilitate. When you're the parent of a teenager—which is hard on anyone's heart. Being a parent is hard. On your credit card. On your sleep. On your time management. On your patience. And ultimately, on your heart. On some days, it's too much with too few outlets. It brings so much joy and good with it, but it is hard. And what I hope to help you do, in this chapter, is to find your way back to your heart.

Let's start with a few questions I want you to think about:

What do you need right now? Physically? Emotionally? Spiritually?

How is your anxiety these days?

When do you feel least anxious?

When do you feel most anxious?

When do you feel most like you?

Five Things to Know about Anxiety and Your Heart

Anxiety is not just a liar . . . anxiety is an *insatiable* liar. Whatever we give that it asks for just makes it hungry for more. If we avoid the things we're anxious about, it makes us feel like we have to keep avoiding them or even avoid more things. If we use safety behaviors that make us feel okay, it requires more safety behaviors to keep us feeling okay. It demands that we sacrifice things we wish we could do and parts of who we are. It's never enough. Anxiety loves control, and once we start giving in, it only screams for more.

The five things I want you to know in this chapter are the five things anxiety is going to try to require of you in this journey of parenting—or even just in this journey of living life this side of heaven. Anxiety craves control, certainty, comfort, predictability, and avoidance. And it wants all of the above immediately and constantly.

1. Anxiety demands control.

As humans, we have a distorted perspective on control. We talk so much about the importance of letting go of it, but we all still somehow spend our days quietly (or loudly) clamoring for it. In case you somehow missed the life memo, control doesn't work. My guess is there's no way you've missed it, now that you're a parent . . . especially if you have kids over the age of two days. Or even more so, twelve years. My colleague David and I talk often about how much we love to speak to parenting conferences where there are parents of teenagers in the room. Young parents often believe that if they just work hard enough and do all the things that people like us say, their kids are going to be successful. Or happy. Or whatever the highest priority is. Parents of teenagers already know differently. They've had enough experiences with their kids melting down at the grocery, embarrassing them in front of their friends when they've "been raised better," and making destructive choices when they certainly know better. All the things. These little people we love are out of our control from the moment they come out of the womb. And it only becomes more evident as they grow.

When have you seen evidence of this in your kids? What about in your life in general? It's not just our kids we can't control. It's the other kids too—maybe especially the ones who are trolling social media. Or the ones driving other cars. Or having our kids over for sleepovers. We can't control the circumstances for the kids we love. Or for ourselves. There is so much we can't do. But one thing we *can* do is pray.

Anne Lamott has a book called *Help, Thanks, Wow*. The reason she titled the book with those three words is because she believes they're the three essential prayers.[1] I love that none of the words implies any control on our part. *Help. Thanks. Wow.* It's evident the control is all in God's hands. We just get to ask and stand in awe and gratitude. In another book, Lamott quotes a woman who said that a lot of the older folks she knows in recovery simply pray "Whatever" at the beginning of the day and "Oh well" at its end.[2] As soon as I read that sentence in her book, it made me laugh. It wasn't until several years later that I heard my mom in the last few months of battling a chronic illness say the words "Oh well" almost every day. It was the phrase she used most often, particularly when talking about her illness. She knew she didn't have any control. And I think she lived with more peace (or at least was trying to) because of it. Anxiety, however, lies to us and tries to tell us different.

Anxiety will tell you that if you check your son's online portal enough and get him the "right" tutor, you can help him pass the sixth grade. Anxiety will tell you that if you invite all the new kids over and work with your daughter on how she interacts, she'll have the "right" friends at her new school. If you do all the "right" things, your son will make good choices. Your daughter will be happy and not have to deal with the anxiety that has crippled you for so much of your life. As my dear friend and the executive director of Daystar, Melissa, would say, control is an illusion. There are a whole lot of "rights" in the previous statements. When we're living under the illusion of our control, we're also living under the illusion that we know best. Maybe even better than God. Anxiety is lying to us yet again. Instead, I love these words from the well-known prayer that originated in the 1930s and still holds true today. It's called the Serenity Prayer, and it begins with the familiar "God, grant me . . ." I'd encourage you to look up the prayer yourself and maybe put it somewhere you'll see regularly. I did for myself, as I've always loved it. But until I found the original, I had never heard how it ended. The final stanza speaks of surrendering to God's will and God making things right, then concludes with this:

> So that I may be reasonably happy in this life,
> And supremely happy with Him forever in the next.[3]

So that you and your children may be reasonably happy in this life . . . The bottom line on the lie of control is that you don't have it anyway. Neither do I. We can let go of the illusion. Primarily because Someone much wiser than you and me does have control. And He's not anxious a bit.

2. Anxiety craves certainty.

Certainty is another form of control, one anxiety will tell you that you have to have in order to feel safe. You want to know that your child will get into the right elementary school. Make the soccer team. Have encouraging friends in high school. What is something you would like certainty about? Think about how you would fill in the blank: *If I only knew _____, I could feel some peace.*

I remember thinking in my twenties, *If God would just put on a billboard what my life is going to look like at forty, I'd be okay. I'm fine with whatever happens. I just want to know.* But the reality is, if He had, I wouldn't have been okay back then. There are pieces of my life that are true post-forty that would have given me way more anxiety than I already had. Mostly because I wouldn't have known the whole picture. I wouldn't have known that, even in the midst of some things I prayed for being unanswered, there was so much good that I could never have dreamed up. I'm glad I didn't know now, looking back. And in reality, certainty wasn't what I longed for in those times. I wanted to know that God had my good in His heart. In His plan. It's what you long for with your kids. That He has their good in mind and is going to bring it to fruition.

I have a friend who says, "The older I get, the less I know. But what I know, I really know." I feel that way a little these days. And I can say with certainty that God has your good and the good of your kids in mind and He will bring it to fruition. In His timing. But what we are certain we need in our timing may be different from His good in His timing.

Certainty can either make us more demanding (of more certainty) and anxious (when we don't get it) or lead us on the long, faltering path toward trust. Anxiety would hold us back, waiting on certainty always. Anxiety would say that we can't take a step until we know the bridge will hold. We can't take a risk until we know the outcome. We can't trust until we know the whole story.

Certainty is another illusion. We don't have certainty in this life—at least not for long. What's the most recent thing you can call to mind that you were certain of? What do you know without a doubt? I want you to write down ten things you're certain of right now.

My guess is that there aren't many things, other than those that are in your control. In fact, that's an exercise I have kids do in my office regularly—and one you can do as well. Draw a circle. In that circle, I want you to write down what you can control. What you're certain of. Mostly, those things have to do with your own actions and reactions, rather than those of others. Outside the circle, I want you to write down the things you can't control. They can be things in general or about a situation that's currently making you anxious.

Anxiety demands certainty. As we give in to anxiety's demands, we become more demanding ourselves. That the others around us will do what we are asking, which is more what our anxiety is asking than we are as our best selves. What is one thing you've been requiring of others lately that is more about anxiety's need for certainty than your own? What could you let go of? One thing I think I know for certain about certainty is that there isn't a lot of it this side of heaven. And the tighter we hold on to get it, the more we strangle out the freedom to be who we long to be and connect with others in ways that bring joy—for them and for us.

3. Anxiety desires comfort.

Anxious kids are pretty obvious in their desperation for comfort. You know this, if you have one. They will loudly and emotionally refuse the things that make them anxious, that cause them to step outside of their comfort zones. Several years ago, I had an extensive surgery that kept me overnight in the hospital. I will never forget coming home to an "emergency call" from a dad whose daughter refused to go to her overnight summer camp. I called the dad back from my bed, which probably was the opposite of what he wanted, as I was still on pain meds and not my most helpful self. But I remember two things: One is the vehemence and tears involved in his daughter's unwillingness to go. The other is my surprise at this dad's boldness to demand that I call him back after just getting home from a major surgery. But his daughter wanted comfort. She wanted the comfort of her own room over the social anxiety she believed would come at camp. And her dad wanted the comfort of talking to his daughter's counselor. It didn't work.

As we talked about before, for your kids to work through their anxiety, they have to do the scary thing. For us to work through our anxiety, we have to do the scary thing. Not make the phone call. Help our kids with a plan to go to camp with coping skills in place. Help them with a plan to get to and stay in school, even when they're anxious. Stop ourselves from checking the online portal. Stop ourselves from micromanaging. Stop ourselves from texting them repetitively to see if they've arrived. The scary thing is not going to bring comfort, even though our anxiety is going to make a lot of noise about how important and necessary comfort is. We and the kids we love need to step into scary things, to retrain our brains and to remind ourselves that we're capable. And that we can trust in Someone who does bring comfort more than any amount of certainty or control ever could.

What is one way you're prioritizing your child's comfort over their courage? How are you letting anxiety win? What's one way you're prioritizing your comfort over your own courage? We often sacrifice one to gain the other. And I would state strongly to the worry monster that comfort is temporary. Courage and trust are lasting.

4. *Anxiety requires predictability.*

As I'm writing this chapter, the meteorologists in Nashville are calling for seven inches of snow starting tonight. But when you read the fine print, they really don't have a clue if it will move north, drop two inches, or accumulate up to a foot. We're also in the midst of the Omicron wave of the COVID pandemic. There is a hashtag trending, #CDCsays, because the number of days to quarantine if you have tested positive for the virus has recently dropped from fourteen days to ten days to five. And there are a variety of jokes online about how the "CDC says you can now run with scissors" and all manner of silly activities. One of my favorites is "The CDC says, 'You got to know when to hold 'em, know when to fold 'em.'" In all seriousness, I can't imagine how difficult the folks at the CDC have had it since this pandemic began. But the reality is, with all of the research that has been done on this virus, they still don't know. We don't know. My hope is that we will by the time you read this book. But as of now, the virus has been a vivid reminder to those of us living in these times that there is just not a lot of predictability around us. Or sometimes even inside of us.

Paul points us to that great truth in Romans 7:15–16, 18–21 in *The Message*:

> What I don't understand about myself is that I decide one way, but then I act another, doing things I absolutely despise. So if I can't be trusted to figure out what is best for myself and then do it, it becomes obvious that God's command is necessary. . . .
> I can will it, but I can't *do* it. I decide to do good, but I don't *really* do it; I decide not to do bad, but then I do it anyway. My decisions, such as they are, don't result in actions. Something has gone wrong deep within me and gets the better of me every time. It happens so regularly that it's predictable.

We ourselves are predictably unpredictable. As are the kids we love and the circumstances of life this side of heaven. I hope you've already heard me say multiple times that you will blow it, and blow it often, as a parent. The wisest, most intentional of parents I know tell me stories within the confidentiality of my office of getting angrier at their kids than they ever imagined they would. As Paul described, you'll have a plan for how you're going to act and then you'll do the opposite. Your kids will too. Plans will change. And you and your kids will change in the midst of them. Life will be predictably unpredictable. But we can have the confidence of One who lives within us who is steady. Hebrews 13:8 says, "Jesus Christ is the same yesterday and today and forever." And Romans 15:3–5 in *The Message* says,

> That's exactly what Jesus did. He didn't make it easy for himself by avoiding people's troubles, but waded right in and helped out. "I took on the troubles of the troubled," is the way Scripture

puts it. Even if it was written in Scripture long ago, you can be sure it's written for *us*. God wants the combination of his steady, constant calling and warm, personal counsel in Scripture to come to characterize *us*, keeping us alert for whatever he will do next. May our dependably steady and warmly personal God develop maturity in you so that you get along with each other as well as Jesus gets along with us all.

Any steadiness or predictability in our lives is found in Him and through Him. He wants the combination of His steady, constant calling and warm, personal counsel in Scripture to come to characterize us, keeping us alert for whatever He will do next. And we sure don't want to miss what comes next because anxiety has told us to avoid it.

5. Anxiety insists on avoidance.

It's easier to talk about what anxiety-producing avoidance looks like in kids. They drop out of the track team. They stop going to school. They don't go to birthday parties, or they eat lunch by themselves at school. And we, sadly, help them avoid those anxiety-producing events. Research says, if you remember, that escape and avoidance are the two primary coping skills parents use most when it comes to their kids' anxiety.[4] We know enough already to realize escape and avoidance don't help. In fact, they only make things worse. The more we avoid, the more the worry monster loudly convinces us we need to avoid—in our kids' lives and, truth be told, in our own as well. Avoidance strengthens anxiety.

It's a little trickier with us. We make the avoidance look good. We know how to gloss over it. We don't necessarily admit to having a little social anxiety. We just "don't feel good," or "we have too much going on these days," or "it's not really one of our gifts." We come up with excuses with the most convincing rationale for getting us off the hook. What's an excuse you use regularly? Obviously, I believe saying no is important at times. We're going to talk more about such self-care toward the end of this chapter. But you intuitively know the difference, when you dig deep, between making choices out of a place of self-care and a place of anxiety. Anxiety is a limiter: You can't do it. You're not ready. You're not _____ enough. And we will never allow ourselves to learn differently if we listen to the limiting lies anxiety tells us. What is one thing you've avoided recently based on your anxiety? What is one thing you'd like to learn to do that might make you a little anxious, but would ultimately make you feel proud and capable and brave? It could be something as small as a cooking class or as adventurous as sky diving. It could be volunteering more. Or taking your child and several friends on a trip somewhere. Applying for a new job. Initiating a trip with friends on your own. I want you to come up with one thing you would like to do if anxiety weren't a factor. I surely believe you can do it. And I think the way you're feeling right now means it's time to try.

Anxiety uses control, certainty, comfort, predictability, and avoidance to limit us. He lies and uses each idea to hold us hostage, requiring more and more of us and giving us nothing back but disappointment with ourselves. Ultimately, he just gives us more of himself—more anxiety, which is not what I want for you. And it's not what I believe you want for yourself or for the kids you love. Let's talk about some things you can do to drown out his insatiable demands.

Five Things to Do to Help Your Anxious Heart

1. Go deeper than the anxiety.

My little Havanese dog, Lucy, sleeps with me every night. Some of you might not be people who let your dog sleep with you. Some of you might not be dog people at all. But I certainly am. If you're not, that's okay. We can still be friends. Lucy not only sleeps beside me, but counsels kids with me every single day. She's featured in my book on anxiety for little girls and has become quite the celebrity at Daystar and beyond. She gets her own fan mail. She's my best friend. When I had the surgery I mentioned earlier, Lucy lived on my bed for two whole weeks. My mom (who stayed with me during my recovery) would take her outside and

Lucy would come right back to my bed. In fact, she would only eat if food was brought to her there. When I took a shower, she would sit outside the shower the entire time. I'll never forget the first time I left the house after my surgery: She wrapped her little front paws around my leg and bit me. I think she was saying, "My job is not done. You aren't allowed out of my sight yet." We don't deserve our dogs, do we? You can imagine that Lucy is one of my primary contexts.

Lucy is thirteen at the time I'm writing this book. A few nights ago, she started breathing funny in the middle of the night. I woke up in a panic and immediately was convinced she was dying. I already had my route to the emergency vet planned when, ten minutes later, she was fine.

But here's the deal. My anxiety over Lucy was secondary. Yes, she is my context. And yes, I had a lot of emotion quickly over something being wrong with her because I love her. But there are some nights and some seasons I would have waited it out without the panic. It wasn't until the next day that I realized I had been carrying a lot of sadness and hadn't stopped to acknowledge it. And I think that sadness came out as anxiety over my little black-and-white furry context.

Our emotions are always indicators that there is more to the story. Psychologist Dan Allender writes, "The reason for looking inside is not to effect direct change of negative emotions to positive emotions. Instead, we are to listen to and ponder what we feel in order to be moved to the far deeper issue of what our hearts are doing with God and others."[5]

We talk often at Daystar about emotions being like a warning light in a car. Their arrival usually means something deeper is going on inside of us. Most psychologists would agree that anger is a secondary emotion, with other feelings at its root. I believe the same is true, for many of us, with anxiety. At the times we're most anxious and have the most need for control to manage that anxiety, there is often something going on that is deeper than the anxiety itself. And we would do well not just to pay attention, but to express it.

If you're new to this idea of feelings and warning lights, you can try a few things I recommend in my office—and that I have to do sometimes myself. I'll often lie in bed feeling disconcerted but not knowing why. I'll try to come up with three feelings I experienced that day and what might have precipitated those feelings. Journaling can also be a great way to get to the heart of what we're feeling. I will often have kids note in a journal any time their anxiety rises above a five on a scale of one to ten and write down two or three other emotions they're feeling in addition to the anxiety. Those feelings are often at anxiety's root for them. We want to take notice and go deeper than the presenting anxiety or anger. But we don't want to stop there. We want to move from understanding the emotions to expressing those same emotions.

2. Share your feelings.

> The opposite of recognizing that we're feeling something is denying our emotions. The opposite of being curious is disengaging. When we deny our stories and disengage from tough emotions, they don't go away; instead, they own us, they define us.
>
> Brené Brown[6]

I believe that anxiety and the healthy expression of emotions have an inverse relationship. The more we make a habit of regularly sharing our feelings, the less anxious we are. The less we talk about those feelings, the more they come out sideways as anxiety. Suppressed emotions still have to go somewhere. When we don't let them out, they often turn inward and manifest as anxiety, anger, or even depression.

But who has time to process those emotions? You're too busy with your kids. Who would you share them with anyway? Who would possibly want to hear this negative voice you have looping around in your head? Dr. Edmund Bourne writes that we withhold feelings because (1) we have a significant need for control and/or (2) we grew up with parents who were overly critical.[7] Either or both of those may be true for you. But I believe any critical voice you heard has now likely become part of your own internal dialogue. It's not necessarily that someone else is telling you that you "shouldn't" feel certain things. You're telling yourself often and loudly enough. I also believe that based on what we know to be true about anxious individuals being kind and conscientious, it may be that you don't believe those feelings are appropriate. Especially anger.

If you're a type A personality, a perfectionist, or an Enneagram 1, our root sin is anger, according to Richard Rohr. "'Anger' is their [a 1's] root sin, although they seldom get directly angry. It is more a low-level resentment because the world is not the way they know it should be! They repress their anger because they see it as something imperfect in themselves."[8] We feel anger isn't appropriate for us. If we become angry, others will see us as the fallible people we are. So we shove it down deeper, only to have it come out—from what I see in counseling—at the kids we love. Or at ourselves and then at the kids we love. It becomes a self-sustaining cycle. We don't admit the anger we feel bubbling beneath the surface of our lives because we don't like it. We don't like who we are when we feel it. And because we don't admit it, anger only gains more power and sometimes more ferocity in its desire to define us. It only creates more anxiety.

One of the things I've noticed over time, particularly with girls, is that anxiety is connected to their intuition. In fact, I believe anxiety is intuition turned on itself. These girls have a gut feeling that someone is being selfish or unkind. Someone is being divisive or even just having an off day. But instead of acknowledging something negative about someone else, it's easier for these conscientious, kindhearted girls to blame themselves. *It must be something about me—because it's surely not them.* I believe the same is true for conscientious, kindhearted adults (ahem). We deny both our intuition and our feelings. We go inward with them, not wanting to be negative or inappropriate, believing those emotions aren't acceptable. And in doing so, we deny part of who we are, part of what God might be trying to tell us, and we perpetuate the anxiety cycle.

It's interesting that nowhere in Scripture does Jesus tell us any emotion not to feel besides fear. Not anger. Not sadness. Not disappointment or frustration. Just fear, which we'll come back to in the last section of the book. He does tell us in our anger not to sin (Ephesians 4:26), which presupposes we will be angry. It's not what we feel, but what we do with those feelings that's the issue. Emotions are scattered throughout Scripture. The Psalms are a great place to find a variety of them and examples of the writers turning toward God with those emotions. My assumption is that God knew how it would impact us to deny our emotions, and therefore He filled Scripture with people who loved Him and failed often, just like you and me, and people who expressed their emotions regularly.

Again, it's not what we feel, but what we do and don't do with those feelings that becomes the problem. Unexpressed emotions not only create anxiety but, according to Ephesians 4 and certainly according to my own life, also cause us to sin.

So here's what I want you to do. Remember that your anxiety and your anger both act as warning lights for something more going on inside of you. Go deeper. Follow the thread to see what really might be at the root of your emotions. Allow yourself to experience your feelings and share them. Write in a journal. Call a trusted friend. Go for a walk with your spouse and talk about what's been happening inside. The people who love you want to know. They want to help share your burden—even if it feels like they have a lot going on externally. (I might hear that excuse from parents from time to time.) Even if it feels like you have a lot going on internally. (That one too.) There are no negative feelings. There are just feelings. And those feelings are meant to be shared and to point you toward something much deeper happening inside of you. And something much deeper that God has called you to as well.

3. Do the scary thing.

Now you get to practice. How do you feel when you read "To work through your fear, you have to do the scary thing"? What scary things does that bring to mind?

Here's the deal: I'm not going to throw you into the deep end without any help. We're going to use a training-wheels approach to scary things. The same as we would do with kids. For example, we have a lot of parents who sign their kids up for our little summer retreat program called Hopetown without their child ever having spent the night away from home. I believe that's a recipe for disaster—for the child and for us! But I encourage parents to have their kids work their way toward Hopetown. First, the parents go out of town and a grandparent stays with them at their own house. Second, the kids stay with the grandparent at the grandparent's house. Next, they stay with another family member, such as an aunt or cousin. Next, they have a sleepover with a close family friend, where the child knows both the child and the parents well. Sleeping away for seven nights doesn't sound nearly as scary when you've successfully slept away for several already. It's a training-wheels approach. We do the same with kids who don't want to sleep in their own beds, who have a fear of going to school, and who struggle with everything in between. Almost every kind of fear we can work toward gradually, step by step, whether we're incorporating gradual behavior toward the desired action or removing gradual behavior toward the desired action. Adding behavior would be the sleepover example. Removing behavior might be more for you, such as checking less frequently your child's online portal for grades or the app that tells you where your teenager is.

In therapy terms, it's called *exposure therapy*. Exposure therapy is a cornerstone of cognitive behavioral therapy.[9] According to the American Psychological Association, therapists "create a safe environment in which to 'expose' individuals to the things they fear and avoid. The exposure to the feared objects, activities or situations in a safe environment helps reduce fear and decrease avoidance."[10] Exposure therapy can take place in our imaginations, which is called imaginal therapy, or in vivo, which are real-life exposures. So if you're afraid of speaking in public and know you have to speak to the PTO soon, your first step could be imagining yourself in front of the group successfully delivering your message.

You may remember from the chapter "Help for Your Body" that the only way to create lasting change in the amygdala is through experience.[11] We have to do the scary thing, gradually and with help. In fact, research says that we need to stay in the scary thing until it's no longer scary to us. In the beginning, however, it will be. For us to create lasting change in the amygdala, it has to be activated. Activate to generate, remember?

So here's what I want you to do: In *Braver, Stronger, Smarter*, I have a drawing of a ladder. I want you to draw a ladder for yourself. On the top rung, write down the scariest of scary things you'd like to work toward. Then step down the ladder, filling in each rung, according to the level of anxiety produced by activities that work toward that scary thing. In the beginning—on the bottom rungs—the activities can be imaginal. With each step, you're going to practice your tools for the body such as breathing and grounding. And your tools for your brain, such as reframing the thought. The goal is to stay on each rung until that activity is no longer anxiety producing . . . which may take weeks or even months. Time doesn't matter; what matters is that you are rewiring your brain.

Let's use another example:

When you worry about your kids, you've noticed that you start to behave obsessively. It's not that you're checking their grades or location on the app, but you're literally checking to make sure the doors in your home are locked. Not related, but that's how anxiety sometimes works. Another type of exposure therapy is called *response prevention*. It's a tool that's helpful when we have obsessive tendencies or actual OCD. So rather than working toward doing something scary, we're working toward not doing something that keeps us from feeling afraid. If you check to make sure your doors are locked three times before going to bed, the first exposure would be imagining yourself not checking before bed, breathing deeply the entire time. Next, you'd allow yourself to check twice. Then once per night. Then every other. You get the idea. Keep reducing the amount you're allowing yourself to check until your amygdala isn't activated during the exposure and the anxiety barely registers for you, if at all. You could even rate your anxiety on a one-to-ten scale each time you complete the exercise.

4. *Practice makes progress.*

It's something we say constantly to parents. Practice doesn't make perfect. I can't think of one thing I can actually do perfectly out of all the things I have practiced in my life. And perfect isn't the goal anyway. When perfection is our goal, anxiety will always be the outcome. Practice makes progress—even in the realm of anxiety.

In fact, research says the primary reason individuals don't overcome their anxiety is because they don't practice. For kids, I believe the primary reason they don't practice is laziness, and maybe a sense of comfort. It's just too hard to do the scary thing. It's easier to lose their tempers and use their parents as their primary coping skill than it is to practice the coping skills they have learned will work. It's too much of a risk to reach out to a new friend or try out for a new sport. In addition, many of them are too young to really understand the power of neuroplasticity and have a hard time imagining the freedom they can find on the other side of anxiety. So instead, they stay comfortable and don't do the work.

We understand the difference practice can make, however. Not only is neuroplasticity fascinating, but it also makes sense. We want things to be different. But I believe we let other excuses creep in. We're too busy. We're prioritizing our kids' mental health over our own. Other things take priority and consume our energy. But research tells us that anxiety left untreated only gets worse.[12] The truth is that this isn't going to go away. I wish it would. But you can beat it with practice. Practice makes progress, and you're certainly worth every bit of effort that practicing will take.

5. *Practice self-care.*

Many of us have read about the fascinating research around growth versus fixed mindsets, developed by Stanford University researcher Dr. Carol Dweck. With a growth mindset, individuals "believe their talents can be developed (through hard work, good strategies, and input from others). . . . They tend to achieve more than those with a more fixed mindset (those who believe their talents are innate gifts)."[13]

Research has found that mindset does impact mental health. In a study of adolescents, a fixed mindset was more often associated with greater mental health problems. Teenagers with a growth mindset, on the other hand, were less likely to experience depression, anxiety, and aggression. For college students, growth mindsets continued to have positive effects on mental health, with students less likely to experience depression, anxiety, and perfectionism.[14] So just the belief that practice does, in fact, make progress encourages our growth and reduces our anxiety.

I've recently read about another mindset that was a little less familiar to me: a kindness mindset. "Performing acts of kindness can help those with social anxiety and social avoidance. It can also help boost confidence and self-esteem," according to a study published in the journal *Motivation and Emotion*.[15] A kindness mindset is simply both the desire and action of doing things for others. The acts of kindness don't have to be extravagant. They can involve simpler tasks, such as encouraging someone, holding a door open, volunteering, or even just saying "thank you." I love the idea that kindness toward others can reduce anxiety. In fact, it reminds me of one of my favorite Scripture passages to share with girls in my office:

> My dear children, let's not just talk about love; let's practice real love. This is the only way we'll know we're living truly, living in God's reality. It's also the way to shut down debilitating self-criticism, even when there is something to it. For God is greater than our worried hearts and knows more about us than we do ourselves.
>
> 1 John 3:18–20 MESSAGE

A kindness mindset operates under the same principle. When we do things for others, we feel better about who we are, reducing our anxiety and stress.

If we go back to Brennan Manning's idea that we ourselves may actually be the "least of these" that Jesus talks about in the Gospels, the same may be true of the kindness mindset. The one you need to be kind to today might just be yourself.

I think, honestly, that much more than helping parents—especially conscientious, try-hard parents (the ones reading this book)—learn to give their kids grace, I'd like to help you learn to give yourself grace. To take care of yourself. I believe that practicing your own self-care has a much more profound impact in the lives of your kids than trying hard to be a good parent. As with all the ideas in the first section, trying hard to be a good parent just doesn't work. It makes you tighter and often angrier and ultimately much more anxious. We only give out of an overflow of what we receive. When you're running on empty, empty is exactly what you have to give.

In fact, I want you to be practicing self-care in three categories: physical, emotional, and spiritual. Caring for yourself physically involves exercise and eating right, going to check-ups, and maintaining the health of your body. Caring for yourself emotionally involves naming and sharing your emotions, taking breaks (such as adult-only vacations and dinners out with your spouse or friends) during the harder (and maybe all) seasons of parenting, and potentially even going to counseling yourself. Caring for yourself spiritually involves being in God's Word, worship, and being in community with other like-minded believers.

I recently met with a couple who came in to talk about their five kids, one of whom was eight years old and on the autism spectrum. They wanted strategies to deal with the chaos that was rampant in their home. What I gave them, instead, was one primary suggestion for the self-care of themselves and their marriage. I think it surprised them that I didn't throw more ideas and techniques their way. (Okay, maybe I had a few more specific ideas, but this was far and away the most important.) I told them I wanted them to go for a ten-minute walk each day without their kids. It was that simple. I knew that those five kids and just the normal pace of life with them had to be wearing, especially when they laughed uncomfortably and told me they didn't take much time for themselves or each other. "There's just no time," they said. My response to them was that I believed those walks without kids would do more for their kids than many of the things they were doing with them. I didn't care if they were having great conversations while they were walking, whether they were praying together or silent. My hope is that they do all three. As a parent, you have to practice self-care. You are giving so much on a daily basis. There is no time for you unless you create it.

In *The Anxiety and Phobia Workbook*, Dr. Bourne says that "without periods of downtime, any stress you experience while dealing with work or other responsibilities tends to become cumulative."[16] Our emotions are indicators of more going on beneath the surface. Strong emotions are, at times, indicators of unmet needs. What needs do you have that you might not acknowledge are currently unmet? What could you do, even in ten minutes, to fulfill those needs?

Let's break it down into categories.

What are three things you could do to take better care of yourself physically?

What are three things you could do to take better care of yourself emotionally?

What are three things you could do to take better care of yourself spiritually?

Maybe for the last question it would be more accurate to ask this: What are three things you could do to allow God to take care of you? Because that's what He wants to do. God cares about your heart. He wants to use every emotion He's given you to draw you to himself. And then He wants to bind up those wounds, bottle up those tears, and bring hope to every worry you've encountered. He doesn't want you to be alone in whatever fears you have right now. About your kids. About your parenting. About your own life. About their future or yours. He is with you and has already gone ahead of you.

One of my favorite verses has always been Zephaniah 3:17. I love the image of God delighting in us and rejoicing over us with singing. Until today, I've never paid attention to the phrase "He will quiet you with His love" (NKJV). That is my prayer for you as we close this chapter. That you and your worries will be quieted by God's love—for you and your kids. That you will know He is greater than your worried heart, and He has so much good headed your way and theirs.

Worry-Free Takeaways

1. Being a parent is hard on your heart . . . and on having a sense of hope.
2. We need more than tools.
3. Anxiety is an insatiable liar. Whatever we give that it asks for just makes it hungry for more.
4. Anxiety demands control. Control doesn't work.
5. Anxiety craves certainty. Certainty can make us more demanding (of more certainty) and anxious (when we don't get it), or it can lead us on the long, faltering path toward trust.
6. Anxiety desires comfort. Comfort is temporary. Courage and trust are lasting.
7. Anxiety requires predictability. Any steadiness or predictability in our lives is found in God and through Him.
8. Anxiety insists on avoidance. Avoidance strengthens anxiety.
9. Go deeper than the anxiety.
10. Share your feelings.
11. Do the scary thing.
12. Practice makes progress, not perfect.
13. Practice self-care.

8

Help for Your Kids

As you've read this book so far, my guess is that you've bounced back and forth between thinking about your kids and your own growing up years. The things you missed and the things you want to be sure to instill. As you know, they are inextricably linked.

So here's what I want you to think about: Based on what you have read so far, what are some of the things you wish you had known growing up regarding emotions and anxiety?

One of the things I love to talk with parents about is that phrase "My mom always said . . ." or "My dad always said . . ." We all have endings to those sentences. For most of us, those answers weren't necessarily intentional on our parents' part. They were an overflow of their world view—their perspective on life or relationships. And sometimes, those perspectives arose out of their own undealt-with issues. I have one friend whose mom always said, "Everyone has an ulterior motive." That is certainly an example of a world view that arose from her issues and one that likely wasn't helpful for my friend.

How would you finish those sentences? What are two or three things your mom or dad always said? How do you feel about those statements? Agree or disagree? Do you find yourself saying them, or at least thinking them?

We know better. We know more than our parents did when we were growing up. We have access to more resources. We know more about anxiety and what causes it. You are doing your best to become the first generation of healthy parents. And my hope, in this book, is to continue to encourage you in that health. So I'm not sure what you wish you had known. But I have five things I wish someone had told you back then. In fact, they're five things I still want you to know today.

Five Things I Want You to Know for You

1. *Whatever you are feeling right now makes sense.*

This statement is probably the statement I say more than anything else in my counseling office . . . to both parents and kids. However, it's not often what we grew up believing. And how many of us were told just the opposite? I have a vivid memory of being in the backseat of the car with a friend when I was little and her trying to tell her dad she was sad. His only response to her was "That's stupid!" It's so vivid to me because I couldn't believe her dad would use that word with her. But I didn't realize the messaging was equally as harmful as the word: *Your feelings not only don't matter, but they're wrong and foolish.* You may have been told something similar. Or it may have been that your feelings were just dismissed. "Oh honey, it's not that big of a deal." "You're fine." "That's nothing to worry about." Or your intuition was negated. "I don't really know what you're talking about." "That's not true. Your dad would never say (or do) that." Maybe you even were told you were too sensitive.

Author Anne Lamott has an entire chapter in her book *Stitches* called the "Overly Sensitive Child."

> If you were raised in the 1950s or 1960s, and grasped how scary the world could be, in Birmingham, Vietnam and the house on the corner where the daddy drank, you were diagnosed as being

the overly sensitive child. There were entire books written on the subject of the overly sensitive child. What the term meant was that you noticed how unhappy or crazy your parents were. . . . You looked into things too deeply, and you noticed things that not many others could see. . . .

As far as I can recall, none of the adults in my life ever once remembered to say, "Some people have a thick skin and you don't. Your heart is really open and that is going to cause pain, but that is an appropriate response to this world. The cost is high, but the blessing of being compassionate is beyond your wildest dreams. However, you're not going to feel that a lot in seventh grade. Just hang on."[1]

Whatever you are feeling right now not only makes sense—it matters. And it is certainly not because something is wrong with you.

2. Your feelings are not meant to act as stumbling blocks but as milestones that reflect something important for you and about the heart of God.

As we established in the last chapter, there is always more to the story. I tell a lot of folks in my office to "follow the thread," especially if they're from the conscientious, trying-to-be-kind-all-the-time school of anxiety. I know many adults who lie in bed every night with a vague sense of worry or dread. In those times, it's important to see what could be underneath the vagueness. I'll tell some of my clients to choose three feelings they might have experienced that day, like in the exercise we talked about earlier. What are three things that could have been hard? Made you sad? Angry? Hurt? Often, when we follow the thread, we find the "more" to the story.

In fact, I believe every home should have a feelings chart hanging on the fridge. In our book *Are My Kids on Track?*, David, Melissa, and I talk about the importance of helping kids build an emotional vocabulary. It's the first of the twelve emotional, social, and spiritual milestones that the book is built on and that we believe every child needs to reach. We talk about each milestone like a muscle, with some kids having more muscles in some areas and other kids having developed more muscles in other areas. We're not very different as adults. Maybe you need to strengthen your own emotional vocabulary muscle. Passing a feelings chart around your dinner table can help—although you obviously want to do the bulk of your emotional processing without young ears nearby. They don't yet have the fortitude to help or the patience to listen long as we talk about our feelings (or maybe even the interest, if they're in their more narcissistic teenage years). But it's still good to practice. Then, do the real processing with your therapist, a friend, or your spouse. Write in your journal. Start with what we would call in therapy the *presenting emotion* and dig underneath. Your emotions are milestones, not stumbling blocks, no matter how they feel. And those emotions are meant to reflect something not only about who God made you to be, but about His heart as well.

For example, I struggle with anger—not that you would ever know, unless you knew me really well. I'm one of the ones who Richard Rohr said seldom gets directly angry. My anger is mostly directed at myself about my perceived failures, but it can also be about injustice, a lack of integrity, or just a lack of organizational skills (I know, I know . . . it's a lot).

I tend to get much angrier when I'm tired. When I haven't had time for my introverted self (yes, I am an introvert, even though I typically look and function like an extrovert). Or it can be when I'm doing something on the frontlines of ministry. All of which happen to a greater degree in the summer, at Hopetown. It wasn't until a few summers ago, when I was smiling on the outside but stomping around again on the inside, angry over some kind of injustice, that it dawned on me that God is angry over injustice too. He was very frustrated with the Pharisees, who didn't seem to quite understand the concept of integrity even though they saw themselves as highly principled people. In the temple, Jesus flipped the tables of the money changers, who were not treating others with fairness and compassion. He didn't sin in His anger, but He sure had it. My anger, at times, is a reflection of God's heart. (At times it's not, but I'm learning to give myself a little credit.) It's not a flaw in me. It's not sin. What I do with that anger can be. But when I realized this truth, it helped me give myself tremendously more grace. And, as always seems to happen, that grace then spilled over to how I saw others. Your anger is the same. Your hurt over your kids' hurt reflects God's compassion. Your anger over injustice in their world reflects His heart for justice in our world. What could your emotions be teaching you right now about the heart of God?

3. Feelings are not facts. They don't have to overwhelm or define you.

As psychologist Susan David says, "Emotions are data, not directives."[2] Or, as a wise dad whose daughter I counseled years ago said, "Your feelings are important, but they are not meant to be the engine of your train. They're meant to be the caboose. They are an integral part, but they are not in charge." Trains wouldn't be trains without cabooses. There is a lot of life in that little red car. But I see many kids today whose cabooses are driving the train. And I would venture to say that for many of us adults living in this age of emotional awareness, our emotions are often in charge as well. It's one of the things that worries me most for both parents and kids.

I guess it's a curse that comes with the blessing of emotional enlightenment. We weren't allowed to experience our feelings growing up. And, all of a sudden, the light turns on and we become aware. Everything looks different. Everything feels different. It's like the way the world shifts during puberty, but without the hormones. I know adults who begin counseling for the first time or just give themselves permission to feel for the first time and everything changes. We discover parts of ourselves and parts of God we never knew existed as we embrace the emotion. For the first time, we become real, as the Skin Horse from *The Velveteen Rabbit* would say. Becoming real is vital in our journey of awareness, connectedness, parenting, and person-ing. Emotions are data, and some of the most important data we'll ever receive because they are meant to point us toward something more. But sometimes, we get stuck. And those feelings become more important than the message underneath.

I met with a mom recently who had awakened to her emotions but had gotten stuck within the swirl of them. When I asked questions about her daughter, she kept finding her way back to talking about herself. Her own sadness. Her own anxiety. She told me about conversations with her daughter where it was obvious that she felt incapable of handling her daughter's emotions as her hands were so full of her own. She felt like a failure as a mom, but the emphasis was more on her failure than her daughter's needs. When I suggested to this mom that her money would be better spent on her own counseling than her daughter's, she politely refused. I think she wanted us to help her daughter work through her issues but didn't want to work on the things in her own life that were perpetuating them. I truly believe she wouldn't have been at Daystar if she hadn't wanted something better for her daughter. But I also believe she was allowing her feelings to drive the train. She was stuck. I remember a teenage girl telling me once, "I don't want to grow. I just want to be understood." And that's exactly what feelings driving the train looks like.

Our personalities have a great deal to do with how we handle our emotions as well. Some personalities have a harder time becoming aware of their emotions. Some have a harder time expressing those emotions. And certain personalities have more of a tendency to blur the lines between fact and feeling. Sometimes I think the more in touch we are with our feelings, the blurrier the line becomes. I'm still on the journey of learning to handle my emotions in healthy ways myself. There is so much grace in this process. And, again, we are flying blind. Many of us didn't have anyone guiding us to the idea that feelings are deeply valuable and that they are not necessarily harbingers of truth.

When was a time you might have confused your feelings with fact? Maybe it was recently, when your adolescent daughter didn't want to spend time with you. You not only felt she didn't like you, but you responded to her as if that message were true. The feeling is valid and important. Being the parent of a teenager is painful at times, as their priorities are often anything other than spending time with their parents; that pain of rejection is real. But the feeling has nothing to do with how your daughter really feels about you. Take it from someone who has counseled thousands of girls just like her. Or maybe feelings and fact became blurred when you were sitting in Bible study hearing other parents talk about what they do for family devotions. You sunk deeper and deeper in your chair, feeling worried that you had somehow neglected your kids spiritually and their lack of faith as adults was going to be all your fault. The feeling is valid and important. The worry and longing for more for them spiritually can drive you to curiosity with them about their faith and action as a family to grow together. Or you can act on the "fact" that you've failed as a parent, and that can drive you deeper into despair. Despair is where we get stuck.

I wish, when I was growing up, that I had learned words to describe my emotions. It wasn't that my parents weren't trying. They just didn't know better because their parents didn't use those kinds of words with them. And I still wish we had talked about feelings around the dinner table. I wish my feelings had been heard and validated, and then I wish someone had helped me differentiate feelings from fact. And, maybe even deeper, helped me differentiate feelings from truth. It's something I try to do with kids in my office on a daily basis. I'll ask questions like "What does that feel like?" And "What do you know to be true?" But I only ask the second question after letting them sit with the first for quite some time.

Your feelings matter so much. They reveal parts of who you are and who God is in a way that nothing else can. And there is truth that is deeper than feeling. It involves hope and redemption and so much grace—for them and for you.

4. Self-care is not selfish.

I saw a mom just this past week in our lobby who said she kept her daughter home from school. She wasn't sick. She said, "I think she just needed a mental health day. That's not a thing at her school, so I decided to make it one." I love that this wise mom knew what her daughter needed and valued the importance of her daughter taking care of herself. My guess is the daughter went back to school refreshed and with more of herself to offer her friends and her studies. And my guess is this mom has never taken a mental health day for herself. What about you? When was the last time you took a mental health day? News bulletin, if you're not there already: No one else is going to tell you to take one—besides me, your own counselor, or your mom. Self-care means you stop waiting for others to give you permission.

I can sometimes get really angry about boundaries. I stomp around (again, all inside my head) thinking, *Why don't others respect my boundaries?* when the problem is that I haven't told them the boundaries are there in the first place. My hints that I'm tired and need a break haven't seemed to come through. Or maybe it's that my boundaries are more spongy than strong.

In our Raising Boys and Girls parenting class, I quote Psalm 144:12: "May our sons in their youth be like plants full grown, our daughters like corner pillars cut for the structure of a palace" (esv). I talk with parents of girls about how your girls are going to have a lot of knocks against their confidence. They're also going to have a lot of knocks against their courage. Girls lead the statistics on anxiety, being twice as likely as boys to suffer from it.[3] I love the comparison to pillars in Psalm 144:12, because when I think of corner pillars, I think not only of their beauty, but of their immense strength. Corner pillars hold up a great deal. Your girls are going to have to hold up so much over the course of their lives. I then look at the moms in the room and say, "You are holding up so much right now. I have no idea what's going on in your life, but I am confident that you are holding up a lot. Even today. More than most people know. We want the girls in our lives to believe they're capable of doing just that." You are holding up a *lot* right now. People depend on your strength twenty-four hours a day, seven days a week. And the likelihood of someone like your five-year-old, your teen, or even your spouse on some days saying, "Why don't you lay that down? I can carry it myself for a while" is pretty close to nil. You're going to have to decide that it's okay to lay it down, and that you are still you when you're not carrying it. And that you're certainly still loved. Because that is the truth.

Take a walk. Write in your journal. Stay up a little later and watch a fun show. Drive through Starbucks and spend the money to buy yourself a coffee. Invest the money in your own therapy. Breathe. Spend time with someone who makes you laugh. You are worth it and . . .

5. You are loved.

> Mostly what God does is love you. Keep company with him and learn a life of love. Observe how Christ loved us. His love was not cautious but extravagant. He didn't love in order to get something from us but to give everything of himself to us. Love like that.
>
> Ephesians 5:2 MESSAGE

It's hard not only to love like that but to understand that we are loved like that when it wasn't our experience at the hands of our family. It may never have been their intention, but the love you received may have been in order for someone else to receive something in return. You may have had a job in your family—to take care of someone else, to keep your family laughing, to keep the peace, to be the responsible one, to make them proud. There are a million jobs you could have had that, whether your parents intended it to or not, became, in your mind, what were required to be loved. Are you aware of any of those? What did you feel you had to do or be to be loved in the family or to not disrupt the system? The system of God doesn't operate that way. Neither does His love. We can't disrupt Him. And His love has no requirements—no conditions.

Because you fulfill so many roles today in the life of your family, it's easy to get those roles mixed up with requirements again. Mostly what God does is love you. He rejoices over you with singing. He takes great delight in you. He quiets you—not with His anger or even His wisdom, but with His love. For you. Simply because of who you are. So much grace.

Five Things I Want You to Do for Them

I want to repeat that last phrase right here. So much grace. And yes, there are things I want you to do for your kids. But those are still under the umbrella of the previous five things. (1) Whatever you are feeling right now makes sense. (2) Your feelings are not meant to act as stumbling blocks but as milestones that reflect something important for you and about the heart of God. (3) Feelings are not facts. They don't have to overwhelm or define you. (4) Self-care is not selfish. (5) You are loved.

In the midst of those truths, here's another I want you to hear: You are the biggest agent of change in your child's fight against anxiety.[4] You. In case that sounds daunting, here's one more: In a seminar I attended with Dan Allender, he talked about how your relationship with your children is one of the only relationships you will ever have that you didn't pick. You didn't get to interview hundreds of kids and decide that Charlie or Bella was right for you. And if you didn't pick, it means Someone much smarter than you or I picked for you. He knew. He knew who each of your children would be . . . even the one who seems to have a knack for pushing your buttons. He knew what they would go through. And He knew you were the right mom or dad for the job. You can do this, and my hope for the rest of this chapter is to help you avoid some of the most common pitfalls anxious parents experience along the journey.

Your anxiety lies to you. About your parenting and about your kids. It limits you. It keeps you from being the parent God wants you to get to be. As you can imagine, I have sat with a lot of intentional, anxious parents over the years. Long enough to see some patterns. Long enough to see some themes in areas of struggle. In areas where anxiety takes over and gets in the way of that intentionality. God is doing a new thing—but when we're anxious, we're often holding on too tight to see it. And that holding on directly impacts the lives of the kids we love. So I've boiled this list of common anxious parenting pitfalls down to five. If I could tell anxious parents just five things that I believe could change the course for them and for the kids they love, these would be the five:

1. *Do your own worry work.*

You remember that if you have anxiety, your kids are seven times more likely to deal with it themselves. And yes, a good portion of that is hardwired into their DNA. But it's also in the way we speak around them, using catastrophic or even just constantly overwhelmed language. It's in the ways we interact with the world in front of them, acting out of our own fear and distrust. It's in the ways we interact with them, perpetuating the escape and avoidance their worry monsters are clamoring for. If you have been finding yourself regularly throughout this book's pages, I want you to do your own worry work.

If you often feel more anxious about whatever is in front of your child than they do.

If you often have your own worst-case scenario, looping thoughts.

If you often have trouble sleeping at night, with images and thoughts of what might happen swirling around in your mind.

If you often find yourself stepping in—fixing, answering, protecting, rescuing, and keeping them from doing the hard thing.

I want you to notice that in every example I used the word *often*. We all do these things sometimes. But the pattern is where the problem lies. So if the word *often* seems to apply to you, then I believe it's time to do your own worry work.

When I wrote my three previous books on anxiety—*Raising Worry-Free Girls*; *Braver, Stronger, Smarter*; and *Brave*—the intention was for those books to be a parent or a girl's first attempt at getting help. We even tell parents who call our office for counseling, "Read the book first. Use the tools recommended. If you don't notice any change within three months, then it's likely time to call us back and come in." I would say the same is true for you. Grab a copy of *The Worry-Free Parent Workbook*. If you feel like anxiety is defining you and keeping you from being the parent you want to be, I want you to not just read this material, but dive into it. I want you to really process and take time to use the workbook. I want you to practice mindfulness. To reframe your thoughts. To share your heart with your people. And if you feel like things still aren't getting better—or if your anxiety is to the point where it's debilitating—I recommend you seek counseling.

Reach out to a few trusted friends for a referral. Call your church. Check with your doctor. To be honest, I don't want you to go with just whomever your insurance will cover. You want to find a therapist who someone else you know has either seen or had experience with and trusts. You are entrusting your heart and, vicariously, the hearts of your kids to that person. You want them to be vetted. You want them to have experience or to be supervised by someone with a lot of experience. You also want them to have a good dose of kindness and strength. You want them to be a person who can bring a lot of grace to your perspective and can also give you a compassionate push when needed. And it helps when you can find someone who believes that faith is foundational to finding hope, healing, and trust in our anxious world. Also, pro tip: The best people are usually worth the wait—unless you're in crisis.

Find a trusted therapist. And stay with it, even when they say hard things. One of my favorite parts of Daystar is that we help kids (and parents) look at both how they have been hurt and how they hurt others. We all have. My counselors, over the years, have helped me understand so much of myself, my past, and how I brought that past into who I am and how I relate to others. They have helped me see that what I need more than anything—more than insight or self-care or tools—is Jesus and His grace. As you continue to discover the same, your load will be lighter, and you'll do less sharing of it with these kids you love so dearly.

2. Let your kids grow and go.

I don't know that there's a lot more to say on this. I believe that despite our best intentions, our anxiety impedes the kids we love. We keep them from growing. We keep them from learning through experience, through struggle and effort and mistakes. The ways most of us likely grew. In fact, I want you to think of one thing you learned through struggle or failure as you were growing up. I also want you to think of an area where you had independence and what you learned from it.

Two of the things that I believe shaped my adult life most were two activities I did independently of my parents. One was a club I was involved in called Y-Teens. Y-Teens was an organization all over Arkansas, at least—maybe further—that promoted leadership and volunteerism. We also had a lot of fun dances where we got to invite boys. I loved Y-Teens and ended up being the citywide vice president my junior year in high school. Y-Teens gave me opportunities to make a difference in the community, forced me to stand up in front of hundreds of peers and sing silly songs and make speeches, and believe that I could invest in girls who were younger than I was. Looking back, I'm not really sure what I had to invest at the time or what I could have brought to the table in speeches. My parents likely wondered the same. But they let me experience and learn to lead. Even though those speeches, in particular, made me a nervous wreck every single time.

The other was an amazing place called Camp Waldemar. I can't imagine what it was like for my sweet, "non-anxious," actually highly anxious mom to watch me board a plane by myself to fly to Texas every summer. She knew I'd be swimming, playing golf, practicing archery, riding horses, and doing all manner of active things that I wasn't necessarily inclined toward or bestowed with the athleticism for. But I did them. I failed and embarrassed myself a few times, but also made a hole in one (chipping, not from the tee box) that helped my team win field day—and certainly surprised the heck out of me. What my mom didn't know was that I would be given opportunities at Waldemar to stretch myself by leading and speaking and doing things like playing the guitar (no business doing that one, either) in front of hundreds of girls. But she and my dad let me grow . . . and go.

It is more than ironic that my everyday life is now leading girls and speaking in front of thousands of parents all over the world—and I even play the guitar at Hopetown. It wasn't ironic. It was God. God was preparing me at thirteen for exactly what He would have me do at fifty-three. And had my parents let their anxiety stop me, I don't know that I would be where I am now.

How can you allow your kids to grow and go today? What could you let them do? Kids need to have things just out of reach, to have to strain on the tiptoes of courage and feel like they did it "all by myself." Not just toddlers, although that is certainly a main way toddlers learn skills. But at every age. Growing and going are how they learn to do things they never imagined they could, how they gain confidence and a sense of purpose, and how they learn that, even in the harder things, God is with them and can use and grow them into who and what He has created them to be.

3. Have warmth.

I hate to type this one out. When writing *Raising Worry-Free Girls*, I came across a statement I mentioned earlier in this book: Anxiety is linked to a lack of parental warmth.[5] It was a hard one to read—and it's an even harder one to say to parents in my office. But since I have read that statement, I have found it to be true. Not always. But many anxious parents lack parental warmth. It's not that you aren't trying. Or that you don't want to be warm. But it's often that you're trying so hard you've lost your warmth. You're so focused on getting it right that you've lost yourself. And you've definitely lost the connection that your child needs.

In 1975, Dr. Edward Tronick from the University of Massachusetts Boston's Infant-Parent Mental Health Program conducted a famous study called the "Still Face Experiment." The results of that study continue to be some of the most replicated findings in developmental psychology. Here's what happened: After three minutes of interacting with a "non-responsive expressionless mother," the infant "rapidly sobers and grows wary. He makes repeated attempts to get the interaction into its usual reciprocal pattern. When these attempts fail, the infant withdraws [and] orients his face and body away from his mother with a withdrawn, hopeless facial expression."[6] The study has been foundational for our learning about attachment and the effects of both maternal and childhood depression, among other things. An article from

The Gottman Institute adds that the baby may not just be experiencing a loss of attachment, but also a loss of agency.

Agency "refers to the subjective awareness that one is initiating, executing, and controlling one's own actions in the world. When we 'still face' our children by ignoring their expressions of emotion, for example, they may experience a loss of agency."[7]

Anxious kids lack agency. Our warmth can help them establish that agency. It helps them not only feel understood and valued, but also helps them feel capable. Dr. Gottman, one of the leaders in the field of attachment theory, outlines the importance of emotion coaching in connecting with children. His five essential steps are these:

- Be aware of your child's emotion
- Recognize your child's expression of emotion as an opportunity for intimacy and teaching
- Listen with empathy and validate your child's feelings
- Help your child learn to label their emotions with words
- Set limits when you are helping your child solve problems or deal with upsetting situations appropriately[8]

Every one of those ideas conveys warmth. When we are too hurried or too worried, however, we often lose ours.

I met with a very perfectionistic dad years ago. His primary objective in counseling for his daughter was that she would learn self-regulation. In sitting with this father, who honestly was trying as hard as any dad I have ever met, I experienced a complete lack of warmth. I also experienced his frustration at his daughter's lack of progress thus far. Because I also met with her, I knew she was trying too. Change is slow with kids, as they don't yet possess the awareness or ability to have the same intentionality we do as adults. In our last conversation together, the father kept outlining the change he wanted to see in his child. And I kept outlining the importance of warmth and connection. It was not what he wanted to hear, and I believe it was the cause of that being our last session together. My hope is that he has found his way to warmth with his daughter. I truly believe it can make a profound difference in how kids feel about themselves and how they interact with the world—both having a direct connection with their anxiety.

Now, if you're reading this and thinking, *Well, I just can't do that one. I'm not a warm person,* I want you to practice. Stand in front of the mirror—seriously—and practice a warm face. Practice a warm tone of voice. Then get down to your child's level, literally, and look them in the eye. Touch them on the shoulder. Hug them, even if it doesn't come naturally. It will, in time. Remind them often that you love them. Laugh with them. And pray. Go back to the truth of Romans 15:5–6 in *The Message.* God can do it. He can help you find your way to warmth and help your kids, through that warmth, find their way back to you and to more courage and confidence in the process.

4. *Offer empathy and questions.*

I can still remember standing in my office, about to walk out the door at the end of a session, and saying to a parent over and over, "Empathy and questions. Empathy and questions. If you hear nothing else from me today, I want you to just offer empathy and questions." This was another try-hard, anxious mom. She was so anxious she barely let me get a word in during our session, with her fears and worries spilling over the entire fifty minutes. She doubted herself and analyzed her actions as a parent constantly, to the degree that she was more focused on herself than on her child. I heard someone say recently that what used to be called "child-rearing" is now called "parenting." Interesting, isn't it? When we focus more on our performance and failures, our attention shifts from our kids to ourselves. My hope is that this book will help you shift the focus back to your kids. That focus on ourselves, in and of itself, is too much pressure.

And so back to empathy and questions. It's what I now recommend daily, if not hourly, in my office. David and I talk about it at every parenting seminar we teach. Remember, anxious kids don't believe they're capable. And anxious parents often have more emotion about whatever their children are facing than their children do. It is easier for anxious kids to let you think and problem-solve for them than to problem-solve for themselves. And the strength of our emotion causes us to step right in and solve those problems. But problem-solving offsets anxiety for kids. Your children need to learn to come up with solutions to the problems and to put those solutions into practice.

Your son comes home frustrated with his track coach. "That sounds really tough, buddy. What do you want to do about it?" Your daughter comes home after her best friend hurt her feelings on the playground, telling her she is no longer allowed to play with the group. "I know that had to really hurt. I'm so sorry. What do you think would help the situation?" With any issue they encounter, our empathy brings the warmth we just talked about. It helps them feel heard, understood, and more connected to us. Kids typically feel alone in whatever they're going through, unless they experience something different. Our empathy reminds them that we're in it with them. And then our questions imply that we believe they're capable of getting out of it. Just asking a question of your child communicates to her that you believe she can come up with the solution. Questions such as "What do you think would help?" "What is your plan?" "How do you want to handle this?" "Who do you want to be in this?" "What do you think God would want you to do?" Questions imply capability, and empathy enhances connection. The two are equally important.

5. Let the bottom 20 percent go.

We talked about this way back in chapter 3. But I believe it's important enough that it bears repeating. It's something I repeat every day in my office. I said it to a mom yesterday. She, of course, is a perfectionist, just like me. We don't tend to let anything go because we don't see detail. So we don't even know, at times, that there is a bottom 20 percent. We also, I believe, start with a *no* more than a *yes*.

When my nephew was born, I tried to do a lot of research on toddler-age boys. I've counseled thousands of children over the years, but toddler boys are not in my wheelhouse. One of the things

I read is that you want to use way more yeses than nos with tod-dlers. When a no is infrequent, it has more weight. We build up more currency with the kids we love when we land more often on yes. Which do you typically start with—yes or no? Try making a conscious effort to start with a yes. I also recommend that you make a list of areas of struggle with your children right now. List them in order of either the frequency of conflict or the degree of your irritation with your child. Lessening the number of total battles decreases the intensity of the individual battle. In other words, choosing to let the bottom 20 percent go makes the top 80 percent less conflictual.

One of my favorite authors, Kelly Corrigan, writes, "Raising people is not some lark. It's serious work with serious repercus-sions. It's air-traffic control. You can't step out for a minute; you can barely pause to scratch your ankle."[9] You're going to be anx-ious. You're going to micromanage and battle 110 percent of the issues on some days. But here's what I want you to remember from this chapter. Put it on your fridge, if it helps.

1. Do your own worry work.
2. Let your kids grow and go.
3. Have warmth.
4. Offer empathy and questions.
5. Let the bottom 20 percent go.

Years from now, I'm not sure how the kids we love will finish the sentence "My mom always said" or "My dad always said" or "My Diddy always said." (Yes, I have an aunt name and it's just the best.) But here's what I hope. I hope they will say, "My mom and dad [or fill in the blank] always loved me. They believed in me. They made me believe I was smart, strong, and brave enough to handle whatever came my way. And when I felt like I wasn't, they reminded me again. My mom and dad always had a sense of hope . . . for me and in God's love and provision for me." And that hope is exactly where we're headed next.

Worry-Free Takeaways

1. Whatever you are feeling right now makes sense.
2. Your feelings are not meant to act as stumbling blocks but as milestones that reflect something important for you and about the heart of God.
3. Feelings are not facts. They don't have to overwhelm or define you.
4. Self-care is not selfish.
5. You are loved.
6. You are the biggest agent of change in your child's fight against anxiety.
7. Do your own worry work.
8. Let your kids grow and go.
9. Have warmth.
10. Offer empathy and questions.
11. Let the bottom 20 percent go.

Hope for the Future

9

Admit Failure. Know Grace.

(A Chapter for the Perfectionist Parent and Maybe Others Too)

I love to meet with parents who are perfectionists or fellow Enneagram 1s. I get it. There is so much to do—and to do well. There is constant pressure inside of us, as well as a constant critic whose voice dogs our every step. We want to do right by the people we love. We want to get all the things right. We don't want to mess up, hurt others, or fail in any way.

I'm going to give you a little inside scoop. The other therapists at Daystar often send the perfectionist parents of the kids they're counseling to me for parent consults. I hate to say it, but it's partly because we're a little hard to give feedback to. In our effort to get so much right, we don't like to be told we're doing wrong. We're defensive. And we can be intimidating in the midst of all that perfectionism and defensiveness. We don't want to be. In fact, if you told us we were, we'd get really mad at ourselves and work hard to change it. But if you are like me, I will hear the feedback, and likely work on the things. But then I might resent you for years. (How's that for making you never want to give me any negative feedback?) But there is one thing that makes all the difference for me: knowing the person speaking to me believes the best about me.

When I know someone sees how hard I'm working—when they believe that I'm doing my best and want the best for whomever is involved, I can hear just about anything. (I think that and apologies are part of my love language.) It's why I'm so glad when the other therapists send me their perfectionists. I get it. You are trying so hard. Every single second of the day. And you likely wake up in the middle of the night with more ideas of how to try hard. I believe parenting is especially hard for perfectionists because not only are the kids we love out of our control, but they often don't believe the best about us. Or at least they stop believing it the closer they get to adolescence. It's why so many parents of teenagers will say, "They were so easy when they were little. I could sit on the floor and play games with them for hours. Now it's just hard." Perfectionist parents are rock stars with littles. They can play on the floor and cook dinner and help with homework and pick up from soccer—all at the same time. But then, somewhere around eleven (or ten or even eight), kids' disrespect begins to creep in. They start to make choices that are different from the choices you want them to make. The eye rolls and the believing the worst about you become not just a fear, but at times, a reality. It is *hard*.

I want us to go back to that idea of sitting in my office. I want you to journal for a few minutes about the things you would say to me if we were. I want to hear about all the things you're carrying. All the pressure you're feeling. The lack of difference it feels like those things make. The lack of change you're seeing in your child. And even more so, the anger you feel toward yourself for not doing and being better.

This chapter is for you.

I'm glad to know more of what you're feeling—or at least as close as we can get through a book. We'll imagine as best we can. (Imagining yourself in a calm, safe place is actually another cognitive behavioral therapy tool for anxiety.) So let's picture it. I'm sitting in my chair, leaning toward you, and smiling. You're on my couch. My little dog, Lucy, is sitting at your feet. I want you to start by taking three deep breaths. Here's what I want you to hear me say first: I see you. I believe the best about you. I know how hard it is to be a perfectionist. And I sure understand how hard it is to be a perfectionist parent. You are trying all the time. Often on your own. Sometimes without much gratitude or awareness from others.

Years ago, a friend who was doing a small-group deep dive into the Enneagram told me that one of my favorite theorists said 1 was the hardest number in the Enneagram to be. She said that all of us have an inner critic, but a 1's inner critic speaks louder and significantly more often. Constantly, in fact, until we learn to strip him of his power. When I heard that, I felt known. I could breathe a little easier. Since that time, I've shared her thoughts with every perfectionist I've met. It's hard to be a 1. And it's even harder to be a 1 parent.

Now that we've established that I'm for you and I get it, let's dig in a little deeper. I want to talk specifically about perfectionist parents: what happens in the lives of your kids, a few things I want you to know, and a few more things I want you to practice. (Not things I want you to do—you've got enough of those.) Just a few things to work toward. Hang on; I'm still for you. And God is for you more than you could ever imagine.

As a perfectionist parent, you live life tightly wound, trying to get it all right. Here's the thing: Your kids need present parents more than perfect parents. And that striving for perfection gives your kids role models who are unattainable and parents who are unreachable. Your kids can't connect with the real you because that you becomes swallowed up in all of the effort. And those kids eventually feel they can't measure up to the impossible standards you set for yourself and therefore must set for them as well.

We've now moved into the hope section of this book—can't you tell?

There is so much hope. For you. For your relationship with the kids you love. And for them. I believe the origins of that hope start with the title of this chapter: Admit failure. Know grace.

Now I want you to write down three ways you've failed in the past week. Yes, I am serious. I know they're there because we all have them. I know you're aware of them, no matter how much you've tried to push them aside. Real hope is only found through honesty. Admit failure. Know grace. In fact, I want you to write not only where you've failed but also how you talked to yourself after that failure. I believe how you talk to yourself causes more harm for you than the failure did in the first place.

I asked my co-workers at Daystar, "If you could tell perfectionist parents anything, what would you say?" I'm going to pepper their answers throughout the rest of this chapter. So let's get started. We perfectionists are fast movers and want to get to the point. Here's to hope that is real and yours for the taking when you admit failure and know grace.

Five Hopeful Things I Want Every Perfectionist Parent to Know

1. *Good parents get it right 50 percent of the time.*

When you first became a parent, you likely heard the word *attachment* quite a bit. Friends gave you books about it. They suggested apps that would help guide you through the process. They even gave you baby gear that would "promote attachment" between parent and child.

In the past several decades, attachment theory has moved to the forefront of a great deal of developmental psychology, particularly when we're talking about a child's first year of life. To put it simply, attachment has to do with how a child interacts with his or her caregivers. A healthy attachment means that the child feels secure in the knowledge that the adults who love him will respond and care for his primary needs such as food, sleep, comfort, et cetera. A study out of Lehigh University in 2019 found that "caregivers need only 'get it right' 50 percent of the time when responding to babies' need for attachment to have a positive impact on a baby."[1]

Yes, you read that correctly. In fact, it's the same statistic we talked about a few chapters ago. **Parents only need to get it right 50 percent of the time!**

Fifty percent is not much. My guess is that you're gunning for one hundred percent, as a perfectionist does in all things. If the 50 percent statistic is true during the only period of time when a child's brain literally doubles in size,[2] we can be fairly confident the same is true throughout their development.

This landmark Lehigh study goes on to say, "Securely attached infants are more likely to have better outcomes in childhood and adulthood."[3] Fifty percent of the time not only makes a difference in their first year, but for the rest of your child's life.

I meet with perfectionist girls who are putting pressure on themselves not to get just 100s on their schoolwork, but to hit 102s and 104s with extra credit. I often ask, "What would a 94 look like?" And then I do my best to convince them to shoot for a 94, which is still an A in almost every school in the country. (Sorry, parents who send their daughters to me for counseling and are pushing for perfection. I'm not your girl.) I also hope you are not reading a push for perfection in the pages of this book. I always want you to know there is so much grace in this journey. Fifty percent leaves room for a lot of grace.

If you had to assign your parenting a percentage today, what would you give it? What are you shooting for? What would the equivalent of a 94 on an exam be? A percentage that helps you believe you are trying and that acknowledges the fact that you are a fallible human being? Lowering your percentage can significantly lower the pressure you feel.

One of my favorite things I read this year was called "The Imperfect-Family Beatitudes," which include,

> Blessed is the weary mother who rises before daybreak for
> no project or prayer book, for no reason but the solace
> of a sleeping house and a tepid cup of instant coffee
> and a fat dog curled on her lap. Hers is the fleeting
> kingdom of heaven. . . .
> Blessed is the fatherless father who surrenders his
> Saturdays to papier-mâché models of the Saturn V
> rocket or sugar-cube igloos or Popsicle-stick replicas of

Fort Ticonderoga, and always to scale. In comforting he
shall be comforted.

Blessed is the mother whose laugh is a carillon, a choir,
an intoxication filling every room in the house and
every dollar-movie theater and every school-play
performance, even when no one else gets the joke. She
will be called a child of God.

Blessed is the winking father who each day delivers his
children to Catholic school with a kiss and the same
advice: "Give 'em hell!" He will be summoned to few
teacher conferences.

Blessed is the braless mother who arrives at the school
pickup line wearing pink plastic curlers and stained
house shoes, and who won't hesitate to get out of the
car if she must. She will never be kept waiting.

Blessed are the parents whose final words on leaving—the
house, the car, the least consequential phone call—are
always "I love you." They will leave behind children
who are lost and still found, broken and, somehow, still
whole.[4]

These parents seem to me like they're on the 50 percent trajectory. But that 50 percent sure does count. They're showing up with all of their braless, imperfect selves to be present in their kids' lives. Take it from a counselor who has worked with tens of thousands of families since 1993. Your children are not longing for a perfect parent. They're longing for you—for you to laugh with them and show up for them and fail in front of them. Even if you make the same mistake more than once. When we let go of the tight grip of perfectionism and allow ourselves the freedom to fail, we experience the joy of connection with the kids we love.

2. Insanity is repeating the same thing over and over again and expecting different results.

I have a small painting of a red barn on my mantel. It's sitting on a stack of books. You'd likely never notice it unless you really looked. A friend painted it for me as a reminder. Several years ago,

I read for the first time a verse in *The Message*. Or maybe it wasn't the first time, but you know how verses do that to you? It was like I had never read these words before:

> Have some of you noticed that we are not yet perfect? (No great surprise, right?) . . . If I was "trying to be good," I would be rebuilding the same old barn that I tore down.
>
> Galatians 2:17–18

How many times do I rebuild that dumb barn of being good and trying to get it right? Enough to qualify myself for the above saying about the definition of insanity. Do I think I'm going to finally speak in public without once tripping over my words? Spend an entire day of counseling without forgetting someone's best friend's name? Or go a day without hurting the feelings of someone I love? Nope. Not a day and likely not an hour. But I keep trying. I've got well-worn "try to be good" pathways all over my brain. And my guess is that you do too. Particularly when it comes to parenting.

A reminder from your friendly Daystar therapists: *Zoom out to the big picture of parenting. If your kid is aware that* (1) *you love them, and* (2) *they can trust you, then relax, because you're doing it right.*

What would it mean for you to zoom out? I believe the focus would move off of you and your parenting and onto your child and raising him or her. I believe zooming out would bring more freedom to be yourself with your child—the you who you like, rather than the you who brings out even more of the inner critic. As a side note, when I'm not taking care of myself, that critic gets even louder.

So I want you to think about a rut you keep falling into—a barn you keep rebuilding as a parent, expecting it to finally be right. What are three things you could stop doing that you believe would make a difference in the freedom you experience in parenting?

3. Practice more "oops" than "shoots."

Let's go back to that idea of how you talk to yourself. I am confident it is significantly harsher than you would ever talk to anyone else in your life.

A reminder from your friendly Daystar therapists: *If you don't learn how to stop criticizing yourself, the criticism will spill over into the lives of your kids. It has to go somewhere.*

Have you found this to be true? I certainly have in my life. The angrier I am at myself, the angrier I inadvertently become with others. Or the angrier I become at the car seat that won't work right or the door that keeps getting stuck or whatever small things go wrong in the presence of others. It still comes out. And they either witness it or bear the brunt of it. That criticism has to go somewhere.

We've got to shut our inner critic down. Or at least go for the 94 percent and muffle him. To do so, we need to recognize the inner critic's voice and then counter it with something different. Have you named your voice yet? If you haven't, I want you to pick out a name right now. Just this week, I told a high school girl who is one of the sweetest, most lovely (not the type to use bad words) girls I know that she could call her critical voice "an ass." Because it is. I feel so angry at her voice, I'd like to call it every curse word I know. I feel the same about yours. And you would probably feel the same about mine. Friends can remind us. But an important part of the process is for you to become angry enough with your own "ass" of a voice to silence him.

The next time you hear the inner critic, I want you to talk back. Remember when we talked in chapter 6 about replacing the thought? In *Braver, Stronger, Smarter*, I call replacing the thought "talking back to the worry monster."[5] Now that you have a name for your inner critic, I want you to practice talking back. With little girls, I tell them they can wag their finger, stomp their foot, and use words they're not allowed to normally. I want them to get angry. So an eight-year-old girl might say to her Worry Monster, "You're stupid. You're not the boss of me. I'm not listening to you, and you're wrong anyway. I can do this." Let's take after her. I want you to get angry with that ass-ish voice in your head. "I am not listening to you. Those words are not truth. You're only robbing me of enjoying my child and enjoying myself. You are wrong." Using our angry voice with our inner critic can help us find a gentler voice to use with ourselves.

I wrote this in my notes in Bible study just a few weeks ago: "My friends in Bible study have been helping me to not be so hard on myself on certain things. I made a mistake last night and forgot something. My first response was an angry 'Shoot!' Followed by a tirade against myself. I realized I need more 'oops' than 'shoots' in my life. 'Oops' feels more like I made a mistake, rather than 'Shoot, I did something wrong.'"

I'm ready. I don't know about you, but I'm tired of being so hard on myself. I have to say that since I turned fifty, I have made a few inches of progress in the right direction. And let me tell you—it feels really good. So much freer. So much more kindness. And I certainly have found that as I have more grace for myself, I have more grace for others.

How can you shift your language? How can you stop rebuilding that same old barn? And how can you start letting every bit of your anger out on the one who actually deserves it? He's trying not only to steal your freedom, but also to keep you from growing. And what he doesn't know (or maybe he does) is that what he's telling you to do is the opposite of what brings real freedom, joy, and spiritual growth.

4. *"We grow spiritually much more by doing it wrong than by doing it right."*[6]

Richard Rohr said these words in his book *Falling Upward*. Rohr, by the way, professes to be an Enneagram 1. He knows of what he speaks. Why do we grow more spiritually by doing it wrong than by doing it right?

Every perfectionist I've ever met is profoundly capable. You think fast. You accomplish more in a day than many people accomplish in a week. You're bright. Hardworking. Strong. Trustworthy. It's part of the problem. Right can come pretty naturally for us—or at least, right in our eyes. We do things—and a lot of things at the same time—well.

Rohr's idea, therefore, feels antithetical for us. But Suzanne Stabile writes, "Integrated [healthy] Ones don't think they have to make everything perfect, and they are able to move from obligation to enthusiasm and from restraint to freedom."[7] Doesn't that sound wonderful? "They understand serenity as being able to hold two opposing views at the same time without having to choose one over the other."[8]

You are good at so many things that the goodness inherently becomes part of your identity. And then you sure better keep it up if you want the others around you to love you. Or to see that you have something to offer. And maybe especially if you want you to feel good about yourself. But we can hold two things. We can do a lot right and get a lot wrong.

We are capable of so much, and that muchness gets in the way of our need for grace. Our desire and our ability to stay in control get in the way of our need for grace as well. Control requires more control. It's an anxiety-producing cycle, as we talked about before. Maybe an anger-producing cycle as well. Here's the truth: You are a mess. You fail often. You get it wrong more than you'd like to admit. Me too. But we can admit it—because there is so much good on the other side. Admit failure. Know grace.

Another one of my favorite statements by Anne Lamott is this: "If I were going to begin practicing the presence of God for the first time today, it would help to begin by admitting the three most terrible truths of our existence: that we are so ruined, and so loved, and in charge of so little."[9]

Let go of the control. Allow yourself to acknowledge the wrong. Admit it to the kids you love. And receive what your heart longs for most: grace.

5. Grace is our deepest need.

Not long ago, Henry, my three-year-old nephew, said something unkind to me. It wasn't anything big. He's three, and his words are driven more by impulsivity than intention. He's also trying on different ways to have power. So he loves to say words like *stinky* and *bad* and any that he thinks wield power over others. As we do with toddlers, I tried to help him see the impact of his words.

"Henry, you hurt Diddy's feelings. That was not a kind thing to say."

He lowered his little head, dropped his shoulders, and said, "I'm sorry, Diddy."

Of course, I immediately felt bad that he felt bad and swooped in with a quick "I forgive you, Henry."

Henry's response was one I hope I never forget. He jumped up and ran to his parents shouting, "She forgives me! She forgives me!"

That story makes me sound a little like I stay angry at Henry or that he gets in trouble often with me. I don't and he doesn't. I believe his response came more as a newcomer to the understanding of grace. Being forgiven was good news of great joy for Henry, as it can be for us. We are forgiven, even when we don't deserve it. And we only experience the impact of that grace when we admit our failure. In fact, we know grace to the degree we know we're sinners.

I attend a liturgical church where we confess our sins publicly and together. The prayer we pray is this:

> Most merciful God,
> we confess that we have sinned against you
> in word, thought, and deed,
> by what we have done,
> and by what we have left undone.
> We have not loved you with our whole heart;
> we have not loved our neighbors as ourselves.
> We are truly sorry and we humbly repent.
> For the sake of your Son Jesus Christ,
> have mercy on us and forgive us;
> that we may delight in your will,
> and walk in your ways,
> to the glory of your Name. Amen.[10]

Then the minister says, "Almighty God have mercy on you, forgive you all your sins through our Lord Jesus Christ, strengthen you in all goodness, and by the power of the Holy Spirit keep you in eternal life."[11] When he prays those words, I lower my head, open my hands, and breathe deeply. I want to open myself up in every way to that forgiveness. I need it.

My open hands serve as a reminder to myself that I bring nothing to the table. I'm letting go of control, of building all the barns, of all the insane decisions, and I'm receiving His grace. Maybe it's how I should start every day: Admitting failure. Receiving grace. We grow more spiritually by getting it wrong than getting it right, because the wrong is where we know we need Jesus.

Our failures deepen our need for Him. Your children's will too. Allow yourself to fail. Fail in front of them. Melissa, in our Modern Parents, Vintage Values parenting seminar talks about how "we can't be Jesus to our kids, but we can need Jesus in front of them." You are going to fail as a parent. When you do, rather than listening to the voice of the inner critic, I want you to listen to the voice of God.

He sees you. He loves you more than you could imagine. He knows how hard you're trying. He's for you. He's for your child. And He wants you to experience all the freedom and connection His grace can bring.

Ten Hopeful Things I Want Every Perfectionist Parent to Practice

(Because I believe you're capable of more than 5.)

I wanted to finish out this chapter with ten more things. They're just ten things to practice. I'm not even going to explain them much, because I want you to spend more time with the things I want you to know than the things I want you to do. Doing comes naturally for you. Knowing and wrestling with the truth of grace is harder. But because I know a hallmark of perfectionism is wanting to grow, I am sharing ten things I want every perfectionist parent to practice. We're going for 94 percent here—not 100. No pressure. Just things to think on and failingly move toward. With God's grace. In hope.

1. Slow down.

Perfectionists move at the speed of light. We're efficient and productive all the way down to our toes. You want us on your team, but you might not want us as your boss. It's easy for us to expect the same proficiency and productivity from others we can accomplish ourselves. I spend a lot of time talking with kids about superhero skills and how just because you're a superhero with a certain skill doesn't mean you won't be frustrated with the superheroes who have different skills.

Your kids are not going to move quickly—literally or figuratively. The rapidity with which we move makes them more anxious, especially if they lean that way already. I'll never forget my sister, at four (and with an adorable lisp I might add), saying, "Thithy, why are you always in thuch a hurry?" Because we 1s are—and I didn't know any better at the time. Slow down. We miss so much in our great speed. And let your kids slow down as well.

Kids don't just move more slowly; they also grow more slowly. Don't rush the change you want to see in your kids. Be aware, and beware having an agenda for milestones you think they're supposed to reach at certain times, skills they're supposed to develop, and characteristics you want to see grow. It all takes time. They take time. And our desire for them to be more than they are right now not only feels like pressure—it feels like disapproval. Enjoy your kids where they are right now.

2. Trust the process.

A reminder from your friendly Daystar therapists: *Focus on meaning over outcome. Try to find meaning in what you are doing, rather than always trying to do it perfectly.*

When we focus on outcome over meaning, we miss the meaning. We get tripped up on micromanaging the kids we love and ourselves. The inner critic becomes louder, and we become smaller. Trust the process. God is impeccable in His timing. He knows exactly what your child needs and when.

Ecclesiastes 3:11 says, "He has made everything beautiful in its time."

His time. It's happening right now, even if you don't see it. Trust the process. His job is to bring that beauty to flourishing fruition in its time. His time. Our worries don't speed Him along. Our job is just to trust and enjoy the process.

3. Savor the moment.

Anxiety lives in the past or the future. Our kids live in the present. When we are sitting next to the kids we love rehashing the mistake we just made or worrying about our (or their) future mistakes, we miss the moment. We miss them.

I've heard grandparents say that they enjoy being grandparents more than they enjoyed being parents. Part of that, I believe, is because they can send their grandkids back home when some of the heavy lifting of discipline is required. But I believe it's also, and maybe even more so, something else.

Age changes our perception of time. We see how fast it goes. We understand the fleetingness of our days and of seasons. Grandparents—I should say grandparents who have the blessing and wisdom to be involved—know that the days of diapers and sippy cups or soccer games and school plays or even learning to drive and beginning to date don't last long. So they savor them. They stop and notice and allow themselves to enjoy these little and big creatures who bring them so very much joy.

Obviously, you can't let go of the discipline. But you can let the bottom 20 percent go. And now you know how to at least start shutting down the worry monster that tries to keep you from being present. Savor the moment. The moment and your kids are worth it. As are you.

4. Assume the best.

If there is one thing I would like to learn in my lifetime, besides how to receive God's love and love others more, it would be to assume the best. I guess the two dovetail each another. It's one of the things I don't do naturally, and I'm guessing you might not either. I believe we see too much. It's another one of our superpowers. We see what's wrong before we see what's right—with the world and often with the people in it. Seeing the worst in people only brings out the worst, because we treat them as if that worst is who they are. Assuming the best brings out the best.

Which way would you say you lean? In viewing yourself? Toward others? Who is someone who believes the best about you and how does it impact you? How can you start assuming the best about yourself? About your kids? I believe there's a trickle-down effect, just as there is with grace. When we assume the best about ourselves instead of allowing the inner critic's voice to win, it's easier to do the same with others. Assume the best—about your kids and about yourself.

5. *Fail in front of them.*

As I've mentioned, I see a lot of kids who have anxiety that comes out as perfectionism. I love that it gives me an opportunity to create some early intervention—to do preventative work against the inner critic who has held you and me hostage for so many years.

I tell those parents that I want them to struggle and fail in front of their kids. I literally want them to say at dinner, "I did the dumbest thing at work today," or "I really hurt one of my friends' feelings." Even to purposefully knock over a glass or drop things. And to say I'm sorry, too, when a failure impacts your kids. When you know that your hero of a mom or dad has failed, it makes your own failure more acceptable. It helps you learn that failure is just a part of life.

Whether your child is a perfectionist or not, they likely see you as someone who doesn't fail. Years ago, I counseled a seventeen-year-old girl who said, "I could never live up to who my mom is. She has more friends than I do. She's so successful. She is smart and somehow is kind to everyone all the time."

You and I both know that her mom wasn't kind to everyone all the time—nor was she all the things her daughter saw her as. She is a fallible human being, but she's also a perfectionist. So her daughter saw what she was trying to present to the world. And that image drove a wedge between the two of them. In fact, it caused her daughter to doubt herself, to believe that she could never become her mom and that her mom expected her to be every bit as kind, strong, smart, and successful as the image she presented. Neither was true. This mom wanted the best for her child. Yet her striving for perfection became a pressure that not only she lived with, but her daughter did as well.

Fail in front of your kids. Spill the milk. Tell embarrassing stories. Talk about how our failure and sin are what open us up to not just our need, but also our gratitude, for grace. And laugh together in the process.

6. Learn to laugh at yourself.

It's another thing I tell parents of little perfectionists. I don't just want you to fail in front of them, but I want you to do something with them that none of you can do well. It could be going to a batting cage, rock climbing, bowling, painting pottery, or learning some type of dance. Kids need to see us struggle and not take ourselves so seriously when we do. And we perfectionists are masters at taking ourselves seriously.

If you are a perfectionist, there is a great likelihood that you'll raise a little perfectionist. Fail in front of him. Struggle with him. One dad I recommended this to said, "Really, you're saying we need to all go do something we suck at together?" Yes. That's exactly what I am saying. I want you to be able to laugh and grow and fail and learn more about each other and about grace in the process. Laughter eases the pressure of perfectionism.

7. See their gifts.

A reminder from your friendly Daystar therapists: *Appreciate the differences.*

My favorite description of the Enneagram is that it identifies the way in which we see the world. Suzanne Stabile writes, "Keeping in mind that none of us can change how we see, we are left with the option of trying to adjust *what we do* with *how we see.*"[12]

As 1s, our default is often to think that how we see is right. It's where we don't reach the serenity Stabile talks about when we hold two things at once. We see things the right way, and until others come to do the same, they're wrong. When we are living in that fixed mindset, our sight is limited. We not only see a certain way—we only see what we see. We don't see the gifts of those who see differently, particularly our kids.

I remember a mom who was a perfectionist (Enneagram 1) raising a highly creative individualist (Enneagram 4) of a daughter. Her daughter, to put it bluntly, made her crazy. I remember her saying to me, "Can't we just somehow parent the 4 out of her?" As a side note, 1s can act like 4s in stress. In other words, this mom acted and thought more like her daughter when she was feeling stressed. So the girl was incredibly triggering for her mom. As a therapist, my hope was to help her appreciate her daughter's gifts. Individualists are highly creative. They are empathetic and intuitive and create beauty in ways most of us can't. But this mom couldn't get past the way she saw to appreciate how her daughter saw differently.

A reminder from your friendly Daystar therapists: *He wasn't created to meet your expectations.*

The therapist who said these words has obviously had a few hard conversations with perfectionist parents. He did clarify that he would only say—or even need to say—those words to a perfectionist in an unhealthy place. When we are unhealthy, we lay our expectations on others, including the kids we love, in a way that blinds us to them and their gifts. We don't appreciate the differences. We want to change them. I remember another dad I worked with who was a 1. He had a daughter who was a challenger, an Enneagram 8. I will never forget him saying to me, "She has so much fight in her. I just want to help her find her way to the right kinds of fights." What a beautiful picture of appreciating the differences in a child. He wanted to help her become the best version of herself, rather than the version he wanted her to be. Appreciate the differences. See their gifts. And then encourage them in those gifts.

8. Encourage.

I'm sure you're tired of hearing me talk about the critic. We certainly have a critic and can be one in the lives of others. We don't mean to be. And then we beat ourselves up for doing it later—or we allow the inner critic to do his work in that arena. It's not only the nos that come more naturally for us, it's the negative. We see what's missing—in the world and other people. So it can be hard not only to see the gifts, but to point them out.

Your child needs your encouragement. He needs you to tell him things he's doing well. To point out the things that you like in her. To remind him he's already got all it takes. To remind her that she's enough. That you love them. Believe in them. Are cheering them on. When we're living with or out of the critic, it's hard to cheer anyone on. But it truly is what your kids want most. For you to see the good. Catch them doing good more than you catch them doing wrong. Even the one who sees so differently from how you do. They long for your encouragement. And they also long for your empathy.

9. Sit with the negative emotion.

"How long do I let my child go on and on about their problems?" When a parent asks me this question, it's usually a giveaway that they're a perfectionist. In a parenting seminar based on our book *Are My Kids on Track?*, I talk about the milestone of regulation. And how many kids these days live their lives at ten on a one-to-ten scale for emotions. They feel big and they use big words to describe those emotions. Often, the kids who use big words have parents who are either over-attending or under-attending. Whatever we pay the most attention to (or what we over-attend) is what's reinforced. A teenage girl told me once that her mom was more nurturing to her when she had panic attacks than any other time. Thus the frequent panic attacks when she was feeling lost or stressed. On the other side are those of us who are type A. As we already established, we are getting a lot done and moving quickly while we're doing it. There is not a lot of time for emotional outbursts. "Come on, come on. There is no time for tears over your hair today. We have to GO!" Sound familiar? As a result, the kids we love sometimes have to use big words just to get us to slow down and pay attention.

We already discussed the importance of empathy and questions. If you have to ask how long you need to sit with a child who is processing their emotions, it's likely that you're not leaning toward them long enough. I'm going to tell on myself here. I sometimes have a hard time with big emotions too. I know . . . funny fact when I'm a therapist. But it's the kids who are stuck in those big emotions who I have a particularly hard time listening to. The kids who repeat themselves over and over and seem to prefer to wallow instead of grow. As Sadness said in the movie *Inside Out*, "I'm too sad to walk," and then when Joy started dragging her around, "This actually feels kind of nice."[13] I am not as good with the Sadnesses of the world. I appreciate their gifts. But I can also get impatient and frustrated and can quickly resort to wanting them to see what I see. Over time, I have learned to make myself sit and listen. Sometimes I'll even watch the clock. I notice inside of myself when I start to feel impatient, and then I make myself wait longer. Considerably longer. I will try to let them process for at least half the session before my one-ness has to stretch its impatient, productive legs. "What do you want to do about that?" "What would you think it would look like to work through that?" Or, as I asked one girl last week, "How do you *want* to feel?" And yes, then I did go on to (kindly and gently, I hope) say, "I'm not really sure you want to get better." Turns out, she didn't.

When I ask the questions too early without empathy, they feel rushed. They feel the agenda I secretly have for them leak its way out of my words. And they, in turn, feel like I don't approve. They feel that I have expectations and that they're not meeting them. That I don't like them. Empathy, on the other hand, creates space for connection. Sitting with them in their negative emotion helps them feel seen and heard. If you have a child with big emotions who likes to wallow from time to time or if you're parenting Sadness, hang in there. Listen for longer than feels comfortable. And then reflect those emotions back, just like you learned in Psych 101. "I can tell you're sad." "I hear how frustrated you are." "I hate this for you." Be in it with them. It's what will ultimately create more connection between you. Then move to the questions.

As a side note, I noticed that I used the word *negative* a few times to describe these big emotions. I talk at length with parents about how emotions aren't negative. They're milestones to point us toward something deeper. But here is my perfectionist perspective seeping out once again—94 percent. We are all still on this journey. Together.

10. Remember that you are doing enough.

It's the last reminder from your friendly Daystar therapists. And it is likely one of the hardest truths for you to grasp. It is for me. But it is true. You are doing enough. Right now. Who you are as a person, and as a parent, with each of your kids.

I recently ran across a meme that said, "Feeling like a bad parent? Quokkas [some kind of koala-looking animal] toss their babies at predators so they can escape." I love another one that says, "Whenever you feel like a bad parent, just remember that the mom from *Home Alone* was halfway to Paris before she realized she was missing her child." You're not doing that. In fact, as a perfectionist, I believe you're trying harder than so many parents out there. You are getting so much right. I promise you that in the long run, what your child remembers most will not be the things you did wrong.

They'll remember that you were with them. That you listened. Laughed together. That you danced in the kitchen after dinner. That you apologized when things went wrong. And that you pointed them toward Jesus.

Dan Allender says, "Hope is the capacity to defy what is now with the promise of what one day will be."[14] You will one day be a perfect parent. But for now, you can trust that you have one. As do your children. He, like me, believes the best about you. He is taking all the good that you bring to your parenting—and there is so much. He's using the good inside of you for His glory and to grow your children. He's also using your failure. He's using your failure to grow not just them, but you. Your life, much more than your words, points your kids toward grace. We can need Jesus in front of them. We can admit failure and know grace. It's what we long for most and where the real freedom and joy are to be found. For us all.

Worry-Free Takeaways

1. Being a perfectionist parent is hard.
2. How you talk to yourself after failure can cause you more harm than the failure did in the first place.
3. Good parents get it right 50 percent of the time.
4. Insanity is repeating the same thing over and over again and expecting different results.
5. Practice more *oops* than *shoots*.
6. We grow spiritually much more by doing it wrong than by doing it right.
7. Slow down.
8. Trust the process.
9. Savor the moment.
10. Assume the best.
11. Fail in front of them.
12. Learn to laugh at yourself.
13. See their gifts.
14. Encourage.
15. Sit with negative emotion.
16. Remember that you are doing enough.

10

Try Softer

Every parent with anxiety I've ever met is trying really hard. I believe if anxious parents could try softer—not give up, but not be so hard on yourselves, not drive and push hard constantly—you would be able to enjoy your kids and yourselves significantly more. The pressure you're living under is only hurting both of you. My hope is you've heard that message already, with a whole lot of grace mixed in.

Try softer is a phrase a wise and dear friend of mine named Heather mentioned to me over lunch years ago.[1] She didn't *tell* me to "try softer"—because she's not the kind of friend who would tell anyone to do anything that directly. She's gentle and insightful in a way that I hope I'm growing more into myself. If what was in my head came out of my mouth, I'd be shouting at myself and everyone around me to "try harder." Okay—I'm being hard on myself. Not all days, but some. When I'm stressed, particularly.

You may have heard this acronym used often in the recovery movement: HALT. It is a reminder not to let ourselves get too hungry, angry, lonely, or tired. Because when we are in any of those states, the try-harder, self-critical voice is much louder. So it's at those times especially that I go back to the words of my friend Heather. She said she was trying to learn two things:

1. To try softer.
2. To let enough be enough.

I'd like to learn those as well. And I would like to help you learn them too. Along with two other things. We're not doing five things in this chapter. Because, you guessed it: We're learning to try softer. But we're going to have four things to think about and to try softly. Four things that I hope will continue this process of freeing you from your anxiety and transforming you into the parent you long to be.

Four Things I Want Us to Learn about Trying Softer

1. *Here's what trying softer can look like.*

Let's talk a little bit about the why of trying softer. How would you say trying hard impacts you? How does it impact your kids? When was a time that trying hard actually made things worse?

I get angry when I try hard. For me, trying hard means I perceive that I'm putting in more work relationally than others. Or professionally. But it's not work that helps my relationships. In fact, it sometimes wears them out—and *always* ends up wearing me out in the long run. It creates expectations, and as you've likely heard, expectations are just preconceived resentments. I can always tell I've moved into an unhealthy place when I have thoughts like *Why do I always have to be the one? Why doesn't anyone try as hard as I do?* (Ugh. I hate typing this out.) I tell myself it's because I want to give and care. But it's often because I want something in return. Trying softer for me looks like not reaching out so much. Not always being the one to initiate. Letting others speak up first. Allowing room for reciprocity. And trusting that the other person cares as much as I do. Their care might just look different.

What about you? Let's do an exercise here. I'm going to assume that there are at least three things you're trying hard with right now because we're all in this anxious boat together. I want us to go back to some of the ideas we learned in chapter 6.

Remember that idea of reframing? Here we go: Your trying hard does *not* mean you're failing as a parent. My trying hard does not mean I'm failing as a friend or coworker (although when I type it out here it sure feels like it). It means I care a lot about the people in my life and want to be connected to them. I want to be the best I can be—in work and in relationship. For you, trying hard doesn't mean not doing a good job as a parent. It doesn't mean you're an overprotective and overcontrolling person (although it might come out that way on your HALT days). What it means is this: You are a really great parent. You love your kids deeply. You want the best for them and your family. You're doing everything you can to ensure that they grow up happy and whole and confident and feeling loved. You (and I) just don't have to try quite as hard.

So I want you to practice trying softer.

Grab *The Worry-Free Parent Workbook* or the journal you've been using recently.

Write out three things you're trying hard with (that you really can let go of).

Now write out what it would look like to try softer.

Next, write out what you think the worry monster is going to tell you when you do.

Finally, write what you can say in response with your kindest, gentlest voice. The same love that is normally directed toward your kids is what I want you to direct toward yourself. It's okay if it doesn't feel natural. Just practice. In fact, I want you to practice this once a week over the next few months. We're growing new try-softer and be-kind-to-yourself circuitry in your brain. It will be challenging, but I promise you that it's worth the effort, for you and the kids you love.

2. Let enough be enough.

When we're anxious, the concept of enough doesn't exist.

We worry too much.

We try too hard.

We ask too many questions.

We overthink.

We overprepare.

We "over" just about everything there is.

We even do too many kind things for other people.

We "never enough" ourselves into a place of exhaustion.

What would it mean for you to let enough be enough? I sit with anxious kids who are gifted intellectually and make all As. But they stay up till two in the morning preparing for tests when they don't need to. They go back over their work again and again. I will often say to them, "I want you to give yourself a time limit. Allow ___ hour(s) per night. At that point, I want you to stop. And then I want you to trust that you have done enough." They are putting in way too much effort for an outcome that doesn't really change.

The majority of you are no longer doing schoolwork. But you are planning family vacations. Or helping your child with a project. You're throwing a baby shower. Or going back over your Christmas list one more time to make sure everyone is taken care of. You're thinking through a friendship that is problematic. Or trying to figure out how to help your child become less anxious or sad, more confident, happier . . . all of the things. You're volunteering and working part- or full-time and raising four kids and still trying to be the room parent for each of your children's classrooms. What would it mean for you to take the same homework challenge I give the kids in my office? What would it mean for you to allow room for *enough*?

Another cognitive behavioral therapy tool I use in my office is called *containment*. With younger kids, I have a worry doll who has a zipper for a mouth. (I know it sounds creepy, but it's actually cute.) The purpose of the doll is that any time a worry comes up the kids can write their worry down and put it in the doll's mouth. Then, when they have their daily "worry time," they sit with a parent, take the worries out, and talk through them. Containment helps a child learn that their worries matter, but that they don't have to be constantly consumed by them. We are "containing" those worries in a doll or box or even prayer house for later. It teaches kids that they have control over their worries, rather than their worries having control over them. Containment might be fun to try with your worried child, or even yourself.

Understanding the concept of enough does the same thing. It helps us learn that we are in control, rather than being controlled by the nagging concern that tells us there is still more to do. We can stop the overpreparing and overplanning and overthinking by just saying, "It's enough."

After I wrote the first draft of this book, I read a wonder of a book by Shauna Niequist called *I Guess I Haven't Learned that Yet*. I know . . . just the title makes me feel a little better about life and myself. Unbeknown to me, she also had written a chapter called "Try Softer." Honored to be in the same company, Shauna. But in that chapter, she reports something one of her son's teachers said that speaks to this concept of enough. "Donna [Shauna's son's teacher] said one of the most important skills you can learn is how to manage your intensity, to dial it down and dial it back up at the right times. The best teachers, she said, are not the ones who arrive at 6:00 a.m. and leave at 6:00 p.m. The best teachers are the ones who go to museums and take art classes and go to the park and throw parties, because when you do all that living, you have something to bring to the classroom."[2] Those teachers let enough be enough . . . as can you.

Think about an area of life where you're having trouble letting enough be enough. Maybe you've taken on too many things. Maybe you're putting too much pressure on yourself to keep up with too many relationships. Maybe it's time to let some things or some people go. Or maybe it's just a pattern of overthinking. Enough.

You might need a friend to help. Sometimes we don't even realize that we've gotten into a pattern of circling the drain over and over. Ask your spouse or a trusted friend if they can help you when you've lost track of enough. It can also help to have a visual reminder. Write *ENOUGH* on a sticky note on your mirror or wear a specific bracelet to remind yourself. I want you to start to gently say "Enough" to yourself in the next few weeks. I want you to let all the effort you have put in be enough.

You have done so much. There is no one asking you to do or think or prepare more and more besides yourself. And my guess is that you'll still have the same outcome with a lot less effort. You've got a long way to go till you get to 50 percent. I know, because you're the kind of person who would pick up this book, that you're doing great. And I don't even have to overthink that one.

3. Embrace the ordinary.

In one of our parenting classes, we show a clip from two different shows to illustrate the difference between today and what things used to be like. Today's show is *Parenthood* (okay, it's not today, but it's a great one that is a little more recent). The older show is *Leave It to Beaver*, which you're probably too young to have heard of. The scene in *Parenthood* has Lorelai—I mean Sarah Braverman—with her daughter, Amber. Amber's hair is dyed black or magenta or some dark shade of blue (it's hard to tell). It appears as if she has spent the night with a boy. The only thing that's really evident is that Sarah is very upset, and Amber is being very rebellious. The scene moves fast, with rapidly shifting camera angles, loud music, lots of yelling, and more than its share of drama. It's over within about forty-five seconds. The *Leave It to Beaver* scene, on the other hand, takes probably six meandering minutes to get the entire message across. It opens on all four members of the Cleaver family gathered around the dining room table, complete with china and a white tablecloth. They have a slow-paced discussion about the school day, with dad jokes, slow camera pans, and canned laughter. Watching the Cleavers feels like a collective sigh of relief. Watching the Bravermans feels like an intense, angsty pinball machine.

If I could choose one word to describe the last decade of life, both as a therapist and as a human, it would be *intense*. (It's not just us who need to learn to dial down the intensity. It's our culture too.) I was just talking to a mom about the intensity of academics and the anxiety they bring kids today. The pressure to get into the right kindergarten. The hours of homework in elementary school. The standardized test prep and the Advanced Placement classes and all the things all the way up the academic scale. As a therapist, I believe it is way too much for these kids—even when they're not putting in more effort than the class requires. The required amount of effort is too much already. I often wish there was something I could do about it. I believe the academic pressure is one of the reasons anxiety rates are on the rise with kids. I keep trying to come up with a solution, where we lobby for less rigorous schools or create petitions for administrations to make a change. I don't know the solution, but I can promise you I'm committed to trying for the sake of our kids. Sadly, however, it's not just academic pressure. It's happening in everything in which they're involved—from sports to plays to arts to leadership activities. It's coming at them from every side. It's too intense.

Their emotional lives have gotten intense as well. Kids no longer say they're worried, as I mentioned earlier. They use the word *anxious*. They're no longer sad. They're "depressed." I meet with kids every week who I believe have googled a diagnosis and memorized it before our meeting. They rattle off the entire list, hoping for me to diagnose them with some issue. These kids don't believe (1) that their emotions are valid without a diagnosis or (2) that anyone will listen to them without one. And we're part of the problem. I met with a dad recently who told me his son had "rejection sensitivity dysphoria." That was a new one for me. I have to say that I think every middle schooler, at some point, has rejection sensitivity dysphoria. But, today, we pathologize everything. Everything and everyone has a label. Anything worth mentioning is in the extreme. Kids can't be a little insecure or awkward or sad. And it can't just be a good day. It has to be the "best day ever." Think about the pressure you feel around birthday parties and trips and helping your son ask a girl to prom. Even that has a name now: prom-posal. Our culture doesn't understand the concept of enough. We've lost sight of the ordinary. And that is, I believe, one of the biggest problems we all face today.

I mentioned before that I attend a liturgical church. It also adheres to a church calendar. You know . . . Advent, Lent, Eastertide seasons. But one of the things I love most about the calendar is that between those great seasons of Lent and Advent and their culminating holidays is something called Ordinary Time. I love just the idea of Ordinary Time. I wish we talked more about it with kids and with each other. Ordinary Time is not intense. It's not extreme in any way. We're not preparing for some lavish celebration. It's just ordinary and serves as a reminder to me that the ordinary is just as important a place to find contentment as the celebratory.

Mother Teresa said, "Do not think that love, in order to be genuine, has to be extraordinary. What we need is to love without getting tired. . . . Be faithful in small things because it is in them that your strength lies."[3] I want you to help your kids learn contentment in the ordinary. The average days. The campouts in the backyard, rather than only the trips to a tropical paradise (although those are nice too). The birthday parties with pizza and three friends, rather than ponies and DJs and skywriting. (Okay— I've never really heard that one.) To teach kids that they don't need a diagnosis to be heard or valued. That they can just be sensitive to rejection because they're a seventh grader. That ordinary is not just okay, but good. As is normal. And average. It's enough. But maybe, for us to teach the kids we love, we need to become content in those areas too. There is so much good and glory in the ordinary—and a whole lot less pressure and anxiety.

4. Rest.

When was the last time you experienced a sense of real rest? Was it your last extraordinary tropical vacation? When your kids all went to summer camp at the same time? Maybe it was before you had kids. My hope for you is for that to change too.

We're trying too hard. Not getting to a place of enough. We're living in intensity and chasing extraordinary way too much. We need rest. You need rest.

We've talked a lot about self-care already in this book. But rest, to me, sounds deeper. It sounds like a place where the ideas of trying softer and getting to enough and embracing the ordinary all come together with one more word: trust. We're going to talk about trust in the last two chapters of this book. I believe real rest is only possible when there's a sense of trust. Trust in yourself and trust in God—that He is taking care of your kids and you. We're going to get there.

But for now, I want you to think about how you could incorporate a little more rest into your life. Rest also happens to be built into our church calendar—not by the church, but by God himself. The Sabbath. I would imagine that a lot of your Sabbaths include soccer games and grocery store runs and last-minute school projects and preparation. That's anything but a true Sabbath. When was the last time you really rested?

I want you to take an hour this week to rest. Consider it therapy homework. Your rest could be a walk outside listening to worship music. It could be a literal nap. It could be reading a non-productive, non-self-help type of book. You know the things that bring you rest. Find one this week and do it. And then why don't you go ahead and do it next week too? I truly believe a little more rest in your life will not only lessen the pressure inside you but will help the intensity around you have less power. It will be a balm for your anxious heart. And it will create more room for play and for trust.

> Let your gentleness be evident to all. The Lord is near. Do not be anxious about anything, but in every situation, by prayer and petition, with thanksgiving, present your requests to God. And the peace of God, which transcends all understanding, will guard your hearts and your minds in Christ Jesus.
>
> Philippians 4:5–7

> Don't fret or worry. Instead of worrying, pray. Let petitions and praises shape your worries into prayers, letting God know your concerns. Before you know it, a sense of God's wholeness, everything coming together for good, will come and settle you down.

It's wonderful what happens when Christ displaces worry at the center of your life.

Philippians 4:6–7 MESSAGE

What happens is that we're able to try softer. Allowing enough to be enough. And seeing God in the ordinary. The Lord is near. And His nearness allows us to rest and to play with these little people we love so deeply.

Worry-Free Takeaways

1. Every parent with anxiety I've ever met is trying really hard.
2. I believe that if anxious parents could try softer—not give up, but not be so hard on yourselves, not drive and push hard constantly—you would be able to enjoy your kids and yourselves significantly more.
3. Try softer. You are a really great parent. You love your kids deeply. You want the best for them and your family. You're doing everything you can to ensure that they grow up happy and whole and confident and feeling loved. You just don't have to try quite as hard.
4. Let enough be enough. It helps us learn that we are in control, rather than being controlled by the nagging concern that tells us there is still more to do. We can stop the overpreparing and overplanning and overthinking by just saying, "It's enough."
5. Embrace the ordinary. Our culture doesn't understand the concept of enough. We've lost sight of the ordinary. And that is, I believe, one of the biggest problems we all face today.
6. Rest. I truly believe a little more rest in your life will not only lessen the pressure inside of you but decrease the power of the intensity around you. Rest will be a balm for your anxious heart. And it will create more room for play and for trust.

11

Trust Your Gut

I recently met with a fifteen-year-old girl at Daystar. "My dad is having an affair," she quietly told me in her first appointment. I hadn't seen this on the intake form her parents filled out, so I wanted to hear more. "I'm so sorry," I started with. "That's got to be really tough. Tell me more about what's going on."

She went on to recount stories of business trips to tropical vacations that her mom no longer went on, although she had for the majority of this girl's life. Errands took much longer than expected. She even saw a hairbrush in her dad's car that she knew did not belong to her mom. He had recently started working out a good bit. He was spending more time online. There was a lot of evidence, and my gut told me that this girl was right.

The parents came up to my office next. "She thinks, for some crazy reason, I'm having an affair," the father quickly told me once they sat down. "I can't imagine why she would ever say such a thing," the mom responded. "He is the best father and husband anyone could ask for."

I did a lot of observing during the rest of this couple's time in my office. I have a strong hunch that he was having an affair—by how he presented himself, by how he related to his wife, and by the things the daughter told me. It all added up. But when this very brave girl went to her mom with her suspicion, her mom immediately told her she was wrong. The mom had no further conversation with her. And apparently did no further reflection of her own. Her daughter's intuition and the mom's feelings were both shut down.

When we, as the grown-ups who love them, invalidate a child's feelings or thoughts, we invalidate their intuition. We tell them their gut is wrong. They don't need to listen to the voice inside of themselves that says, "Wait." "Stop." "There is more to this story." "This is not safe." After all these years of working with kids, I believe that invalidating their intuition is profoundly harmful to a child. I worry so much for this girl in her dating relationships as she gets older. She has been told by the people she is supposed to trust most not to trust herself.

Intuition gets us through life. It's how we know what and who is safe. It's how we know when to stop, when to move, and when to proceed with caution. Intuition tells us what to do and who to be in any given situation, if we have the confidence to trust it and to trust ourselves.

As I was writing this chapter, I asked parents on social media if they trusted themselves as parents. An overwhelming 82 percent said yes. I'm going with my gut here—but I don't believe a lot of them. Or you, if that's your answer right now. Or maybe I'm invalidating your feelings with that statement. Let me say it differently. It's not my experience sitting with parents in counseling that they truly trust their guts. In counseling, I experience the opposite. I tend to think 82 percent don't trust their gut. Maybe it's because the parents I sit with have children in counseling for one reason or another, and very likely for a reason that makes those parents anxious. For them, the voice of worry may be louder than the voice of their gut. Maybe it's because the parents I meet with feel broken, and with brokenness comes an introspection that many of us lack on our good days. Maybe it's just because a counseling office with someone you trust is a safer space to share than the internet. But I'm going to go ahead and assume that on some days—maybe most days—it's hard for you to trust your gut.

I believe your gut, outside of your faith in God, is the most important tool you have as a parent. It's your parental superpower.

In addition to asking parents whether they trusted themselves, I also asked why or why not. The overwhelming majority who didn't recounted a story from their childhood of hurt at the hands of their parents. Two simple answers, in both directions, stood out to me most. One woman said she didn't trust herself because "I didn't grow up with good parents." In other words, her feelings and thoughts were likely invalidated—thus, invalidating her trust in herself. Another mom, who happens to be one of the best moms and grandmothers (and cousins—because she's mine) I know said that she did trust herself as a parent, "Because I had wonderful parents and learned from them." Her parents weren't perfect. They were part of my family too. But they did all they could to help her know that what she thought and felt was important. They helped her feel heard in a way that communicated that the voice inside of her mattered. And because that voice mattered to them, it mattered to her as well.

You may not have had that experience. Many of us did not. Your voice still matters. For some parents who don't trust their gut, I think they believe it's because their gut hasn't grown up quite yet. It hasn't developed inside of them. That couldn't be further from the truth. You still have the superpower. You just haven't learned to listen to or trust it. If I were sitting with you right now, I would quietly tell you over and over to trust the gut that God has given you. And here are some suggestions as to how to do just that.

Five Ways to Learn to Trust Your Gut

1. Quiet the voice of worry.

Learning to hear our intuition does take time. And practice. It's not that we have to practice developing intuition. It's that we have to practice hearing it. Our worry speaks to us so loudly. It captivates our focus and causes us to question not only what the voice is saying, but if there is, in fact, a voice at all. So that's where we start. We need to quiet the noisy, insistent, consuming voice of worry.

What do you remember so far that has helped you quiet your worry monster? My hope is that you're already practicing: Calm your body. Reset your amygdala. Name the worry. Talk back to it. Reframe the thought. Share your feelings—even the ones that are tougher to talk about. Do the things that fill you up. Do brave things. Rest. Spend time with your people—little and big. Admit failure. Know grace. Try softer. And be in the moment.

2. Be in the moment.

> The real enemies of our life are the "oughts" and the "ifs." They pull us backward into the unalterable past and forward into the unpredictable future. But real life takes place in the here and the now. God is a God of the present. God is always in the moment, be that moment hard or easy, joyful or painful. . . . That's why Jesus came to wipe away the burden of the past and the worries for the future. He wants us to discover God right where we are, here and now.
>
> —Henri Nouwen[1]

Last year, I had a meeting with a mom whom I have known for years. I've walked closely with two of her children, as well as her and her husband. She came to sit down with me after her husband died unexpectedly. At the time, one of her four children was making concerning choices she never would have imagined or hoped for. Another had walked away from his faith and into a destructive lifestyle. This mom was struggling, as you can imagine.

After catching me up on how she and all her kids were doing, she said, "You know, Sissy, I've recently become convicted. I realized that worry had ransomed my thoughts and heart. I was getting ahead of myself, and I was getting ahead of God. What I learned is that I was just borrowing tomorrow's manna." I must have looked at her perplexed because she went on to remind me of the story of Exodus 16. The Israelites were wandering through the desert—and doing lots of worrying about starving, I might add. To take care of them, God gave them all the manna they needed. For that day and that day only. He never ceased to care for them. But they only had enough manna to last them for the day. And then they had to trust Him all over again for enough manna for the next. When she said she was borrowing tomorrow's manna, she meant that she was not trusting that God would care for her beyond today. She was living with a fearfulness of the future that kept her from being in the present. And that present is exactly where we have to be to hear the voice of our intuition. In fact, it's what her intuition—or the Holy Spirit—was telling her.

3. Pray.

When I'm training new counselors, I tell them often that the most important thing they can do is to learn to trust their gut. It's what will tell them what questions to ask, how to respond, and what direction to go next with their clients. I want them to trust their intuition much more than they trust all their years of training. But only because I believe the voice inside of them comes from Someone much wiser than any counselor has ever been. Or I should say, I believe that voice is the wisest Counselor of all—the one Jesus promised in John 14 when He was leaving the disciples, who had to be worried about the prospect of life without Him.

> And I will pray the Father, and he will give you another Counselor, to be with you for ever, even the Spirit of truth, whom the world cannot receive, because it neither sees him nor knows him; you know him, for he dwells with you, and will be in you.
>
> John 14:16–17 RSV

I don't just tell them to trust their intuition. I tell them to pray like crazy that their intuition is led by the Holy Spirit. I would tell you the same.

At the beginning of this year in my Bible study, we decided we were going to talk more about the Holy Spirit. Each of us went around the room talking about our experience with Him and how we would describe our relationship. It was during that conversation that I connected the dots a step further.

If you're anything like me, you can believe truth and have hope more easily for others than for yourself. I know the Holy Spirit leads me in counseling, but I sometimes struggle to believe the same to be true for my own personal life. All of a sudden, that morning in Bible study, it made sense to me in a new way. I was reminded of the voice that wakes me up at night with some kind of clarity, that I hear when I'm praying or driving or in the shower that reminds me of truth. That is the voice of God's Spirit telling me how to respond and what direction to go next.

Talk to Him. Pray that God would speak to you in the depths of who you are. One of my favorite things to hear in counseling is a parent saying, "Well, I've always prayed that he'd get caught. And something told me to grab his phone and check it." God answers prayer, as you know. And I have heard hundreds of versions of that same story—where God has led parents to not only catch their kids, but to have a depth of insight that obviously came from Someone much wiser than you or I. We just need to listen.

4. *Listen.*

Prayer is first of all listening to God. It's openness. God is always speaking; he's always doing something. Prayer is to enter into that activity. . . . Convert your thoughts into prayer. As we are involved in unceasing thinking, so we are called to unceasing prayer. The difference is not that prayer is thinking about other things, but that prayer is thinking in dialogue. It is a move from self-centered monologue to a conversation with God.

Henri Nouwen[2]

Listening is hard. It's much easier to pray all the things we want. To even allow our prayers to just be the voice of our worry monsters spoken out loud. Thinking unceasingly sounds a lot to me like the one-loop roller coaster at the fair. But God calls us to convert those thoughts, those loops, to unceasing prayer. When we pray, we practice the sharing of our thoughts with God, but we also offer them openhanded in dialogue.

I want you to do something right now for the next ten minutes. Set a timer to help you know when the time is up. Now close your eyes. Take three deep, slow belly breaths. Now, with or without words, offer your worries to God. Imagine something you're worried about in the lives of your kids right now. Imagine yourself taking that worry from your heart, pulling it out with your fist tight. Then, turn your hands palms up, and offer it to God. Tell Him your fears and why you're afraid. And then sit. I want you to sit and listen for at least five minutes to see where you hear God's response.

Just as in our relationships, the more often we hear a voice, the more quickly we recognize it. Practice praying and listening openhanded regularly. Set a timer, if that helps. Sit in silence and wait. Wait until you hear God's voice or sense in some small way what He's trying to tell you.

According to theologian Winnie-the-Pooh, "If the person you are talking to doesn't appear to be listening, be patient. It may simply be that he has a small piece of fluff in his ear."[3] We get the fluff out of our ears by quieting the other voices and creating space to listen. Keep listening until you learn to recognize His voice. And keep trusting too.

5. Keep trusting.

I have a few Enneagram 6s in my life. They're known as the questioners or the loyalists. Sixes love a committee. Whether it is which outfit to wear, which restaurant to try, or which school their children should attend, many 6s want the opinion of not just one other person, but an entire group of people. What I often find myself wanting to tell them—and to tell you, if you lean toward listening to others more than the voice inside—is that the Holy Spirit speaks most directly to you. He does not typically speak to the committee for you.

You will be tempted to trust a lot of voices more than your own. You'll have committees who are happy to tell you exactly which school your child should attend. You might have your own parents tell you what you should be doing to change your child's behavior. You'll have children who tell you what you should do to change your behavior. You'll have other parents of kids the same age as yours tell you when your child should get their own phone or social media account and why. And you'll even have parenting experts who will tell you exactly what you need to do to raise a happy child by tomorrow. Trust yourself more. More than the committee. More than the other parents. More than your own parents—or kids, for sure. I can't tell you how often I've had parents over the years say, "No, my child told me it was a friend's alcohol they asked them to hide." Let me clarify this right here: It is never a friend's alcohol in your child's room—or car. However, I think the parents of these smart, conniving kids already know the truth. They just trust their child more than their own gut. Trust yourself more than the voices around you and, yes, even the parenting experts who write really helpful parenting books. God speaks most directly to you about your life and about the lives of your kids. Obviously, I believe in the power of other voices and that God can speak insightful, impactful truth to us through voices we trust. But when we get the fluff out of our own ears and make space for dialogue with Him, I believe He speaks to us the loudest and clearest about our own lives and our own families.

One of my favorite authors and C. S. Lewis's mentor, George MacDonald, said, "My prayers, my God, flow from what I am not; I think thy answers make me what I am."[4] God has given you a superpower of intuition. It is one of the greatest gifts you will receive in your life as a parent. And as a person. It is also one of the greatest gifts to your kids. Listen to it. Trust it. God will use that intuition to deepen your understanding of your kids, of yourself, and of His immense love for you both.

Worry-Free Takeaways

1. I believe your gut, outside of your faith in God, is the most important tool you have as a parent.
2. Quiet the voice of worry.
3. Be in the moment.
4. Pray.
5. Listen.
6. Keep trusting.
7. God speaks most directly to you about your life and about the lives of your kids.

12

Trust God

Years ago, I had the incredible privilege of taking a writing course at Regent University in Vancouver from two of my heroes: Madeleine L'Engle and Luci Shaw. I have loved L'Engle's writing for most of my life and had recently come to love Shaw's as well. It was one of my favorite things I've ever done. And so many things they said that week have stayed with me through the years.

Madeleine L'Engle said that she believed waking up and falling asleep are holy moments. She said that our concerns, consciousness, and busyness can't filter out the voice of God at those times—and so we hear Him more clearly. (Sounds a little like learning to listen to our gut, doesn't it?) I have found that to be true. So many of my most creative thoughts— book ideas or titles, creative gifts for others, or just insights into my life—have come in those moments. My other holy listening moments seem to be when I'm not in charge and can simply listen. I have a feeling the same is true for you. I had one of those moments at Hopetown this past summer.

One morning, I was sitting outside under the canopy of trees listening to Melissa teach the kids, relishing not having to be responsible for the moment. Okay, I guess I wasn't really listening (don't tell her), because I found myself reflecting on the past year. I started jotting down to the side of my notes things I learned over the year—and am learning still. Here's what they were:

1. So many things don't matter (that I give a lot of weight).
2. Frustration isn't worth it—or fun.
3. Hurried me isn't the best me. Slow down.
4. It's not that others aren't trying. It's just that they see other things. Thank goodness.

I am definitely learning these things, still. We talked earlier about trusting the process, and I am living evidence that this process takes a long time. I am still learning at fifty-one that hurried me isn't the best me. The process is slow, as am I. But in the midst of that process, I have a whole lot of trust.

A few summers ago at Hopetown, when I *was* listening, Melissa said something to the kids I'll never forget: Courage isn't the antidote to anxiety. Trust is. Now, I don't mean superficial, platitude-type trust. And neither did she. I mean the kind of trust that life lays open through struggle and sorrow and suffering, of trying hard and still not quite getting there. Past the layers of worry. Past the layers of control we try to take when we are worried. Past the layers of our will that get in the way of His will.

I recently read on a social media account (that shall remain nameless) this statement: "I relinquish my outcomes and trust that all things are working out in my favor." It stopped me in my tracks. That's not the kind of trust we're talking about in this chapter. I wish I could trust that all things are working in my favor. "My favor" implies to me the things I want to happen. The things I think should happen in my life and others' lives, including, but not limited to, my taking Henry to Disney World tomorrow and winning the lottery. Both. Maybe at the same time. I wish that were true, but I don't really believe things will work out in my favor. At least not in the short-sighted favor I often have in mind for myself. However, I still have trust that God will work things out, ultimately, for my good and His glory. And, in that knowledge, I wholeheartedly believe that I can surrender.

The reason I can surrender is solely because of God. Without Him, I could not. I'm too grabby and controlling on my own. But I can surrender because I know He who I have believed is much wiser than I am, and I am convinced He is able to guard that which, and those people whom, I have entrusted to Him (2 Timothy 1:12). It's what makes surrender possible. In other words, I could never surrender if I didn't believe that (1) I was surrendering to Someone good and trustworthy, (2) that Someone was going to take care of my people, and finally (3) that Someone, in His goodness, was going to take care of me. His goodness may not look like I would expect or even want in my life or the lives of others. But I can trust that He is still good. And that He will move me out of all the pressure, fear, worry, grabbiness, and trouble I often find myself stuck in. He is moving me slowly as I learn to trust.

Five Byproducts of Learning to Trust

And One to Grow (and Go) On

I want to go back to the name Jesus gave the Holy Spirit in John 14: "But the Counselor, the Holy Spirit, whom the Father will send in my name, will teach you all things and remind you of everything I have told you" (John 14:26 csb).

Jesus' mention of the Holy Spirit, in that moment, is a part of a discussion He was having with the disciples about what was to come. The disciples didn't understand because He was, at the time, still with them. By the time we get to Luke 24, however, Jesus has died and risen from the grave, unbeknown to the grieving disciples, who believe Him dead.

Mary Magdalene, Joanna, Mary the mother of James, and several other women went to the disciples to tell them they found the tomb empty. In Luke's account, Peter then ran to look as well and came home perplexed at the sight of the empty tomb.

Just as [two of Jesus' followers] were telling about it, Jesus himself was suddenly standing there among them. "Peace be with
you," he said. But the whole group was startled and frightened,
thinking they were seeing a ghost!

    "Why are you frightened?" he asked. "Why are your hearts
filled with doubt? Look at my hands. Look at my feet. You can
see that it's really me. Touch me and make sure that I am not a
ghost, because ghosts don't have bodies, as you see that I do."
As he spoke, he showed them his hands and his feet.

vv. 36–40 NLT

Jesus then eats bread in front of them to prove that He is real.
He reminds them of the truth of His words in the Gospel of John
and the promise that is coming to fulfillment before their eyes.
Then we pick back up with "And now I will send the Holy Spirit"
(v. 49 NLT). It's Jesus' last conversation with the disciples before
He is taken up to heaven.

    I want you to insert yourself into this scene. Can you imagine
being one of the disciples on that Easter morning? The grief you
would have felt over His death and then the fear over where His
body had gone? Of course, it would be easy to try to blame others, insisting that someone had stolen Him. It would help you feel
control in a moment when you feel so incredibly out of control
that it doesn't even seem real. Then, what appears to be a ghost
is in front of you—the ghost of Jesus. Seriously, we can be over-
spiritual and assume that if we were to see the ghost of Jesus, we
would fall down in worship. But most likely, we would be quaking
in our sandals. We would be terrified. So Jesus starts by speaking
directly to that fear. He gives us context.

1. *From context to context*

About a month ago, just as I was in the thick of research for this
book, I was invited to be on a podcast. Amanda Bible Williams and
Raechel Myers reached out to ask if I'd be a guest on the *She Reads
Truth* podcast to talk about anxiety as a part of their series Do Not
Fear. I was honored and immediately replied yes. The nervousness

came promptly upon hitting send on the email. What do I have to say on a podcast about the Bible? I can talk about anxiety all day long, but I have not gone to seminary. I am not a Bible scholar. And I haven't devoted my life to teaching the Bible, as these wise and amazingly gracious women have, I might add. But God always takes care of us.

In the first five minutes, Amanda brought up the word *context*. The two of them began to talk about how every time Scripture tells us "Do not fear," it is always followed by context. In other words, He gives us a reason not to fear. Every single time. I was stunned that they used the same word I had been reading over and over in my research on anxiety. He gave me a new context in that moment.

Anxiety is always searching for context. Worry finds and attaches to context in the things that matter most to us: Whether that's our failure, our worst-case scenario, our *you have no business being on this podcast* thoughts, or our fears about the kids we love. But Jesus moves us from context to context. He replaces the context of our anxiety with the context of His truth. He graciously and consistently gives us the why behind not having to worry.

Read for yourself:

> But the angel said to them, "Do not be afraid. I bring you good news that will cause great joy for all the people."
>
> Luke 2:10

> Do not be afraid, little flock, for your Father has been pleased to give you the kingdom.
>
> Luke 12:32

> So don't be afraid; you are worth more than many sparrows.
>
> Matthew 10:31

> So do not fear, for I am with you: do not be dismayed, for I am your God. I will strengthen you and help you; I will uphold you with my righteous right hand.
>
> Isaiah 41:10

Do not fear, for I have redeemed you; I have summoned you by name; you are mine.

Isaiah 43:1

Even though I walk through the darkest valley, I will fear no evil, for you are with me; your rod and your staff, they comfort me.

Psalm 23:4

The LORD is my light and my salvation—whom shall I fear? The LORD is the stronghold of my life—of whom shall I be afraid?

Psalm 27:1

God is our refuge and strength, an ever-present help in trouble. Therefore we will not fear.

Psalm 46:1–2

For I am the LORD your God who takes hold of your right hand and says to you, Do not fear; I will help you.

Isaiah 41:13

Peace I leave with you; my peace I give you. I do not give to you as the world gives. Do not let your hearts be troubled and do not be afraid.

John 14:27

He will cover you with his feathers, and under his wings you will find refuge; his faithfulness will be your shield and rampart. You will not fear the terror of night, nor the arrow that flies by day.

Psalm 91:4–5

Do not be afraid of them; the LORD your God himself will fight for you.

Deuteronomy 3:22

Say to those with fearful hearts, "Be strong, do not fear; your God
will come, he will come with vengeance; with divine retribution
he will come to save you."

Isaiah 35:4

"So then, don't be afraid. I will provide for you and your children." And he reassured them and spoke kindly to them.

Genesis 50:21

See? Every time He tells us not to fear, he follows it up with a
reason. Context. As we start to believe His words, trust His contexts, our contexts will start to dissipate. His kind words can become the truth we tell ourselves, rather than the worried thoughts
that loop endlessly in our anxious minds.

With the kids, I often have them choose a favorite Scripture
about fear and then memorize it as a way to replace the worried
thoughts. I'd love for you to do the same with one of the verses
above. And then, when those worried thoughts come, you auto-
matically have true context to keep the worries from taking hold.

2. From grabbiness to gratitude

We cling to that which makes us feel secure. We cling to our
ideas. We cling to our possessions. We cling to our people. We grab
hold and we hold tight. The more anxious we become, the more
tightly we grab and cling. The more we try to have control. It doesn't
work. Think back on something you've held tightly to in the past: a
possession, a feeling, a person. Grabbing only serves to squeeze the
life and the good out of that which we want to keep. The grabbier
we get, the more we sabotage it. But God can move us from grabbiness to gratitude. Through trust and with a whole lot of practice.

In one of my favorite stories about life raising a teenager, Anne
Lamott outlined not only the hardships but where she found hope
and help:

> The usual things helped: some distance, prayer, chocolate. Talk-
> ing to the parents of older kids was helpful for me, since parents

of kids the same age as yours won't admit how horrible their children are. . . . I taped things to the wall that give me some light to see by. One pink card says, "Breathe, Pray, Be Kind, Stop Grabbing." Another card says something I heard recently, that you can either practice being right, or practice being kind. Screaming in the car helped.[1]

Stop grabbing. Be kind. Breathe. Pray. Go back to God's context. Right after the reminder that God will provide for our children in Genesis, it says God "reassured them and spoke kindly to them." Kindness always has the effect of helping me unclench my fists. Kindness helps us find our way back to gratitude. And that gratitude is another way to reframe the worried thought.

Instead of, *I'm so afraid my son is going to fail this test he's poured all of this time and energy into. I've got to cling tight and help,* you can think, *I'm so grateful my son cares about his schoolwork. I have never seen him invest so much of himself in his grades. I'm going to trust him and trust that his school is as committed to his academic life as I am.*

Instead of, *I'm so afraid my daughter is never going to make friends. I'm the only person she talks to,* you can think, *I'm so grateful that my daughter and I are as close as we are. Most girls at this age don't want to talk to their moms at all.* These are both actual conversations I've had in my office.

The gratitude doesn't negate the concern. But the concern doesn't have to overtake the gratitude. When we flip the thought to one of gratitude, the gratitude becomes stronger than the anxiety or even just the worrisome things we have going on. There is so much good God is doing still, if we can loosen our grip and look for it.

Grabbiness causes us to sabotage. Gratitude becomes self-fulfilling. The more grateful we are, the less we have to hold tight; and then the more grateful we become. Gratitude brings about more gratitude and is even known to reduce anxiety, from a clinical standpoint. It's an idea that I talked about at length in *Raising Worry-Free Girls.* Gratitude and anxiety cannot coexist.[2]

To be grateful is to recognize the love of God in everything He has given us—and He has given us everything. Every breath we draw is a gift of His love, every moment of existence is a grace, for it brings with it immense graces from Him. Gratitude therefore takes nothing for granted, is never unresponsive, is constantly awakening to new wonder and to praise of the goodness of God. For the grateful person knows that God is good, not by hearsay but by experience. And that is what makes all the difference.

Thomas Merton[3]

3. From fear to reminders of His faithfulness

Have you heard the song "Goodness of God"? The version performed by CeCe Winans has been one of my most frequently played songs this past year. It's also one of our favorites to sing at Hopetown. If you haven't heard it, go listen now. Really . . . I'd love for you to hear her beautiful, powerhouse of a voice singing of the goodness of God: "All my life you have been faithful."[4] As Merton said,

> For the grateful person knows that God is good not by hearsay, but by experience.[5]

What is your experience? How many of the things you've worried about in the past year have come true? How many good things have happened that you never worried about because you never would have imagined them? I'd love for you to make a list of each of those things now. Which list is longer? What have you seen just by remembering?

A few chapters ago, we talked about being good detectives as a cognitive behavioral therapy tool. When we are good detectives, we use the evidence of what happened in the past to tell us what will likely happen in the future. Then we're able to dispute the anxious thoughts with what we know to be true. When I go back and look at God's faithfulness in the past, it helps me not to fear the future. All my life He *has* been faithful . . . even if that faithfulness looked different from how I would have imagined. I still see it. And because of it, I can live with more gratitude for my past and more of a sense of wonder in the present.

4. *From worry to wonder*

> The old grief, by a great mystery of human life, gradually passes into quiet tender joy.
>
> Fyodor Dostoevsky[6]

My mom was one of the biggest worriers I've ever known. We jokingly referred to her as Chicken Little because the sky was always falling. Two years ago, my mom died of chronic obstructive pulmonary disease. Since that time, I have been waiting for the "quiet tender joy" Dostoevsky wrote of in *The Brothers Karamazov*. I glimpse it in moments, but not nearly as much as I'd like. I still miss the heck out of her. The quiet, tender joy is not here yet, but I can see it. I have a knowingness deep inside me that what Dostoevsky said is true. It feels like a future promise. Right now, I'm still in the present.

When I think back on the last eight months of Mom's life, I can almost see two different themes playing out. At times, they were side by side. At times, they met and were woven together. In one, my sister and I were constantly worried. Worried doesn't even do it justice. Terrified is a better word. We were told that April that she was dying and likely wouldn't make it until Christmas. We were shocked. But we were also determined to have as much time with her as possible. I remember conversation after conversation with Lisa, our dear nurse from Alive Hospice, about how much longer Mom had. I wanted a literal date, even though I knew that wasn't possible. What I really wanted was control. I remember worrying about the little things—sobbing, quite literally, to Mom about how I wouldn't be able to hang paintings without her. (She was my favorite decorator.) And worrying about the big things too. At the time, my grandmother was not doing so well either, and I knew she wouldn't last long.

One night, my mom and I were sitting side by side eating pizza at the counter in the house she shared with my sister, brother-in-law, and nephew, Henry. It was in the final two weeks of her life, although I didn't know it at the time. In between bites, I started sobbing. "Mom, I just don't know what I'm going to do without you. You won't be here. Marian [my grandmother] won't be here. I'm going to be like the matriarch of our family. I want to take care of Kathleen, Aaron, and Henry [who was only a year old at the time] the way you would want me to. What do you want me to do for Henry? What is most important to you?" (As a side note, my mom and I didn't talk this way with each other very often—as in, maybe never. She wasn't really one to share her feelings, other than how much she loved us.) She paused for a few minutes and looked at me with all of the seriousness and strength she could muster with her oxygen tube around her nose. "Have a candy drawer. Henry needs a candy drawer in your house where he can get candy whenever he wants it." Seriously. That was my mom's response to my intense fear about how to care for our family without her. You can bet your bottom dollar I've got a well-stocked candy drawer in my house today.

That story is more of a reflection to me of the second theme I felt so significantly during that time: wonder. As I look back on all that I was worried about every single day of those long and too-short months, I am filled with a sense of wonder. I have never experienced God moving as obviously and profoundly as I did during that seven-month period.

The fall after I graduated from college, my parents divorced. In all of the division of life and assets, my mom had to give up the lake house she had loved and even found for our family when I was a kid. The spring we found out Mom was so sick, a lake house next to Hopetown came up for sale. Through a strange series of events, my sister, her husband, and I were able to buy it. We didn't take possession till July, although the three of us were all working at Hopetown for the entire summer. (Aaron is the director of boys at Hopetown. Kathleen owns a boutique in Nashville but spends most of the summer at Hopetown with us.) The entire month of June I was worried about Mom. I kept anxiously wondering if I should leave Hopetown and all my responsibilities as director there and just move home to be with her. But in July, she moved to the lake house with us. She spent the last summer of her life sharing a room with her only grandchild, and a house with both of her beloved daughters. In their room, Mom and Henry would wake up every morning at the same time. From my room, I could hear him babbling and her responding. She would sit on the edge of her bed, oxygen tank nearby, with her hand on his back, reading and talking to him. The last night of Hopetown, before coming home to Nashville, she looked at Kathleen and said, "I never dreamed our family would have a lake house again." Wonder. God moved her from worry to wonder in just seven months. And He moved us right along with her for every day of those seven months as we trusted Him to get us through the darkest season of our lives to date. When I think back, I did a lot of desperate praying. But I don't remember making a conscious decision to trust. It was simply my only option.

As a side note, the very first morning we were home from that summer at Hopetown, Kathleen and I got a text from Mom asking for one of us to take her to the hospital. She declined rapidly from that point until December 18, when we lost her. I think that entire summer may have been a taste of wonder for her—and a sweet foretaste of the fact that one day, we'll all live together again. But this time, with Henry and her soon-to-be grandson named Witt. And my guess is that our houses will all be close together around a lake.

I heard someone say once that wonder is where gratitude and joy meet. I have so much gratefulness for that time. And such quiet joy, even now, in writing this—with, as you can imagine, tears streaming down my face. In the end, maybe our bitter tears will turn to quiet joy. And certainly, our worries will turn to wonder.

In trust, we look back on our past with gratitude. We allow a sense of wonder in our present, even in the midst of what can feel like worry and sorrow. And we can look forward to the promise of a future where there will be no more tears, no more worry, and no more pressure.

5. *From pressure to promise*

My hope is that you're already starting to experience some of the ways God moves us as we trust Him. I hope you're not reading this with a list of all the things you're supposed to be and do as a parent. I would never want you to receive my words that way. You've got enough pressure already.

Instead, my hope is that this book is helping you breathe a little more freely and deeply. I hope that as you have come to understand more about your past, you're able to give yourself more grace in the knowledge that you've been doing the best you can so far—and can have gratitude for God's faithfulness in all He has already done in and through you. I hope that as you gain more practical help and knowledge, you can be anchored to the present with confidence in who you are as a parent and a sense of wonder in the worry-free moments you get to have with your kids. And I hope that as you look toward the future, you feel less pressure and are more aware of the promise of what's to come. God will take care of your kids. He brings truth and grace and hope to even the scariest of our contexts. And His promises are always fulfilled.

> But to love God is not a goal we have to struggle toward on our own because what at its heart the Gospel is all about is that God himself moves us toward it even when we believe he has forsaken us.
>
> The final secret, I think, is this: that the words "You shall love the Lord your God" become in the end less a command than a promise.
>
> Frederick Buechner [7]

Since I have read it, this has been one of my all-time favorite quotes by my all-time favorite writer. Because in it, a command that felt like pressure my whole life became a promise. I will love God not because I rose to the pressure and tried hard and accomplished it, but because in the end, He is all I really have. He is moving me from pressure to promise. As the sign says in my office, He doesn't ask me to try harder. He just makes me new. He makes you new. As a parent and as a person. He is moving you right now. And He is bringing all that He has promised to completion.

Let's do another experiment. I want you to pull out your journal again. Make two columns. On one side, write *From* and on the other write *To*. Then I want you to write down some of the transformation that has already taken place inside you. I'm that confident it's happening. And I trust Him and you enough to know there's even more good and glory to come.

6. *From trouble to trust*

The verse I have used as a foundation for all my anxiety books so far is John 16:33. You know the one . . . "In this world you will have trouble. But take heart! I have overcome the world."

Part of why I used John 16:33 is because I believed that kids needed to learn to expect trouble. I still do, but the past few years have shifted my perspective. Pre-pandemic, I don't think they expected trouble. They thought their lives should be as fun, friend-filled, and flawless as their social media posts implied. When trouble hit, they didn't have the resilience to meet it. They thought that something was wrong with their world on the outside or with themselves on the inside. They also weren't learning what it meant to trust in the midst of trouble.

Now we have all lived through collective trouble. We've had to develop resilience and flexibility. We've had to learn to trust . . . in each other and in the things that truly matter. We haven't had any option. As a result, I think your kids are going to be stronger emotionally and spiritually than kids have been in generations. We have all learned together more of what it means to take heart and trust—not because of our power or control, but because of Him.

> Through Jesus we discover, by faith, absolute trust: that which we turn over to God is secure. He is not careless or absent-minded

with the precious treasure of our lives. God takes care of that which we give him. . . .

*I commit myself and those I live with into your safekeeping, dear Father. Permit no evil to ruin our faith, no testing to damage our obedience, no unbelief to diminish our love, **no anxieties to weaken our hope**. You bought us with a great price; now keep us for eternity. Amen.*

Eugene Peterson (emphasis added)[8]

Anxiety does weaken our hope. It lies to us, limits us, and tries to keep us from trusting God. It causes us to distrust not only Him, but also ourselves. However, with trust, God moves us from context to context. He moves us from grabbing to gratitude. From fear to reminders of His faithfulness. From worry to wonder. From pressure to promise. And from trouble to trust. Gratitude, faithfulness, wonder, promise, and trust sure sound a whole lot like the stuff hope is made of to me.

I want you to hear from me one more time that you are doing a great job. I want you to gently remind yourself of that truth often after you close the pages of this book. Even Mr. Rogers said, "It's not possible to be a parent without having times of worry."[9] We can reframe that worry knowing that you only worry because you're a good parent. Because you care so deeply about the little and big people in your life. They themselves are reminders of God's faithfulness in the past, the wonder of His presence and provision today, and His promises for all of our futures as we trust in Him. Your kids want to be in each of those spaces with you. They want to laugh and play and enjoy themselves and the parent you truly are created and free to be. It's who you are. Okay— one more exercise. Write down ten good things that are true about you that you've learned or been reminded of through this book. There is so much good to remember and experience as God continues to grow us toward being worry-free in and because of Him.

The Lord bless you and keep you; the Lord make his face shine on you and be gracious to you; the Lord turn his face toward you and give you peace.

Numbers 6:24–26

And may He remind you that your face is a reflection of His. Your kindness. Your strength. Your courage. Your love and heart for your child are but a minute reflection of His immense love for you both. His love is our past and our future. And it's enough to carry us, with wonder, through our worry-free present. You've got this. Because He's got you.

Worry-Free Takeaways

1. We are all still in the slow process of becoming the people God has called us to be.
2. Courage isn't the antidote to anxiety. Trust is.
3. God moves us from context to context. Anxiety is always searching for context. Through Scripture, God moves us from the context of worry to the context of truth. He graciously and consistently gives us the why behind not having to worry.
4. God moves us from grabbiness to gratitude. Grabbiness causes us to sabotage. Gratitude becomes self-fulfilling. The more grateful we are, the less we have to hold tight, and the more grateful we become. Gratitude brings about more gratitude.
5. God moves us from fear to reminders of His faithfulness. When I go back and look at God's faithfulness in the past, it helps me not to fear the future.
6. God moves us from worry to wonder. In trust, we look back on our past with gratitude. We allow a sense of wonder in our present, even in the midst of what can feel like worry and sorrow.

7. God moves us from pressure to promise. He doesn't ask you to try harder. He just makes you new. As a parent and as a person. He is moving you right now. And He is bringing all that He has promised to completion.
8. God moves us from trouble to trust. We can trust in the midst of trouble because of and through Him.
9. You are doing a great job.

Acknowledgments

One of the things I've learned in the last few years about my personality through the Enneagram is that, as a 1, I'm in what's referred to as "the dependent stance."[1] When I first read that, I was a little disgruntled. In so many ways, I think of myself as a highly independent person. But then someone explained it to me in a way that made sense. Those of us in the dependent stance like to have a reference point outside of ourselves. We have a trusted few we can go to with questions—questions such as, "Did that sound okay to you?" "Is there anything I need to do differently?" I do, in fact, have those kinds of questions a lot. In this world of writing (and person-ing), I have a few go-to people for my questions—people whose hearts I trust deeply, who are on my team in a way in which I know they will tell me the truth about myself but continue to see and remind me of the good. I don't really mind being dependent when these are the amazing folks I get to depend on:

Jeff Braun, Jana Muntsinger, and Lisa Jackson are three of my favorite teammates. You all push me not only to be a better writer, but to trust my own gut and God more in the process. Also, to Sharon Hodge and Hannah Ahlfield for wisely sifting through so many words and being particularly encouraging while you do! To Deirdre, Becca, Mycah, Stephanie, and the entire Bethany House team, you all do an amazing job championing your people. I'm so privileged to be one of them!

Amanda Young and Amy Cato, our writing—our podcasting—our speaking—our existing as *Raising Boys and Girls* would not be possible without the time and energy and heart you two pour into our ministry on a daily basis. I am deeply indebted to (and dependent on) the two of you.

To Annie, Fallon, Kelli, and the TSF team, it is a PLEASURE to be a part of your family. Thanks for believing in *Raising Boys and Girls*! Jess and Marcus, always grateful to share Fridays and tacos and this podcasting adventure with your brilliance!

To my favorite friends at Daystar (our entire staff): Mary, Paige, Susan, Kerry, Aaron, Katie, Kenneth, Melissa, Emma, Allye, Amy, Rachel, Jenny, Shannon, David, David, Sherman, Tommy, and Don, it is a true honor to walk alongside you in this important work of caring for families. You guys are my heroes. I'm grateful every day for the privilege of calling you friends.

To my Wednesday morning Bible study girls: Melissa, Pace, Heather, Jackie, Lauren, Kristi, Emily, and Susan, thank you for being trusted sources of truth, hope, and grace to me every single week. I know Jesus better because of who each of you are in my life.

Melissa and David, I continue to be so grateful to share this journey of offering help and hope alongside you. I can't imagine better co-workers or friends.

To my extended Arkansas family: the Longs, the Allens, my godparents, Tootie and Buddha, Robin, Ashley, you all remind me constantly of how important it is to be deeply known and loved—and to do the same for others. My life is surely richer for having all of you in it.

Dad and Jane, thank you both for all the ways you've loved and supported and cheered me on over the years. I'm grateful for all that I've learned from and gotten to experience on adventures with you, and I look forward to many more to come.

Kathleen and Aaron, thanks for letting me tag along in all the ways. I'm so proud of you both—and honored to be your big sister.

Henry and Witt, you fill me with a sense of wonder every single day . . . the wonder of how fun and brave and kind and smart and all around amazing the two of you are. And that I have the immense gift of being your Diddy. God sure knew what He was doing when he picked all four of you to be my family.

Notes

Introduction

1. Reid Wilson and Lynn Lyons, *Anxious Kids, Anxious Parents: 7 Ways to Stop the Worry Cycle and Raise Courageous and Independent Children* (Deerfield Beach, FL: Health Communications, Inc., 2013), 35.

Chapter 1: Understanding Worry and Anxiety

1. Sun Tzu, *The Art of War* (Minneapolis: Filiquarian Publishing edition, 2006), 15.

2. Edmund J. Bourne, *The Anxiety & Phobia Workbook*, rev. and updated ed. (Oakland, CA: New Harbinger Publications, Inc., 2020), 8.

3. U.S. Department of Health and Human Services, "What Are the Five Major Types of Anxiety Disorders?," https://www.hhs.gov/answers/mental-health-and-substance-abuse/what-are-the-five-major-types-of-anxiety-disorders/index.html.

4. "2018 Children's Mental Health Report" (At a Glance section), Child Mind Institute, https://childmind.org/awareness-campaigns/childrens-mental-health-report/2018-childrens-mental-health-report/.

5. Claire McCarthy, "Anxiety in Teens Is Rising: What's Going On?" American Academy of Pediatrics, November 20, 2019, https://www.healthychildren.org/English/health-issues/conditions/emotional-problems/Pages/Anxiety-Disorders.aspx.

6. Ron J. Steingard, "Mood Disorders and Teenage Girls," Child Mind Institute, https://childmind.org/article/mood-disorders-and-teenage-girls/.

7. Tamar E. Chansky, *Freeing Your Child from Anxiety: Practical Strategies to Overcome Fears, Worries, and Phobias and Be Prepared for Life—from Toddlers to Teens*, rev. and updated ed. (New York: Harmony Books, 2014), 28–29.

8. Reid Wilson and Lynn Lyons, *Anxious Kids, Anxious Parents: 7 Ways to Stop the Worry Cycle and Raise Courageous and Independent Children* (Deerfield Beach, FL: Health Communications, Inc., 2013), 26.

9. "Any Anxiety Disorder," National Institute of Mental Health, https://www.nimh.nih.gov/health/statistics/any-anxiety-disorder.

10. "Anxiety Disorders," Office on Women's Health, https://www.womenshealth.gov/mental-health/mental-health-conditions/anxiety-disorders.

11. "The Most Common Mental Illness: Myths and Facts About Anxiety," *UPMC Health Beat*, Western Behavioral Health, May 28, 2020, https://share.upmc.com/2020/05/myths-and-facts-about-anxiety/.

12. "The Most Common Mental Illness."

13. "Anxiety Disorders: Identification and Intervention," Molina Healthcare, citing the Anxiety and Depression Association of America, https://www.molinahealthcare.com/providers/nv/medicaid/resources/bh_toolkit/anxiety.aspx.

14. Judson Brewer, *Unwinding Anxiety: New Science Shows How to Break the Cycles of Worry and Fear to Heal Your Mind* (New York: Avery, 2021), 17.

15. Brewer, *Unwinding Anxiety*, 17.

16. Kendra Cherry, "What Is Neuroplasticity?," *Verywell Mind*, September 19, 2022, https://www.verywellmind.com/what-is-brain-plasticity-2794886.

17. Daniel J. Siegel and Tina Payne Bryson, *The Yes Brain: How to Cultivate Courage, Curiosity, and Resilience in Your Child* (New York: Bantam Books, 2018), 17.

18. Seth Gillihan, *Cognitive Behavioral Therapy Made Simple: 10 Strategies for Managing Anxiety, Depression, Anger, Panic and Worry* (Emeryville, CA: Althea Press, 2018), 132.

19. Sissy Goff, *Brave: A Teen Girl's Guide to Beating Worry and Anxiety* (Minneapolis, MN: Bethany House, 2021), 24.

20. Kendra Cherry, "What Is the Confirmation Bias?," *Verywell Mind*, October 11, 2022, https://www.verywellmind.com/what-is-a-confirmation-bias-2795024.

21. Bridgett Flynn Walker, *Anxiety Relief for Kids: On-the-Spot Strategies to Help Your Child Overcome Worry, Panic & Avoidance* (Oakland, CA: New Harbinger Publications, 2017), 20.

22. *Pooh's Grand Adventure: The Search of Christopher Robin*, 1997, written by Carter Crocker and Karl Geurs, distributed by Walt Disney Home Video, United States.

23. Dan Allender, To Be Told Conference, West End Community Church, Nashville, TN, Saturday, March 31, 2019.

Chapter 2: Understanding Ourselves

1. Richard Rohr, *Things Hidden: Scripture as Spirituality* (London: Society for Promoting Christian Knowledge, 2016), 25.

2. Sissy Goff, *Raising Worry-Free Girls: Helping Your Daughter Feel Braver, Stronger, and Smarter in an Anxious World* (Minneapolis, MN: Bethany House, 2019), 52.

3. Reid Wilson and Lynn Lyons, *Anxious Kids, Anxious Parents: 7 Ways to Stop the Worry Cycle and Raise Courageous and Independent Children* (Deerfield Beach, FL: Health Communications, Inc., 2013), 26.

4. Wilson and Lyons, *Anxious Kids, Anxious Parents*, 26.

5. Tamar E. Chansky, *Freeing Your Child from Anxiety: Practical Strategies to Overcome Fears, Worries, and Phobias and Be Prepared for Life—from Toddlers to Teens*, rev. and updated ed. (New York: Harmony Books, 2014), 32–33.

6. Chansky, *Freeing Your Child from Anxiety*, 32–33.

7. Edmund J. Bourne, *The Anxiety & Phobia Workbook*, rev. and updated ed. (Oakland, CA: New Harbinger Publications, Inc., 2020), 41, 42.

8. Catherine M. Pittman and Elizabeth M. Karle, *Rewire Your Anxious Brain: How to Use the Neuroscience of Fear to End Anxiety, Panic & Worry* (Oakland, CA: New Harbinger Publications, Inc., 2015), 6.

9. 2008 Presidential Task Force on Posttraumatic Stress, "Children and Trauma, Update for Mental Health Professionals: Disorder and Trauma in Children and Adolescents," American Psychological Association, https://www.apa.org/pi/families/resources/children-trauma-update.

10. Chansky, *Freeing Your Child from Anxiety*, 34.

11. Bourne, *The Anxiety & Phobia Workbook*, 39, 40.

12. Bourne, *The Anxiety & Phobia Workbook*, 39, 40.

13. David A. Clark and Aaron T. Beck, *The Anxiety and Worry Workbook: The Cognitive Behavioral Solution* (New York: The Guilford Press, 2012), 41, 51.

14. "Obsessive Compulsive Disorder, Overview," National Institute of Mental Health, https://www.nimh.nih.gov/health/topics/obsessive-compulsive-disorder-ocd.

15. Cathy Creswell, Monika Parkinson, Kerstin Thirlwall, and Lucy Willetts, *Parent-Led CBT for Child Anxiety: Helping Parents Help Their Kids* (New York: The Guilford Press, 2017), 42.

16. Elizabeth Wagele and Renee Baron, *The Enneagram Made Easy: Discover the 9 Types of People* (New York: HarperSanFrancisco, 1994), 12.

17. Sarah Bessey, *A Rhythm of Prayer: A Collection of Meditations for Renewal* (New York: Convergent, 2021), 133.

18. Anne Lamott, *Operating Instructions: A Journal of My Son's First Year* (New York: Anchor Books, 2005), 22.

19. Bourne, *The Anxiety & Phobia Workbook*, 1.

20. C. S. Lewis, *The Horse and His Boy* (New York: Macmillan, 1954), 187. *The Horse and His Boy* by CS Lewis, © copyright 1955, CS Lewis Pte Ltd. Extract used with permission.

21. Dan Allender, To Be Told Conference, West End Community Church, Nashville, TN, Saturday, March 31, 2019.

22. Brad Montague, *Becoming Better Grownups: Rediscovering What Matters and Remembering How to Fly* (New York: Avery, 2020), 154.

Chapter 3: How Anxiety Impacts You

1. Sarah B. Johnson, Robert W. Blum, and Jay N. Giedd, "Adolescent Maturity and the Brain: The Promise and Pitfalls of Neuroscience Research in Adolescent Health Policy," *The Journal of Adolescent Health: Official Publication of the Society for Adolescent Medicine* 45, no. 3 (September 2009): 216–221, https://doi.org/10.1016/j.jadohealth.2009.05.016.

2. Melissa Trevathan and Sissy Goff, *Raising Girls* (Grand Rapids, MI: Zondervan, 2007), 19.

3. Chansky, *Freeing Your Child from Anxiety*, 203.

4. Bob Goff (@bobgoff), Twitter, October 31, 2021, https://twitter.com/bobgoff/status/1454813613575737348.

Chapter 4: How Your Anxiety Impacts Your Kids

1. Reid Wilson and Lynn Lyons, *Anxious Kids, Anxious Parents: 7 Ways to Stop the Worry Cycle and Raise Courageous and Independent Children* (Deerfield Beach, FL: Health Communications, Inc., 2013), 26.

2. Shawn Achor and Michelle Gielan, "Make Yourself Immune to Secondhand Stress," *Harvard Business Review*, September 2, 2015, https://hbr.org/2015/09/make-yourself-immune-to-secondhand-stress.

3. Achor and Gielan, "Secondhand Stress."

4. Judson Brewer, *Unwinding Anxiety: New Science Shows How to Break the Cycles of Worry and Fear to Heal Your Mind* (New York: Avery, 2021), 22–23.

5. Achor and Gielan, "Secondhand Stress."

6. "Projection," *Psychology Today*, https://www.psychologytoday.com/us/basics/projection.

7. "Backhoe," *Wikipedia*, https://en.wikipedia.org/wiki/Backhoe.

8. Madeline Levine, *Ready or Not: Preparing Our Kids to Thrive in an Uncertain and Rapidly Changing World* (New York: Harper, 2020), 109.

9. Sissy Goff, *Raising Worry-Free Girls: Helping Your Daughter Feel Braver, Stronger, and Smarter in an Anxious World* (Minneapolis, MN: Bethany House, 2019), 74–75.

10. Kate Bayless, "What Is Helicopter Parenting?" *Parents*, September 16, 2022, Parents.com, https://www.parents.com/parenting/better-parenting/what-is-helicopter-parenting/.

11. Ann Dunnewold, *Even June Cleaver Would Forget the Juice Box* (Deerfield Beach, FL: Health Communications, Inc., 2007), 58.

12. "7 Signs You Might Be a Helicopter Parent," *WebMD*, https://www.webmd.com/parenting/ss/slideshow-helicopter-parent.

13. Anna Sillman, "Stressed-Out Parents at Ritzy Summer Camps Are Driving Staff Nuts Over Kids' Photos," *Business Insider*, July 21, 2021, https://www.businessinsider.com/sleepaway-camp-photo-drama-tyler-hill-2021-7.

14. Nicole B. Perry as quoted in "Helicopter Parenting May Negatively Affect Children's Emotional Well-Being, Behavior," American Psychological Association, APA.org, June 18, 2018, https://www.apa.org/news/press/releases/2018/06/helicopter-parenting.

15. Bayless, "What Is Helicopter Parenting?"

16. Katherine and Jay Wolf, *Suffer Strong: How to Survive Anything by Redefining Everything* (Grand Rapids, MI: Zondervan, 2020), 215.

Chapter 5: Help for Your Body

1. Catherine M. Pittman and Elizabeth M. Karle, *Rewire Your Anxious Brain: How to Use the Neuroscience of Fear to End Anxiety, Panic & Worry* (Oakland, CA: New Harbinger Publications, Inc., 2015), 118.

2. "Understanding the Stress Response: Chronic Activation of this Survival Mechanism Impairs Health," July 6, 2020, Harvard Health Medical Publishing, Harvard Medical School, https://www.health.harvard.edu/staying-healthy/understanding-the-stress-response.

3. Mayo Clinic Staff, "Chronic Stress Puts Your Health at Risk," July 8, 2021, Mayo Clinic, https://www.mayoclinic.org/healthy-lifestyle/stress-management/in-depth/stress/art-20046037.

4. Pittman and Karle, *Rewire Your Anxious Brain*, 5.

5. Pittman and Karle, *Rewire Your Anxious Brain*, 17, 19.

6. Pittman and Karle, *Rewire Your Anxious Brain*, 14.

7. Pittman and Karle, *Rewire Your Anxious Brain*, 34–35.

8. Pittman and Karle, *Rewire Your Anxious Brain*, 25.

9. Pittman and Karle, *Rewire Your Anxious Brain*, 42.

10. Pittman and Karle, *Rewire Your Anxious Brain*, 32.

11. Pittman and Karle, *Rewire Your Anxious Brain*, 45.

12. Pittman and Karle, *Rewire Your Anxious Brain*, 85.

13. Edmund J. Bourne, *The Anxiety & Phobia Workbook*, rev. and updated ed. (Oakland, CA: New Harbinger Publications, Inc., 2020), 2.

14. Robert M. Sapolsky, "How to Relieve Stress," *Greater Good Magazine*, University of California, Berkeley, March 22, 2012, https://greatergood.berkeley.edu/article/item/how_to_relieve_stress.

15. Daniel J. Siegel and Tina Payne Bryson, *The Yes Brain: How to Cultivate Courage, Curiosity, and Resilience in Your Child* (New York: Bantam Books, 2018), 17.

16. Pittman and Karle, *Rewire Your Anxious Brain*, 6.

17. Joseph LeDoux, *Synaptic Self: How Our Brains Become Who We Are* (New York: Penguin Books, 2002), 3.

18. Pittman and Karle, *Rewire Your Anxious Brain*, 31.

19. Pittman and Karle, *Rewire Your Anxious Brain*, 50.

20. *Raising Boys & Girls Podcast*, "Intentional Conversations: Dr. Tina Payne Bryson," February 2, 2021.

21. Pittman and Karle, *Rewire Your Anxious Brain*, 126.

22. Bessel A. van der Kolk, *The Body Keeps the Score: Brain, Mind, and Body in the Healing of Trauma* (New York: Penguin Books, 2014), 206.

23. Jessica Migala, "Meet Your Chill Center," *Women's Health*, December 2021. https://apple.news/ApvbWimqeSq-CqIARYyp5Rg.

24. Migala, "Meet Your Chill Center."

25. Catherine M. Pittman, "Rewire the Anxious Brain: Using Neuroscience to End Anxiety, Panic and Worry," March 13, 2017, digital seminar, https://catalog.pesi.com/item/19659/?_ga=2.223424467.918260906.1591987936-1079570723.1539110393.

26. Lori Keong, "This Breathing Exercise Will Help You Keep Calm and Carry On," *Marie Claire*, December 22, 2016, https://www.marieclaire.com/health-fitness/a24265/breath-exercises-for-keeping-calm/.

27. Seth J. Gillihan, *Cognitive Behavioral Therapy Made Simple: 10 Strategies for Managing Anxiety, Depression, Anger, Panic, and Worry* (Emeryville, CA: Althea Press, 2018), 5.

28. Judson Brewer, *Unwinding Anxiety: New Science Shows How to Break the Cycles of Worry and Fear to Heal Your Mind* (New York: Avery, 2021), 46.

29. Gillihan, *Cognitive Behavioral Therapy Made Simple*, 92.

30. Gillihan, *Cognitive Behavioral Therapy Made Simple*, 92.

31. Gillihan, *Cognitive Behavioral Therapy Made Simple*, 92

32. Gillihan, *Cognitive Behavioral Therapy Made Simple*, 92.

33. Pittman and Karle, *Rewire Your Anxious Brain*, 96.

34. Pittman and Karle, *Rewire Your Anxious Brain*, 99.

35. Pittman and Karle, *Rewire Your Anxious Brain*, 107.

36. Brewer, *Unwinding Anxiety*, 86.

37. Brewer, *Unwinding Anxiety*, 86.

38. Mayo Clinic Staff, "Mindfulness Exercises," Mayo Clinic, https://www.mayoclinic.org/healthy-lifestyle/consumer-health/in-depth/mindfulness-exercises/art-20046356.

39. Liz Mineo, "With Mindfulness, Life's in the Moment," *Harvard Gazette*, April 17, 2018, https://news.harvard.edu/gazette/story/2018/04/less-stress-clearer-thoughts-with-mindfulness-meditation/.

40. Pittman and Karle, *Rewire Your Anxious Brain*, 143.

41. Pittman and Karle, *Rewire Your Anxious Brain*, 145.

42. Pittman and Karle, *Rewire Your Anxious Brain*, 6.

43. Fiona MacDonald, "Here's What Happens to Your Body When You Check Your Smartphone Before Bed," ScienceAlert.com, July 26, 2015, https://www.sciencealert.com/watch-here-s-what-happens-to-your-body-when-you-check-your-smartphone-before-bed.

44. "How Smartphones Affect Your Sleep," with Dr. Dan Seigel, Science Insider, *YouTube*, https://www.youtube.com/watch?v=_1V0rDSTC9I.

45. Pittman and Karle, *Rewire Your Anxious Brain*, 151.

46. Uma Naidoo, "Nutritional Strategies to Ease Anxiety," Harvard Health Publishing, Harvard Medical School, August 28, 2019, https://www.health.harvard.edu/blog/nutritional-strategies-to-ease-anxiety-201604139441.

47. Tanya Zuckerbrot, "Eat to Beat Stress: 10 Foods That Reduce Anxiety," *Men's Journal*, https://www.mensjournal.com/food-drink/eat-to-beat-stress-10-foods-that-reduce-anxiety.

48. Sharon Lee Song, "Take Time for Breath Prayer," *Christianity Today*, February 6, 2018, https://www.christianitytoday.com/women-leaders/2018/february/take-time-for-breath-prayer.html?paging=off.

49. Sarah Bessey, *A Rhythm of Prayer: A Collection of Meditations for Renewal* (New York: Convergent, 2020), 57–58.

50. Gillihan, *Cognitive Behavioral Therapy Made Simple*, 5.

Chapter 6: Help for Your Mind

1. Jena E. Pincott, "Wicked Thoughts," *Psychology Today*, September 1, 2015, https://www.psychologytoday.com/us/articles/201509/wicked-thoughts.

2. Kelly Billodeau, "Managing Intrusive Thoughts," Harvard Health Publishing, October 1, 2021, https://www.health.harvard.edu/mind-and-mood/managing-intrusive-thoughts.

3. Billodeau, "Managing Intrusive Thoughts."

4. Billodeau, "Managing Intrusive Thoughts."

5. Kirsten Nunez, "What Is the ABC Model in Cognitive Behavioral Therapy?," *Healthline*, April 17, 2020, https://www.healthline.com/health/abc-model#how-it-works.

6. Catherine M. Pittman and Elizabeth M. Karle, *Rewire Your Anxious Brain: How to Use the Neuroscience of Fear to End Anxiety, Panic & Worry* (Oakland, CA: New Harbinger Publications, Inc., 2015), 53.

7. Judith S. Beck, *Cognitive Behavior Therapy: Basics and Beyond*, second ed. (New York: Guilford Press, 2011), 34.

8. David D. Burns, *Feeling Great: The Revolutionary New Treatment for Depression and Anxiety* (Eau Claire, WI: PESI Publishing and Media, 2020), 65.

9. Burns, *Feeling Great*, 65.

10. Seth J. Gillihan, *Cognitive Behavioral Therapy Made Simple: 10 Strategies for Managing Anxiety, Depression, Anger, Panic, and Worry* (Emeryville, CA: Althea Press, 2018), 56–57.

11. Judson Brewer, *Unwinding Anxiety: New Science Shows How to Break the Cycles of Worry and Fear to Heal Your Mind* (New York: Avery, 2021), 88.

12. Brewer, *Unwinding Anxiety*, 89.

13. Brewer, *Unwinding Anxiety*, 90.

14. Louisa C. Michl, et al., "Rumination as a Mechanism Linking Stressful Life Events to Symptoms of Depression and Anxiety: Longitudinal Evidence in Early Adolescents and Adults," *Journal of Abnormal Psychology*, vol. 122, no. 2 (May 2013): 339–52, https://www.ncbi.nlm.nih.gov/pmc/articles/PMC4116082/.

15. Brewer, *Unwinding Anxiety*, 236.

16. Pittman and Karle, *Rewire Your Anxious Brain*, 54.

17. Pittman and Karle, *Rewire Your Anxious Brain*, 190.

18. Pittman and Karle, *Rewire Your Anxious Brain*, 170.

19. "What Is Cognitive Behavioral Therapy?," Clinical Practice Guideline for the Treatment of Posttraumatic Stress Disorder, American Psychological Association, July 2017, https://www.apa.org/ptsd-guideline/patients-and-families/cognitive-behavioral.

20. Pittman and Karle, *Rewire Your Anxious Brain*, 161.

21. Gillihan, *Cognitive Behavioral Therapy Made Simple*, 62.

22. Pittman and Karle, *Rewire Your Anxious Brain*, 60.

23. Edmund J. Bourne, *The Anxiety & Phobia Workbook*, rev. and updated ed. (Oakland, CA: New Harbinger Publications, Inc., 2020), 189–190.

24. Bourne, *The Anxiety & Phobia Workbook*, 197.

25. Pittman and Karle, *Rewire Your Anxious Brain*, 186.

26. "Turning Toward the Good," Center for Action and Contemplation, February 18, 2016, https://cac.org/turning-toward-the-good-2016-02-18/.

27. Ben Tinker, "The Modern Problem with Pursuing Perfection," *CNN*, January 9, 2018, https://www.cnn.com/2018/01/09/health/perfection-mental-health-study-intl/index.html.

28. Tinker, "Pursuing Perfection."

29. Brennan Manning, *The Ragamuffin Gospel* (Colorado Springs, CO: Multnomah, 2005 edition), 173–174.

30. Gail Pitt, *Consolation and Desolation: Discernment of Spirits* (Nashville, TN: self-published, 2020).

31. Charlie Mackesy, *The Boy, the Mole, the Fox and the Horse* (New York: HarperOne, 2019), 44

Chapter 7: Help for Your Heart

1. Anne Lamott, *Help, Thanks, Wow: The Three Essential Prayers* (New York: Riverhead Books, 2012), back cover.

2. Anne Lamott, *Almost Everything: Notes on Hope* (New York: Riverhead Books, 2018), 62.

3. "Serenity Prayer," Wikipedia, https://en.wikipedia.org/wiki/Serenity_Prayer.

4. David A. Clark and Aaron T. Beck, *The Anxiety and Worry Workbook: The Cognitive Behavioral Solution* (New York: The Guilford Press, 2012), 41, 51.

5. Dr. Dan B. Allender and Dr. Tremper Longman III, *The Cry of the Soul: How Our Emotions Reveal Our Deepest Questions about God* (Colorado Springs, CO: NavPress, 1994), 15.

6. Brené Brown, *Rising Strong: How the Ability to Reset Transforms the Way We Live, Love, Parent, and Lead* (New York: Random House, 2015, 2017), 50.

7. Edmund J. Bourne, *The Anxiety & Phobia Workbook*, rev. and updated ed. (Oakland, CA: New Harbinger Publications, Inc., 2020), 285.

8. Richard Rohr, "The Enneagram (Part 1)," *Richard Rohr's Daily Meditation*, May 28, 2014, https://myemail.constantcontact.com/Richard-Rohr-s-Meditation--Type-One --The-Need-to-Be-Perfect.html?soid=1103098668616&aid=Airf17xQKeA.

9. Bridget Flynn Walker, *Anxiety Relief for Kids: On-the-Spot Strategies to Help Your Child Overcome Worry, Panic & Avoidance* (Oakland, CA: New Harbinger, 2017), 20.

10. "What Is Exposure Therapy?," American Psychological Association, APA.org., https://www.apa.org/ptsd-guideline/patients-and-families/exposure-therapy.

11. Catherine M. Pittman, "Rewire the Anxious Brain: Using Neuroscience to End Anxiety, Panic and Worry," March 13, 2017, digital seminar, https://catalog.pesi.com /item/19659/?_ga=2.223424467.918260906.1591987936-1079570723.1539110393.

12. Sissy Goff, *Raising Worry-Free Girls: Helping Your Daughter Feel Braver, Stronger, and Smarter in an Anxious World* (Minneapolis, MN: Bethany House, 2019), 31.

13. Carol Dweck, "What Having a 'Growth Mindset' Actually Means," Harvard Business Review, January 13, 2016, https://hbr.org/2016/01/what-having-a-growth -mindset-actually-means.

14. "Is Growth Mindset the Answer to Students' Mental Health Problems?," *InnerDrive*, https://blog.innerdrive.co.uk/is-growth-mindset-the-answer-to-students -mental-health-problems.

15. Steven Handel, "How a Kindness Mindset Helps You Overcome Social Anxiety," *The Emotion Machine*, https://www.theemotionmachine.com/how-a-kindness-mindset -helps-you-overcome-social-anxiety/.

16. Bourne, *The Anxiety & Phobia Workbook*, 105.

Chapter 8: Help for Your Kids

1. Anne Lamott, *Stitches: A Handbook on Meaning, Hope and Repair* (New York: Riverhead Books, 2013), 26–28.

2. Susan David (@SusanDavid_PhD), "Emotions are data, not directives," Twitter, February 2, 2021, 1:02 p.m., https://mobile.twitter.com/susandavid_phd/status /1356679327744724992.

3. Ron J. Steingard, "Mood Disorders and Teenage Girls," Child Mind Institute, https://childmind.org/article/mood-disorders-and-teenage-girls/.

4. Cathy Creswell, Monika Parkinson, Kerstin Thirlwall, and Lucy Willetts, *Parent-Led CBT for Child Anxiety: Helping Parents Help Their Kids* (New York: The Guilford Press, 2017), 3.

5. Tamar E. Chansky, *Freeing Your Child from Anxiety: Practical Strategies to Overcome Fears, Worries, and Phobias and Be Prepared for Life—from Toddlers to Teens*, rev. and updated ed. (New York: Harmony Books, 2014), 203.

6. Jason Goldman, "Ed Tronick and the 'Still Face Experiment'," Science Blogs, October 18, 2010, https://scienceblogs.com/thoughtfulanimal/2010/10/18/ed-tronick -and-the-still-face#google_vignette.

7. Gottman Institute Editorial Team, "The Research: The Still Face Experiment," The Gottman Institute, 2022, https://www.gottman.com/blog/research-still-face -experiment.

8. Gottman Institute, "Still Face Experiment."

9. Kelly Corrigan, *Glitter and Glue: A Memoir* (New York: Ballantine Books), 213.

Chapter 9: Admit Failure. Know Grace.

1. Lehigh University, "'Good Enough' Parenting Is Good Enough, Study Finds," *Science Daily*, May 8, 2019, https://www.sciencedaily.com/releases/2019/05/190508134511.htm.

2. "Brain Development," *First Things First*, https://www.firstthingsfirst.org/early-childhood-matters/brain-development/.

3. Lehigh University, "Good Enough."

4. Margaret Renkl, "The Imperfect-Family Beatitudes, Birmingham, 1972" from *Late Migrations: A Natural History of Love and Loss.* Copyright © 2019 by Margaret Renkl. Reprinted with the permission of The Permissions Company, LLC on behalf of Milkweed Editions, www.milkweed.org.

5. Sissy Goff, *Braver, Stronger, Smarter: A Girl's Guide to Overcoming Worry and Anxiety* (Minneapolis, MN: Bethany House, 2019).

6. Richard Rohr, *Falling Upward: A Spirituality for the Two Halves of Life* (San Francisco, CA: Jossey-Bass, 2011), xxii.

7. Suzanne Stabile, *The Journey Toward Wholeness: Enneagram Wisdom for Stress, Balance, and Transformation* (Downers Grove, IL: InterVarsity Press, 2021), 125.

8. Stabile, *Journey Toward Wholeness*, 125.

9. Anne Lamott, *Help, Thanks, Wow: The Three Essential Prayers* (New York: Riverhead Books, 2012), 27.

10. *Book of Common Prayer* (New York: The Seabury Press, 1979), 116–117.

11. *Book of Common Prayer*, 117.

12. Suzanne Stabile, *The Path Between Us: An Enneagram Journey to Healthy Relationships* (Downers Grove, IL: IVP Books, 2018), 4.

13. *Inside Out*, directed by Pete Docter, Pixar, Walt Disney Pictures, June 19, 2015.

14. Dan Allender, To Be Told Conference, West End Community Church, Nashville, TN, Saturday, March 31, 2019.

Chapter 10: Try Softer

1. The phrase has since gained in popularity and is even the title of a 2020 book on anxiety by Aundi Kolber.

2. Shauna Niequist, *I Guess I Haven't Learned That Yet: Discovering New Ways of Living When the Old Ways Stop Working* (Grand Rapids, MI: Zondervan Books, 2022), 198.

3. Mother Teresa, as quoted in Donald Altman, *Clearing Emotional Clutter: Mindfulness Practices for Letting Go of What's Blocking Your Fulfillment and Transformation* (Novato, CA: New World Library, 2016), 133–134.

Chapter 11: Trust Your Gut

1. Henri J. M. Nouwen, *Here and Now: Living in the Spirit* (New York: The Crossroad Publishing Company, 1994), 18.

2. Henri Nouwen in Richard Foster and Henri Nouwen, "How Can a Spiritual Leader Keep His or Her Faith Vital?," Christian Bible Studies, *Christianity Today*, March 20, 2012, https://www.christianitytoday.com/biblestudies/bible-answers/spirituallife/spiritualleader.html?start=1.

3. Joan Powers, inspired by A. A. Milne, *Pooh's Little Instruction Book* (New York: Dutton, 1995), back matter.

4. C. S. Lewis, *George MacDonald: An Anthology* (New York: HarperCollins, 1946, 1973), 157.

Chapter 12: Trust God

1. Anne Lamott, *Plan B: Further Thoughts on Faith* (New York: Riverhead Books, 2005), 94.

2. Sissy Goff, *Raising Worry-Free Girls* (Minneapolis, MN: Bethany House, 2019), 191.

3. Thomas Merton, *Thoughts in Solitude* (New York: Farrar, Straus & Giroux, 1956, 1999), 33.

4. Jenn Johnson, Jason Ingram, Ben Fielding, Ed Cash, and Brian Johnson, © 2018 Fellow Ships Music, So Essential Tunes (Admin by Essential Music Publishing), SHOUT! Music Publishing (Admin by Capitol CMG Publishing), Alletrop Music (Admin. by Music Services, Inc.), Bethel Music Publishing.

5. Merton, *Thoughts in Solitude*, 33.

6. Fyodor Dostoevsky, *The Brothers Karamazov* (New York, Toronto: Alfred A. Knopf, 1927, 1992), 292.

7. Frederick Buechner, *A Room Called Remember: Uncollected Pieces* (San Francisco: HarperSanFrancisco, 1984), 45.

8. Eugene Peterson, *A Year with Jesus: Daily Readings and Meditations* (San Francisco: HarperSanFrancisco, 2006), 301, emphasis added.

9. Fred Rogers, *A Beautiful Day in the Neighborhood* (*Movie Tie-In*): *Neighborly Words of Wisdom from Mister Rogers* (Penguin Books, 1994), 124.

Acknowledgments

1. Suzanne Stabile, *The Journey Toward Wholeness: Enneagram Wisdom for Stress, Balance, and Transformation* (Downers Grove, IL: InterVarsity Press, 2021), 200.

Sissy Goff, LPC-MHSP, is the director of child and adolescent counseling at Daystar Counseling Ministries in Nashville, Tennessee, where she works alongside her counseling assistant/pet therapist, Lucy the Havanese. Since 1993, she has been helping girls and their parents find confidence in who they are and hope in who God is making them to be, both as individuals and families. Sissy cohosts the popular podcast *Raising Boys and Girls*, is a sought-after speaker for parenting events, and is the author of twelve books, including the bestselling *Raising Worry-Free Girls* and *Braver, Stronger, Smarter*, for elementary-aged girls, and *Brave*, for teenage girls.

More from SISSY GOFF

In a world fraught with worry and anxiety, veteran counselor Sissy Goff offers practical advice on how you can instill bravery and strength in your daughter, helping her understand why her brain is often working against her when she starts to worry and what she can do to fight back.

Raising Worry-Free Girls

This illustrated guide for girls ages 6 to 11 will help your daughter see how brave, strong, and smart God made her. Through easy-to-read stories and writing and drawing prompts, she will learn practical ways to fight back when worries come up and will feel empowered knowing she is deeply loved by a God who is bigger than her fears.

Braver, Stronger, Smarter

This teen-friendly guide—for girls ages 13 to 18—from counselor Sissy Goff will help your daughter understand anxiety's roots and why her brain is often working against her when she worries. In this book filled with stories and self-discovery exercises, she will find more of her voice and her confidence, discovering the brave girl God made her to be.

Brave

You May Also Like . . .

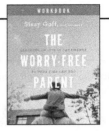

In this thoughtful companion workbook to *The Worry-Free Parent*, veteran counselor and parenting expert Sissy Goff invites you to make the teaching and truths in the book more personal and practical for you and your family. Here are the tools you need to grab hold of peace, embrace grace, and become the person, parent, and family you truly long to be.

The Worry-Free Parent Workbook